History of the American Peoples, 1840-1920:

A Primary Source Reader

Second Edition

John Majewski

University of California at Santa Barbara

KENDALL/HUNT PUBLISHING COMPANY
4050 Westmark Drive   Dubuque, Iowa 52002

Cover image from Corel.

Copyright © 2001, 2006 by Kendall/Hunt Publishing Company

ISBN 978-0-7575-2685-5

Printed in the United States of America
10 9 8 7 6 5

Contents
History of the American Peoples, 1840-1920

☆ Part III: The Rise of Big Business and the Settlement of the West

☆ Part IV: The Progressive Era

Part I:
Republican America,
1830-1850

DOCUMENT 1

Andrew Jackson Vetoes the Second Bank of the United States

Context: Congress created the Second Bank of the United States in 1816, granting a charter (a legislative act officially authorizing operations) for twenty years. Nicholas Biddle, president of the Bank, decided to preempt possible opposition and sought a new charter four years before the original one was due to expire. With the support of his Whig allies—including Henry Clay—the new charter was passed by Congress. President Andrew Jackson, however, vetoed the bill in 1832. Jackson's veto became the primary issue in the election of 1832, in which Jackson handily defeated Clay.

Questions to Consider: Why did Jackson regard the Bank as "dangerous to the liberties of the people"? Do you consider Jackson's aggressive rhetoric a reasonable assessment of the bank's political and economic impact? How did the message reflect Jackson's strong sense of nationalism? Should historians interpret Jackson's veto message as a broad attack against the market revolution as a whole?

Andrew Jackson, "Veto Message" (July 10, 1832)

The bill "to modify and continue" the act entitled "An act to incorporate the subscribers to the Bank of the United States" was presented to me on the 4th July instant. Having considered it with that solemn regard to the principles of the Constitution which the day was calculated to inspire, and come to the conclusion that it ought not to become a law, I herewith return it to the Senate, in which it originated, with my objections.

A bank of the United States is in many respects convenient for the Government and useful to the people. Entertaining this opinion, and deeply impressed with the belief that some of the powers and privileges possessed by the existing bank are unauthorized by the Constitution, subversive of the rights of the States, and dangerous to the liberties of the people, I felt it my duty at an early period of my Administration to call the attention of Congress to the practicability of organizing an institution combining all its advantages and obviating these objections. I sincerely regret that in the act before me I can perceive none of those modifications of the bank charter which are necessary, in my opinion, to make it compatible with justice, with sound policy, or with the Constitution of our country.

The present corporate body, denominated the president, directors, and company of the Bank of the United States, will have existed at the time this act is intended to take effect twenty years. It enjoys an exclusive privilege of banking under the authority of the General Government, a monopoly of its favor and support, and, as a necessary consequence, almost a monopoly of the foreign and domestic exchange. The powers, privileges, and favors bestowed upon it in the original charter, by increasing the value of the stock far above its par value, operated as a gratuity of many millions to the stockholders.

. . . It is not our own citizens only who are to receive the bounty of our Government. More than eight millions of the stock of this bank are held by foreigners. By this act the American Republic proposes virtually to make them a present of some millions of dollars. For these gratuities to foreigners and to some of our own opulent citizens the act secures no equivalent whatever. They are the certain gains of the present stockholders under the operation of this act.

Every monopoly and all exclusive privileges are granted at the expense of the public, which ought to receive a fair equivalent. The many millions which this act proposes to bestow on the stockholders of the existing bank must come directly or indirectly out of the earnings of the American people. It is due to them, therefore, if their Government sells monopolies and exclusive privileges, that they should at least exact for them as much as they are worth in open market. The value of the monopoly in this case may be correctly ascertained. The twenty-eight millions of stock would probably be at an advance of 50 per cent, and command in market at least $42,000,000, subject to the payment of the present bonus. The present value of the monopoly, therefore, is $17,000,000 and this the act proposes to sell for three millions, payable in fifteen annual installments of $200,000 each.

This act . . . seems to be predicated on the erroneous idea that the present stockholders have a prescriptive right not only to the favor but to the bounty of Government. It appears that more than a fourth part of the stock is held by foreigners and the residue is held by a few hundred of our own citizens, chiefly of the richest class. For their benefit does this act exclude the whole American people from competition in the purchase of this monopoly and dispose of it for many millions less than it is worth. This seems the less excusable because some of our citizens not now stockholders petitioned that the door of competition might be opened, and offered to take a charter on terms much more favorable to the Government and country.

If our Government must sell monopolies, it would seem to be its duty to take nothing less than their full value, and if gratuities must be made once in fifteen or twenty years let them not be bestowed on the subjects of a foreign government nor upon a designated and favored class of men in our own country. It is but justice and good policy, as far as the nature of the case will admit, to confine our favors to our own fellow- citizens, and let each in his turn enjoy an opportunity to profit by our bounty. In the bearings of the act before me upon these points I find ample reasons why it should not become a law.

. . . By documents submitted to Congress at the present session it appears that on the 1st of January, 1832, of the twenty-eight millions of private stock in the corporation, $8,405,500 were held by foreigners, mostly of Great Britain. The amount of stock held in the nine Western and South-western States is $140,200, and in the four Southern States is $5,623,100, and in the Middle and Eastern States is about $13,522,000. The profits of the bank in 1831, as shown in a statement to Congress, were about $3,455,598; of this there accrued in the nine Western States about $1,640,048; in the four Southern States about $352,507, and in the Middle and Eastern States about $1,463,041. As little stock is held in the West, it is obvious that the debt of the people in that section to the bank is principally a debt to the Eastern and foreign stockholders; that the interest they pay upon it is carried into the Eastern States and into Europe, and that it is a burden upon their industry and a drain of their currency, which no country can bear without inconvenience and occasional distress.

In another of its bearings this provision is fraught with danger. Of the twenty-five directors of this bank five are chosen by the Government and twenty by the citizen stockholders. From all voice in these elections the foreign stockholders are excluded by the charter. In proportion, therefore, as the stock is transferred to foreign holders the extent of suffrage in the choice of directors is curtailed. Already almost a third of the stock in foreign hands and not represented in elections. It is constantly passing out of the country, and this act will accelerate its departure. The entire control of the institution would necessarily fall into the hands of a few citizen stockholders, and the ease with which the object would be accomplished would be a temptation to designing men to secure that control in their own hands by monopolizing the remaining stock. There is danger that a president and directors would then be able to elect themselves from year to year, and without responsibility or control manage the whole concerns of the bank during the existence of its charter. It is easy to conceive that great evils to our country and its institutions might flow from such a concentration of power in the hands of a few men irresponsible to the people. . . . Their power would be great whenever they might choose to exert it; but if this monopoly were regularly renewed every fifteen or twenty years on terms proposed by themselves, they might seldom in peace put forth their strength to influence elections or control the affairs of the nation. But if any private citizen or public functionary should interpose to curtail its powers or prevent a renewal of its privileges, it can not be doubted that he would be made to feel its influence.

. . . It is maintained by the advocates of the bank that its constitutionality in all its features ought to be considered as settled by precedent and by the decision of the Supreme Court. To this conclusion I can not assent. Mere precedent is a dangerous source of authority, and should not be regarded as deciding questions of constitutional power except where the acquiescence of the people and the States can be considered as well settled. . . . The bank is professedly established as an agent of the executive branch of the Government, and its constitutionality is maintained on that ground. Neither upon the propriety of present action nor upon the provisions of this act was the Executive consulted. It has had no opportunity to say that it neither needs nor wants an agent clothed with such powers and favored by such exemptions. There is nothing in its legitimate functions which makes it necessary or proper. Whatever interest or influence, whether public or private, has given birth to this act, it can not be found either in the wishes or necessities of the executive department, by which present action is deemed premature, and the powers conferred upon its agent not only unnecessary, but dangerous to the Government and country.

It is to be regretted that the rich and powerful too often bend the acts of government to their selfish purposes. Distinctions in society will always exist under every just government. Equality of talents, of education, or of wealth can not be produced by human institutions. In the full enjoyment of the gifts of Heaven and the fruits of superior industry, economy, and virtue, every man is equally entitled to protection by law; but when the laws undertake to add to these natural and just advantages artificial distinctions, to grant titles, gratuities, and exclusive privileges, to make the rich richer and the potent more powerful, the humble members of society—the farmers, mechanics, and laborers—who have neither the time nor the means of securing like favors to themselves, have a right to complain of the injustice of their Government. There are no necessary evils in government. Its evils exist only in its abuses. If it would confine itself to equal protection, and, as Heaven does its rains, shower its favors alike on the high and the low, the rich and the poor, it would be an unqualified blessing. In the act before me there seems to be a wide and unnecessary departure from these just principles.

Nor is our Government to be maintained or our Union preserved by invasions of the rights and powers of the several States. In thus attempting to make our General Government strong we make it weak. Its true strength consists in leaving individuals and States as much as possible to themselves—in making itself felt, not in its power, but in its beneficence; not in its control, but in its protection; not in binding the States more closely to the center, but leaving each to move unobstructed in its proper orbit.

Experience should teach us wisdom. Most of the difficulties our Government now encounters and most of the dangers which impend over our Union have sprung from an abandonment of the legitimate objects of Government by our national legislation, and the adoption of such principles as are embodied in this act. Many of our rich men have not been content with equal protection and equal benefits, but have besought us to make them richer by act of Congress. By attempting to gratify their desires we have in the results of our legislation arrayed section against section, interest against interest, and man against man, in a fearful commotion which threatens to shake the foundations of our Union. It is time to pause in our career to review our principles, and if possible revive that devoted patriotism and spirit of compromise which distinguished the sages of the Revolution and the fathers of our Union. If we can not at once, in justice to interests vested under improvident legislation, make our Government what it ought to be, we can at least take a stand against all new grants of monopolies and exclusive privileges, against any prostitution of our Government to the advancement of the few at the expense of the many, and in favor of compromise and gradual reform in our code of laws and system of political economy.

I have now done my duty to my country. If sustained by my fellow-citizens, I shall be grateful and happy; if not, I shall find in the motives which impel me ample grounds for contentment and peace. In the difficulties which surround us and the dangers which threaten our institutions there is cause for neither dismay nor alarm. For relief and deliverance let us firmly rely on that kind Providence which I am sure watches with peculiar care over the destinies of our Republic, and on the intelligence and wisdom of our countrymen. Through His abundant goodness and their patriotic devotion our liberty and Union will be preserved.

ANDREW JACKSON

DOCUMENT 2

Godey's Lady's Book
Promotes Domestic Ideology

Context: During the first half of the nineteenth century, scores of advice books, women's magazines, and sentimental novels outlined the tenets of domestic ideology. Domestic ideology held the women possessed talents and virtues bested suited for the home. In contrast to men, who were often portrayed as cold, calculating, and competitive, domestic ideology viewed women as pious, sentimental, and caring. *Godey's Lady's Book*, which circulated among northern middle-class women, was a particularly well known exponent of domestic ideology.

Questions to Consider: How would you describe the tone of these selections? In what ways did domestic ideology limit women's power within society? (Notice that one selection explicitly mentions the women's rights movement). In what ways might women use domestic ideology to exert more influence in political and social matters? In what ways do the selections suggest that nineteenth-century Americans were concerned about the strength of republican "virtue" in their society?

"Female Education" (December, 1830)

A YOUNG lady may excel in speaking French and Italian; may repeat a few passages from the volume of extracts; play like a professor, and sing like a siren; have her dressing-room decorated with her own drawing tables, stands, flower pots, screens and cabinets; nay, she may dance like Semphronia herself, and yet we shall insist, that she may have been very badly educated. I am far from meaning to set no value whatever on any or all of these qualifications; they are all of them elegant, and many of them tend to the perfecting of a polite education. These things, in their measure and degree may be done; but there are others which should not be left undone. Many things are becoming, but "one thing is needful." Besides, as the world seems to be fully apprised of the value of whatever tends to embellish life, there is less occasion here to insist on its importance. But, though a well-bred young lady may lawfully learn most of the fashionable arts, yet, let me ask, does it seem to be the true end of education, to make women of fashion dancers, singers, players, painters, actresses, sculptors, gilders, varnishers, engravers, and embroiderers?

Most men are commonly destined to some profession, and their minds are, consequently, turned each to its respective object. Would it not be strange if they were called out to exercise their profession, or set up their trade, with only a little general knowledge of the trades and professions of all other men, and without any previous definite application to their own peculiar calling? The profession of ladies, to which the bent of their instruction should be turned, is that of daughters, wives, mothers, and mistresses of families. They should be, therefore, trained with a view to these several conditions, and be furnished with ideas, and principles, and qualifications, and habits, ready to be applied and appropriated, as occasion may demand, to each of these respective situations.

Though the arts; which merely embellish life, must claim admiration, when a man of sense comes to marry, it is a companion whom he wants, and not an artist. It is not merely a creature who can paint and play, and sing, and draw, and dress, and dance: it is a being who can comfort and counsel him; one who can reason, and reflect, and feel, and judge, and discourse, and discriminate; one who can assist him in his affairs, lighten his cares, soothe his sorrows, purify his joys, strength his principles, and educate his children. Such is the woman who is fit for a wife, a mother, and a mistress of a family.

"Editors' Table" (February 1841)

"And savage winter rules the year."

THERE is no month when this iron sceptre is so heavily felt as during the present one. February is cold, rugged, inhospitable, and if it were not for St. Valentine's day, would scarcely relax his frozen features with a smile through his whole reign. . . . And yet his one glorious day—the birthday of Washington –is it not sufficient to hallow this month to the Americans as one of the most important in our history? There seems something in the very gloom and atmosphere of the season, congenial with the greatness won by a good man—for such superiority is almost always gained by sacrifices and sufferings severe as the blighting storm; through enmities and envyings bitter as the cold wind laden with frost and snow. And this discipline it is which forms the true hero.

"In the rough school of billows, clouds, and storms,
Nursed and matur'd, the pilot learns his art;
Thus Fate's dread ire, by many a conflict forms
The lofty spirit and enduring heart."

These are the sentiments which this month naturally inspires, and which every American mother should strive to impress on the hearts of her children. The mother of Washington, by training her son in habits of truth, obedience, temperance, industry, and self-denial, laid the foundation of his greatness in the goodness of his character. Providence directed that his talents and energies, as they unfolded, should be devoted to the service of his country, and this gave him fame—but had he never emerged from private life he would still have' been that noblest work of God—an honest man. And such, it should be the ambition of every mother to make her son—a Washington at home.

There are so many helps, as they are called, in education now-a-days, that parents are in danger of taking up the idea that their care is not really essential, or may be dispensed with at their pleasure. This is a great, and often proves a fatal mistake. True, the common schools will do much for the intellect, Sabbath schools for the knowledge of morals—but it is at home that the heart is trained to reverence that which is good, to love, and cherish the pure affections and feelings, which make the happiness of a virtuous life. And these flowers of the human soul, which, in childhood begin to open, require to be tended by the hand of maternal love. Yes, the mother's eye, which is the sunlight of the little being just beginning to grope its way through this dark "cold world of ours," must point the path, her smile must be the reward of the first efforts to duty; and her conversation, and example are the seals which stamp, for good or for evil, the character of her child.

Some reformers there are who are zealously urging the cause of "Woman's Rights." We are anxious she should be instructed to perform her duties. If she will faithfully discharge the latter, she need not trouble herself about the former. Will a good son consent that his mother—that any mother should be wronged or oppressed?

Let all mothers train up their sons to be good men, and we should have good legislators, who would speedily reform what is now unjust and injurious in our laws. And remember that good son will make good husbands and fathers, thus securing and perpetuating the happiness, and improvement of social and domestic life.

We did not anticipate the homily we have given, when beginning this paper—but the month is congenial to sober thought. We hope it will awaken such in the hearts of our readers, and that each fond mother, as she bends over the cradled sleep of her babe will resolve that, as far as lies in her power, her children shall be trained to do good.

"Remarkable Women" (November 1834)

IT is worthy of notice that those women whose excellencies have obtained the esteem of posterity, have invariably united to their more remarkable qualities, the gentleness and delicacy characteristic of the sex. Had they not done so, they would, indeed, scarcely have been loved; and love is a sentiment, with regard to the future as well as the present, which ought to be the chief ambition of a woman to excite. She should desire to be remembered, not only with admiration, but with tenderness; and, therefore, in her, nothing can compensate for the absence of those qualities which call forth affection. In looking back, then, upon our celebrated women, it is with pleasure that we remark, that kindness gave the polish to their characters. They were not the stern mentors of society; on the contrary, they were as distinguished for mildness as for any other virtue; and we feel, that besides being the objects of our esteem, they would have been, had we known them, the companions of our choice. Their humility is no less deserving of praise. There has always been an absence of pretension in superior women, which is consistent with our preconceived notions of what they ought to be, and with our own actual observation. The position which they occupy is conceded to them, not because they assume it, but because it naturally belongs to them. And the influence they exert is of a quiet and gentle kind. In considering the lives of the most illustrious among them, we cannot but be struck with the power they possessed of swaying opinion.

Contrast, for instance, the influence of Lady Russell and Mrs. Hutchinson [prominent religious writers and leaders] with ordinary women. The latter may be, indeed, allowed the control in all minor matters, may be supreme in their domestic arrangements, may be petted and indulged; but if their minds can take no higher range, they will either not be consulted in things of greater moment, or their opinion will have no weight. Yet lady Russell and Mrs. Hutchinson never obtruded their advice, or made any show of their power—their counsel was asked because it was needed, and followed because it was found to be of value. The influence of such women has not been confined to domestic life, but has embraced and adorned an ample sphere. To say nothing of the effect of their example, the success that has sometimes attended them as authors, may be considered a gratifying tribute to their usefulness. Society will acknowledge the debt it owes to those of them who, as moral and religious writers, have attracted public attention, and so materially affected the tone and habits of their sex. Of this, perhaps, the most eminent example has shed its lustre on our own day.

Sarah Grimké Calls for Greater Equality

Context: While most men and women accepted the dictates of domestic ideology, a few radical reformers rejected it. Sarah and Angelina Grimké were from a wealthy South Carolina family that owned many slaves. When visiting Philadelphia, Pennsylvania in 1819, Sarah converted to Quakerism, a religion that stressed plain dress, orderly habits, and individual conscience. Some years later she convinced Angelina to convert as well. Although the Quakers were a relatively small religious group, their unwavering opposition to slavery made them extremely influential within the abolitionist movement. The Grimkés became speakers for the American Anti-Slavery Society and advocates of women's rights.

Questions to Consider: What specific reforms did Sarah Grimké advocate to improve the condition of women in the United States? Did her arguments completely dismiss domestic ideology, or did she merely seek to reform it? Why do you think she focused so much of her attention on slave women in a letter addressing the rights of all women?

Sarah M. Grimké, "On the Condition of Women in the United States" (Brookline, 1837)

My Dear Sister,

During the early part of my life, my lot was cast among the butterflies of the fashionable world; and of this class of women, I am constrained to say, both from experience and observation, that their education is miserably deficient; that they are taught to regard marriage as the one thing needful, the only avenue to distinction; hence to attract the notice and win the attentions of men, by their external charms, is the chief business of fashionable girls. They seldom think that men will be allured by intellectual acquirements, because they find, that where any mental superiority exists, a woman is generally shunned and regarded as stepping out of her "appropriate sphere," which, in their view, is to dress, to dance, to set out to the best possible advantage her person, to read the novels which inundate the press, and which do more to destroy her character as a rational creature, than any thing else. Fashionable women regard themselves, and are regarded by men, as pretty toys or as mere instruments of pleasure; and the vacuity of mind, the heartlessness, the frivolity, which is the necessary result of this false and debasing estimate of women, can only be fully understood by those who have mingled in the folly and wickedness of fashionable life; and who have been called from such pursuits by the voice of the lord Jesus, inviting their weary and heavy laden souls to come unto Him and learn of Him, that they may find something worthy of their immortal spirit, and their intellectual powers; that they may learn the high and holy purposes of their creation, and consecrate themselves unto the service of God; and not, as is now the case, to the pleasure of man.

There is another and much more numerous class in this country, who are withdrawn by education or circumstances from the circle of fashionable amusements, but who are brought up with the dangerous and absurd idea, that marriage is a kind of preferment; and that to be able to keep their husband's house, and render his situation comfortable, is the end of her being. Much that she does and says and thinks is done in reference to this situation; and to be married is too often held up to the view of girls as the sine qua non of human happiness and human existence. For this purpose more than for any other, I verily believe the majority of girls are trained. This is demonstrated by the imperfect education which is bestowed upon them, and the little pains taken to cultivate their minds, after they leave school, by the little time allowed them for reading, and by the idea being constantly inculcated, that although all household concerns should be attended to with scrupulous punctuality at particular seasons, the improvement of their intellectual capacities is only a secondary consideration, and may serve as an occupation to fill up the odds and ends of time. In most families, it is considered a matter of far more consequence to call a girl off from making a pie, or a pudding, than to interrupt her whilst engaged in her studies. This mode of training necessarily exalts, in their view, the animal above the intellectual and spiritual nature, and teaches women to regard themselves as a kind of machinery, necessary to keep the domestic engine in order, but of little value as the intelligent companions of men.

Let no one think, from these remarks, that I regard a knowledge of housewifery as beneath the acquisition of women. Far from it: I believe that a complete knowledge of household affairs is an indispensable requisite in a woman's education—that by the mistress of a family, whether married or single, doing her duty thoroughly and understandingly, the happiness of the family is increased to an incalculable degree, as well as a vast amount of time and money saved. All I complain of is, that our education consists so almost exclusively in culinary and other manual operations. I do long to see the time, when it will no longer be necessary for women to expend so many precious hours in furnishing "a well spread table," but that their husbands will forego some of their accustomed indulgences in this way, and encourage their wives to devote some portion of their time to mental cultivation, even at the expense of having to dine sometimes on baked potatoes, or bread and butter. . . .

The influence of women over the minds and character of children of both sexes, is allowed to be far greater than that of men. This being the case by the very ordering of nature, women should be prepared by education for the performance of their sacred duties as mothers and as sisters. . . .

There is another way in which the general opinion, that women are inferior to men, is manifested, that bears with tremendous effect on the laboring class, and indeed on almost all who are obligate to earn a subsistence, whether it be by mental or physical exertion—I allude to the disproportionate value set on the time and labor of men and of women. A man who is engaged in teaching, can always, I believe, command a higher price for tuition than a woman—even when he teaches the same branches, and is not in any respect superior to the woman. This I know is the case in boarding and other schools with which I have been acquainted, and it is so in every occupation in which the sexes engage indiscriminately. As for example, in tailoring, a man has twice, or three times as much for making a waistcoat or pantaloons as a woman, although the work done by each may be equally good. In those employments which are peculiar to women, their time is estimated at only half the value of that of men. A woman who goes out to wash, works as hard in proportion as a wood sawyer, or a coal heaver, but she is not generally able to make more than half as much by a day's work. The low remuneration which women receive for their work, has claimed the attention of a few philanthropists, and I hope it will continue to do so until some remedy is applied for this enormous evil. I have known a widow, left with four or five children, to provide for, unable to leave home because her helpless babes demand her attention, compelled to earn a scanty subsistence, by making coarse shirts at 12 1/2 cents a piece, or by taking in washing, for which she was paid by some wealthy persons 12 1/2 cents per dozen. All these things evince the low estimation in which woman is held. There is yet another and more disastrous consequence arising from this unscriptural notion—women being educated, from earliest childhood, to regard themselves as inferior creatures, have not that self-respect which conscious equality would engender, and hence when their virtue is assailed, they yield to temptation with facility, under the idea that it rather exalts than debases them, to be connected with a superior being.

There is another class of women in this country, to whom I cannot refer, without feelings of the deepest shame and sorrow. I allude to our female slaves. Our southern cities are wheeled beneath a tide of pollution; the virtue of female slaves is wholly at the mercy of irresponsible tyrants, and women are bought and sold in our slave markets, to gratify the brute lust of those who bear the name of Christian. In our slave States, if amid all her degradation and ignorance, a woman desires to preserve her virtue unsullied, she is either bribed or whipped into compliance, or if she dares resist her seducer, her life by the laws of some of the slave States may be, and has actually been sacrifice to the fury of the disappointed passion. Where such laws do not exist, the power which is necessarily vested in the master over his property, leaves the defenseless slave entirely at his mercy, and the suffering of some females on this account, both physical and mental, are intense. Mr. Gholson, in the House of Delegates of Virginia, in 1832, said, "He really had been under the impression that he owned his slaves. He had lately purchased four women and ten children, in whom he thought he had obtained a great bargain; for he supposed they were his own property, as were his brood mares." But even if any laws existed in the United States, as in Athens formerly, for the protection of female slaves, they would be null and void, because the evidence of a colored person is not admitted against a white, in any of our Courts of Justice in the slave States. "In Athens, if a female slave had cause to complain of any want of respect to the laws of modesty, she could seek the protection of the temple, and demand a change of owners; and such appeals were never discountenanced, or neglected by the magistrates." In Christian America, the slave has no refuge from unbridled cruelty and lust.

S. A. Forrall, speaking of the state of morals at the South, says, "Negresses when young and likely, are often employed by the planter, or his friends, to administer to their sensual desires. This frequently is a matter of speculation, for it the offspring, a mulatto, be a handsome female, 800 or 1000 dollars may be obtained for her in the New Orleans market. It is an occurrence of no uncommon nature to see a Christian father sell his own daughter, and the brother his own sister." The following is copied by the *N. Y. Evening Star* from the *Picayune*, a paper published in New Orleans. "A very beautiful girl, belonging to the estate of John French, a deceased gambler at new Orleans, was sold a few days since for the round sum of $7,000. An ugly-looking bachelor named Gouch, a member of the Council of one of the Principalities, was the purchaser. The girl is a brunette; remarkable for her beauty and intelligence, and there was considerable contention, who should be the purchaser. She was, however, persuaded to accept Gouch, he having made her princely promises." I will add but one more from the numerous testimonies respecting the degradation of female slaves, and the licentiousness of the South. It is from the Circular of the Kentucky Union, for the moral and religious improvement of the colored race. "To the female character among our black population, we cannot allude but with feeling of the bitterest shame. A similar condition of moral pollution and utter disregard of a pure and virtuous reputation, is to be found only without the pale of Christendom. That such a state of society should exist in a Christian nation, claiming to be the most enlightened upon the earth, without calling forth any particular attention to its existence, though ever before our eyes and in our families, is a moral phenomenon at once unaccountable and disgraceful."

Nor does the colored woman suffer alone: the moral purity of the white woman is deeply contaminated. In the daily habit of seeing the virtue of her enslaved sister sacrificed without hesitancy or remorse, she looks upon the crimes of seduction and illicit intercourse without horror, and although not personally involved in the guilt, she loses that value for innocence in her own, as well as the other sex, which is one of the strongest safeguards to virtue. She lives in habitual intercourse with men, whom she knows to be polluted by licentiousness, and often is she compelled to witness in her own domestic circle, those disgusting and heart-sickening jealousies and strifes which disgraced and distracted the family of Abraham. In addition to all this, the female slaves suffer every species of degradation and cruelty, which the most wanton barbarity can inflict; they are indecently divested of their clothing, sometimes tied up and severely whipped, sometimes prostrated on the earth, while their naked bodies are torn by the scorpion lash.

> The whip on WOMAN's shrinking flesh!
> Our soil yet reddening with the stains
> Caught from her scourging warm and fresh.

Can any American woman look at these scenes of shocking licentiousness and cruelty, and fold her hands in apathy and say, "I have nothing to do with slavery"? She cannot and be guiltless.

I cannot close this letter, without saying a few words on the benefits to be derived by men, as well as women, from the opinions I advocate relative to the equality of the sexes. Many women are now supported, in idleness and extravagance, by the industry of their husbands, fathers, or brothers, who are compelled to toil out their existence, at the counting house, or in the printing office, or some other laborious occupation, while the wife and daughters and sisters take no part in the support of the family, and appear to think that their sole business is to spend the hard bought earnings of their male friends. I deeply regret such a state of things, because I believe that if women felt their responsibility, for the support of themselves, or their families it would add strength and dignity to their characters, and teach them more true sympathy for their husbands, than is now generally manifested—a sympathy which would be exhibited by actions as well as words. Our brethren may reject my doctrine, because it runs counter to common opinions, and because it wounds their pride; but I believe they would be "partakers of the benefit" resulting from the Equality of the Sexes, and would find that woman, as their equal, was unspeakably more valuable than woman as their inferior, both as a moral and an intellectual being.

Thine in the bonds of womanhood,

Sarah M. Grimké

DOCUMENT 4

The Seneca Falls Convention
Advocates Complete Equality

Context: Elizabeth Cady Stanton and Lucretia Mott were among two of the women excluded from an 1840 abolitionist conference held in London. They vowed to organize their own conference which would advance the cause of women's rights. Eight years later, they succeeded in organizing a highly successful convention in Seneca Falls, New York. Although many luminaries of the abolitionist movement attended the convention—including the black abolitionist Frederick Douglass—Stanton and Mott were the key organizers. The Seneca Falls conference launched the women's rights movement based on complete equality, including the particularly radical demand of women's suffrage.

Questions to consider: Why did Stanton chose the form of the Declaration of Independence to state her position? What specific assumptions of domestic ideology did Stanton attack? Why did the call for women's right to vote generate the most heated debate among the delegates?

The First Convention Ever Called to Discuss the Civil and Political Rights of Women
(Seneca Falls, N.Y., July 19, 20, 1848).

WOMAN'S RIGHTS CONVENTION

A Convention to discuss the social, civil, and religious condition and rights of woman will be held in the Wesleyan Chapel, at Seneca Falls, N. Y., on Wednesday and Thursday, the 19th and 20th of July current; commencing at 10 o'clock A. M.

During the first day the meeting will be exclusively for women, who are earnestly invited to attend. The public generally are invited to be present on the second day, when Lucretia Mott, of Philadelphia, and other ladies and gentlemen, will address the Convention. *

DECLARATION OF SENTIMENTS

When, in the course of human events, it becomes necessary for one portion of the family of man to assume among the people of the earth a position different from that which they have hitherto occupied, but one to which the laws of nature and of nature's God entitle them, a decent respect to the opinions of mankind requires that they should declare the causes that impel them to such a course.

We hold these truths to be self-evident: that all men and women are created equal; that they are endowed by their Creator with certain inalienable rights, that among these are life, liberty, and the pursuit of happiness; that to secure these rights governments are instituted, deriving their just powers from the consent of the governed. Whenever any form of government becomes destructive of these ends, it is the right of those who suffer from it to refuse allegiance to it, and to insist upon the institution of a new government, laying its foundation on such principles, and organizing its powers in such form as to them shall seem most likely to effect their safety and happiness. Prudence, indeed, will dictate that governments long established should not be changed for light and transient causes; and accordingly, all experience hath shown that mankind are more disposed to suffer, while evils are sufferable, than to right themselves by abolishing the forms to which they were accustomed. But when a long train of abuses and usurpations, pursuing invariably the same object evinces a design to reduce them under absolute despotism, it is their duty to throw off such government, and to provide new guards for their future security. Such has been the patient sufferance of the women under this government, and such is now the necessity which constrains them to demand the equal station to which they are entitled.

The history of mankind is a history of repeated injuries and usurpations on the part of man toward woman, having in direct object the establishment of an absolute tyranny over her. To prove this, let facts be submitted to a candid world.

He has never permitted her to exercise her inalienable right to the elective franchise.

He has compelled her to submit to laws, in the formation of which she had no voice.

He has withheld from her rights which are given to the most ignorant and degraded men both natives and foreigners.

---

* This call was published in the Seneca County Courier , July 14, 1848, without any signatures. The movers of this Convention, who drafted the call, the declaration and resolutions were Elizabeth Cady Stanton, Lucretia Mott, Martha C. Wright, Mary Ann McClintock, and Jane C. Hunt.

Having deprived her of this first right of a citizen, the elective franchise, thereby leaving her without representation in the halls of legislation, he has oppressed her on all sides.

He has made her, if married, in the eye of the law, civilly dead.

He has taken from her all right in property, even to the wages she earns.

He has made her, morally, an irresponsible being, as she can commit many crimes with impunity, provided they be done in the presence of her husband. In the covenant of marriage, she is compelled to promise obedience to her husband, he becoming, to all intents and purposes, her master—the law giving him power to deprive her of her liberty, and to administer chastisement.

He has so framed the laws of divorce, as to what shall be the proper causes of divorce; in case of separation, to whom the guardianship of the children shall be given; as to be wholly regardless of the happiness of women—the law, in all cases, going upon a false supposition of the supremacy of man, and giving all power into his hands.

After depriving her of all rights as a married woman, if single and the owner of property, he has taxed her to support a government which recognizes her only when her property can be made profitable to it.

He has monopolized nearly all the profitable employments, and from those she is permitted to follow, she receives but a scanty remuneration.

He closes against her all the avenues to wealth and distinction, which he considers most honorable to himself. As a teacher of theology, medicine, or law, she is not known.

He has denied her the facilities for obtaining a thorough education—all colleges being closed against her.

He allows her in Church, as well as State, but a subordinate position, claiming Apostolic authority for her exclusion from the ministry, and, with some exceptions, from any public participation in the affairs of the Church.

He has created a false public sentiment, by giving to the world a different code of morals for men and women, by which moral delinquencies which exclude women from society, are not only tolerated but deemed of little account in man.

He has usurped the prerogative of Jehovah himself, claiming it as his right to assign for her a sphere of action, when that belongs to her conscience and to her God.

He has endeavored, in every way that he could, to destroy her confidence in her own powers, to lessen her self-respect, and to make her willing to lead a dependent and abject life.

Now, in view of this entire disfranchisement of one-half the people of this country, their social and religious degradation, in view of the unjust laws above mentioned, and because women do feel themselves aggrieved, oppressed, and fraudulently deprived of their most sacred rights, we insist that they have immediate admission to all the rights and privileges which belong to them as citizens of the United States.

In entering upon the great work before us, we anticipate no small amount of misconception, misrepresentation, and ridicule; but we shall use every instrumentality within our power to effect our object. We shall employ agents, circulate tracts, petition the state and national legislatures, and endeavor to enlist the pulpit and the press in our behalf. We hope this Convention will be followed by a series of Conventions, embracing every part of the country.

Firmly relying upon the final triumph of the Right and the True, we do this day affix our signatures to this declaration.

Lucretia Mott, Elizabeth Cady Stanton, Eunice Newton Foote, Mary Ann McClintock, Martha C. Wright, Jane C. Hunt, Amy Post, Catharine A. F. Stebbins, Mary H. Hallowell, Charlotte Woodward, Sarah Hallowell

Richard P Hunt, Samuel D. Tilman, Elisha Foote, Frederick Douglass, Elias J. Doty, James Mott, Thomas McClintock

This Declaration was unanimously adopted and signed by 32 men and 68 women.

RESOLUTIONS

Whereas the great precept of nature is conceded to be, "that man shall pursue his own true and substantial happiness." Blackstone, in his Commentaries, remarks, that this law of Nature being coeval with mankind, and dictated by God himself, is of course superior in obligation to any other. It is binding over all the globe, in all countries, and at all times; no human laws are of any validity if contrary to this, and such of them as are valid, derive all their force, and all their validity, and all their authority, mediately and immediately, from this original; therefore,

Resolved, That such laws as conflict, in any way, with the true and substantial happiness of woman, are contrary to the great precept of nature, and of no validity; for this is "superior in obligation to any other."

Resolved, That all laws which prevent woman from occupying such a station in society as her conscience shall dictate, or which place her in a position inferior to that of man, are contrary to the great precept of nature, and therefore of no force or authority.

Resolved, That woman is man's equal—was intended to be so by the Creator—and the highest good of the race demands that she should be recognized as such.

Resolved, That the women of this country ought to be enlightened in regard to the laws under which they live, that they may no longer publish their degradation, by declaring themselves satisfied with their present position, nor their ignorance, by asserting that they have all the rights they want.

Resolved, That inasmuch as man, while claiming for himself intellectual superiority, does accord to woman moral superiority, it is pre-eminently his duty to encourage her to speak, and teach, as she has an opportunity, in all religious assemblies.

Resolved, That the same amount of virtue, delicacy, and refinement of behavior, that is required of woman in the social state, should also be required of man, and the same transgressions should be visited with equal severity on both man and woman.

Resolved, That the objection of indelicacy and impropriety, which is so often brought against woman when she addresses a public audience, comes with a very ill-grace from those who encourage, by their attendance, her appearance on the stage, in the concert, or in feats of the circus.

Resolved, That woman has too long rested satisfied in the circumscribed limits which corrupt customs and a perverted application of the Scriptures have marked out for her, and that it is time she should move in the enlarged sphere which her great Creator has assigned her.

Resolved, That it is the duty of the women of this country to secure to themselves their sacred right to the elective franchise.

Resolved, That the equality of human rights results necessarily from the fact of the identity of the race in capabilities and responsibilities.

Resolved, therefore, That, being invested by the Creator with the same capabilities, and the same consciousness of responsibility for their exercise, it is demonstrably the right and duty of woman, equally with man, to promote every righteous cause, by every righteous means; and especially in regard to the great subjects of morals and religion, it is self-evidently her right to participate with her brother in teaching them, both in private and in public, by writing and by speaking, by any instrumentalities proper to be used, and in any assemblies proper to be held; and this being a self-evident truth, growing out of the divinely implanted principles of human nature, any custom or authority adverse to it, whether modern or wearing the hoary sanction of antiquity, is to be regarded as a self-evident falsehood, and at war with the interests of mankind.

The only resolution which met opposition was the 9th, demanding the right of suffrage which, however, after a prolonged discussion was adopted. All of the meetings throughout the two days were largely attended, but this, like every step in progress, was ridiculed from Maine to Louisiana.

The First and Closing Paragraphs of Mrs. Stanton's Address, Delivered at Seneca Falls, N.Y., July 19, 20, 1848:

I should feel exceedingly diffident to appear before you at this time, having never before spoken in public, were I not nerved by a sense of right and duty, did

I not feel the time had fully come for the question of woman's wrongs to be laid before the public, did I not believe that woman herself must do this work; for woman alone can understand the height, the depth, the length, and the breadth of her own degradation. Man cannot speak for her, because he has been educated to believe that she differs from him so materially, that he cannot judge of her thoughts, feelings, and opinions by his own. Moral beings can only judge of others by themselves. The moment they assume a different nature for any of their own kind, they utterly fail. The drunkard was hopelessly lost until it was discovered that he was governed by the same laws of mind as the sober man. Then with what magic power, by kindness and love, was he raised from the slough of despond and placed rejoicing on high land.

Let a man once settle the question that a woman does not think and feel like himself, and he may as well undertake to judge of the amount of intellect and sensation of any of the animal creation as of woman's nature. He can know but little with certainty, and that but by observation.

Among the many important questions which have been brought before the public, there is none that more vitally affects the whole human family than that which is technically called Woman's Rights. Every allusion to the degraded and inferior position occupied by women all over the world has been met by scorn and abuse. From the man of highest mental cultivation to the most degraded wretch who staggers in the streets do we meet ridicule, and coarse jests, freely bestowed upon those who dare assert that woman stands by the side of man, his equal, placed here by her God, to enjoy with him the beautiful earth, which is her home as it is his, having the same sense of right and wrong, and looking to the same Being for guidance and support. So long has man exercised tyranny over her, injurious to himself and benumbing to her faculties, that few can nerve themselves to meet the storm; and so long has the chain been about her that she knows not there is a remedy.

The whole social, civil and religious condition of woman is a subject too vast to be brought within the limits of one short lecture. Suffice it to say, for the present, wherever we turn, the history of woman is sad and dark, without any alleviating circumstances, nothing from which we can draw consolation.

The world has never yet seen a truly great and virtuous nation, because in the degradation of woman the very fountains of life are poisoned at their source. It is vain to look for silver and gold from mines of copper and lead. It is the wise mother that has the wise son. So long as your women are slaves you may throw your colleges and churches to the winds. You can't have scholars and saints so long as your mothers are ground to powder between the upper and nether millstone of tyranny and lust. How seldom, now, is a father's pride gratified, his fond hopes realized, in the budding genius of his son. The wife is degraded, made the mere creature of caprice, and the foolish son is heaviness to his heart. Truly are the sins of the fathers visited upon the children to the third and fourth generation. God, in his wisdom, has so linked the whole human family together, that any violence done at one end of the chain is felt throughout its length, and here, too, is the law of restoration, as in woman all have fallen, so in her elevation shall the race be recreated. "Voices" were the visitors and advisers of Joan of Arc. Do not "voices" come to us daily from the haunts of poverty, sorrow, degradation and despair, already too long unheeded. Now is the time for the women of this country, if they would save our free institutions, to defend the right, to buckle on the armor that can best resist the keenest weapons of the enemy—contempt and ridicule. The same religious enthusiasm that nerved Joan of Arc to her work nerves us to ours. In every generation God calls some men and women for the utterance of truth, a heroic action, and our work to-day is the fulfilling of what has long since been foretold by the Prophet Joel, II, xxviii; "And it shall come to pass afterward that I will pour out my spirit upon all flesh, and your sons and your daughters shall prophecy." We do not expect our path will be strewn with the flowers of popular applause, but over the thorns of bigotry and prejudice will be our way, and on our banners will beat the dark storm clouds of opposition from those who have entrenched themselves behind the stormy bulwarks of custom and authority, and who have fortified their position by every means, holy and unholy. But we will steadfastly abide the result. Unmoved we will bear it aloft. Undauntedly we will unfurl it to the gale, for we know that the storm cannot rend from it a shred, that the electric flash will but more clearly show to us the glorious words inscribed upon it, "Equality of Rights."

Part II:
Race, Slavery, and Civil War

DOCUMENT 5

Amos Kendall Justifies Censorship of the Mail

Context: In 1835, abolitionists flooded South Carolina with mail designed to convince slaveholders of slavery's immorality. Before the mail could reach its intended recipients, South Carolinians broke into the Charleston Post Office and burned the abolitionist literature. Far from decrying such actions, Postmaster General Amos Kendall supported South Carolinians in his official report. Like most Jacksonians, Kendall was a strong supporter of state's rights and slavery.

Questions to Consider: Why did Kendall believe that the abolitionist mailings endangered public safety? How did Kendall interpret the Constitution in regards to the power of the states? What parts of the Constitution did Kendall ignore or downplay?

Postmaster General Amos Kendall's Report on the Delivery of Abolition Materials in the Southern States (1835)

A new question has arisen in the administration of this [Post Office] Department. A number of individuals have established an association in the Northern and Eastern States and raised a large sum of money, for the purpose of effecting the immediate abolition of Slavery in the Southern States. One of the means reported to has been the printing of a large mass of newspapers, pamphlets, tracts, and almanacs, containing exaggerated, and in some instances, false accounts of the treatment of slaves, illustrated with cuts [pictures] calculated to operate on the passions of the colored men, and produce discontent, assassination, and servile war. These they attempted to disseminate throughout the slaveholding states, by the agency of the public mails.

As soon as it was ascertained that the mails contained these productions, great excitement arose, particularly in Charleston, S.C., and to ensure the safety of the mail in its progress Southward, the postmaster at that place agreed to retain them in his office until he could obtain instructions from the Postmaster General. In reply to his appeal, he was informed, that it was a subject upon which the Postmaster General had no legal authority to instruct him. The question again came up from the Postmaster at New York, who had refused to send the papers by the steamboat mail to Charleston, S.C. He was also answered that the Postmaster General possessed no legal authority to give instructions on the subject; but as the undersigned had no doubt that the circumstances of the case justified the detention of the papers, he did not hesitate to say so. Important principles are involved in this question, and it merits the grave consideration of all departments of the Government.

It is universally conceded, that our States are united only for certain purposes. There are interests, in relation to which they are believed to be as independent of each other as they were before the constitution was formed. The interest which the people of some of the States have in slaves, is one of them. No State obtained by the union any right whatsoever over slavery in any other State, nor did any State lose any of its power over it, within its own borders. On this subject, therefore, if this view be correct, the States are still independent, and may fence round and protect their interest in slaves, by such laws and regulations as in their sovereign will they may deem expedient.

Nor have the people of one State any more right to interfere with this subject in another State, than they have to interfere with the internal regulations, rights of property, or domestic police, of a foreign nation. If they were to combine and send papers among the laboring population of another nation, calculated to produce discontent and rebellion, their conduct would be good ground of complaint on the part of that nation; and, in case it were not repressed by the United States, might be, if perseveringly persisted in, just cause of war. The mutual obligations of our several States to suppress attacks by their citizens on each others' reserved rights and interests, would seem to be greater, because by entering into the Union, they have lost the right of redress which belongs to nations wholly independent. Whatever claim may be set up, or maintained, to a right of free discussion within their own borders of the institutions and laws of other communities, over which they have no rightful control, few will maintain that they have a right, unless it be obtained by compact or treaty, to carry on such discussions within those communities, either orally, or by the distribution of printed papers, particularly if it be in violation of their peculiar laws, and at the hazard of their peace and existence. The constitution of the United States provides that "the citizens of each State shall be entitled to all privileges and immunities of citizens in the several

States," but this clause cannot confer on the citizens of one State, higher privileges and immunities in another, than the citizens of the latter themselves posses. It is not easy, therefore, to perceive how the citizens of the Northern States can possess or claim the privilege of carrying on discussions within the Southern States, by the distribution of printed papers, which the citizens of the latter are forbidden to circulate by their own laws.

Neither does it appear that the United States acquired, by the constitution, any power whatsoever over this subject except a right to prohibit the importation of slaves after a certain date. On the contrary, that instrument contains evidences, that one object of the Southern States, in adopting it, was to secure to themselves a more perfect control over this interest, and cause it to be respected by the sister States. In the exercise of their reserved rights, and for the purpose of protecting this interest, and ensuring the safety of their people, some of the States have passed laws, prohibiting under heavy penalties, the printing or circulation of papers like those in question, within their respective territories. It has never been alleged that these laws are incompatible with the constitution and laws of the United States. Nor does it seem possible that they can be so, because they relate to a subject over which the United States cannot rightfully assume any control under that constitution, either by law or otherwise. If these principles be sound, it will follow that the State laws on this subject, are, within the scope of their jurisdiction, the supreme laws of the land, obligatory alike on all persons, whether private citizens, officers of the State, or functionaries of the General Government.

The constitution makes it the duty of the United States "to protect each of the States against invasion; and, on application of the Legislature, or of the Executive, (when the Legislature cannot be convened) against domestic violence" There is no quarter whence domestic violence is so much to be apprehended, in some of the States, as from the servile population, operated upon by mistaken or designing men. It is to obviate danger from this quarter, that many of the State laws, in relation to the circulation of incendiary papers, have been enacted. Without claiming for the General Government the power to pass laws prohibiting discussions of any sort, as a means of protecting States from domestic violence, it may safely be assumed, that the United States have no right, through their officers or departments, knowingly to be instrumental in producing within the several states, the very mischief which the constitution commands them to repress. It would be an extraordinary construction of the powers of the general Government, to maintain that they are bound to afford the agency of their mails and post offices, to counteract the laws of the States, in the circulation of papers calculated to produce domestic violence; when it would, at the same time, be one of their most important constitutional duties to protect the States against the natural, if not necessary consequences produced by that very agency.

The position assumed by this Department, is believed to have produced the effect of withholding its agency, generally, in giving circulation to the obnoxious papers in the Southern States. Whether it be necessary more effectually to prevent, by legislative enactments, the use of the mails, as a means of evading or violating the constitutional laws of the States in reference to this portion of their reserved rights, is a question which, it appears to the undersigned, may be submitted to Congress, upon a statement of the facts, and their own knowledge of the public necessities.

George Fitzhugh Attacks Wage Labor

Context: As the abolitionists stepped up their attack on slavery, southerners took to the offensive. Rather than apologize for slavery, they defended the institution as a positive good, both for whites and the slaves themselves. George Fitzhugh, a slaveholder from Virginia, was one of the best known proponents of the positive defense of slavery. Fitzhugh's attack against wage labor, in particular, provoked outrage among many northerners.

Questions to Consider: Why did Fitzhugh equate wage slavery with "moral cannibalism"? According to Fitzhugh, why were slaves generally happier than wage workers? According to Fitzhugh's logic, should all workers—white as well as black—welcome enslavement?

George Fitzhugh, *Cannibals All!* (1859)
Chapter 1: The Universal Trade

We are, all, North and South, engaged in the White Slave Trade, and he who succeeds best, is esteemed most respectable. It is far more cruel than the Black Slave Trade, because it exacts more of its slaves, and neither protects nor governs them. We boast, that it exacts more, when we say, "that the profits made from employing free labor are greater than those from slave labor." The profits, made from free labor, are the amount of the products of such labor, which the employer, by means of the command which capital or skill gives him, takes away, exacts or "exploits" from the free laborer. The profits of slave labor are that portion of the products of such labor which the power of the master enables him to appropriate. These profits are less, because the master allows the slave to retain a larger share of the results of his own labor, than do the employers of free labor. But we not only boast that the White Slave Trade is more exacting and fraudulent (in fact, though not in intention,) than Black Slavery; but we also boast, that it is more cruel, in leaving the laborer to take care of himself and family out of the pittance which skill or capital have allowed him to retain. When the day's labor is ended, he is free, but is overburdened with the cares of family and household, which make his freedom an empty and delusive mockery. But his employer is really free, and may enjoy the profits made by others' labor, without a care, or a trouble, as to their well-being. The negro slave is free, too, when the labors of the day are over, and free in mind as well as body; for the master provides food, raiment, house, fuel, and everything else necessary to the physical well-being of himself and family. The master's labors commence just when the slave's end. No wonder men should prefer white slavery to capital, to negro slavery, since it is more profitable, and is free from all the cares and labors of black slave-holding.

Now, reader, if you wish to know yourself—to "descant on your own deformity"—read on. But if you would cherish self-conceit, self-esteem, or self-appreciation, throw down our book; for we will dispel illusions which have promoted your happiness, and shew you that what you have considered and practiced as virtue, is little better than moral Cannibalism. But you will find yourself in numerous and respectable company; for all good and respectable people are "Cannibals all," who do not labor, or who are successfully trying to live without labor, on the unrequited labor of other people: Whilst low, bad, and disreputable people, are those who labor to support themselves, and to support said respectable people besides. Throwing the negro slaves out of the account, and society is divided in Christendom into four classes: The rich, or independent respectable people, who live well and labor not at all; the professional and skillful respectable people, who do a little light work, for enormous wages; the poor hard–working people, who support every body, and starve themselves; and the poor thieves, swindlers and sturdy beggars, who live like gentlemen, without labor, on the labor of other people. The gentlemen exploit, which being done on a large scale, and requiring a great many victims, is highly respectable—whilst the rogues and beggars take so little from others, that they fare little better than those who labor.

But, reader, we do not wish to fire into the flock. "Thou art the man!" You are a Cannibal! and if a successful one, pride yourself on the number of your victims, quite as much as any Feejee chieftain, who breakfasts, dines and sups on human flesh. And your conscience smites you, if you have failed to succeed, quite as much as his, when he returns from an unsuccessful foray. Probably, you are a lawyer, or a merchant, or a doctor, who have made by your business fifty thousand dollars, and retired to live on your capital. But, mark! not to spend your capital. That would be vulgar, disreputable, criminal. That would be, to live by your own labor; for your capital is your amassed labor. That would be, to do as common working men do; for they take the pittance which their employers leave them, to live on. They live by labor; for they exchange the results of their own labor for the products of other people's labor. It is, no doubt, an honest, vulgar way of living; but not at all a respectable way. The respectable way of living is, to make other people work for you, and to pay them nothing for so doing—and to have no concern about them after their work is done. Hence, white slave–holding is much more respectable than negro slavery—for the master works nearly as hard for the negro, as he for the master. But you, my virtuous, respectable reader, exact three thousand dollars per annum from white labor, (for your income is the product of white labor,) and make not one cent of return in any form. You retain your capital, and never labor, and yet live in luxury on the labor of others. Capital commands labor, as the master does the slave. Neither pays for labor; but the master permits the slave to retain a larger allowance from the proceeds of his own labor, and hence "free labor is cheaper   than slave labor." You, with the command over labor which your capital gives you, are a slave owner—a master, without the obligations of a master. They who work for you, who create your income, are slaves, without the rights of slaves. Slaves without a master! Whilst you were engaged in amassing your capital, in seeking to become independent, you were in the White Slave Trade. To become independent, is to be able to make other people support you, without being obliged to labor for them. Now, what man in society is not seeking to attain this situation? He who attains it, is a slave owner, in the worst sense. He who is in pursuit of it, is engaged in the slave trade. You, reader, belong to the one or other class. The men without property, in free society, are theoretically in a worse condition than slaves. Practically, their condition corresponds with this theory, as history and statistics every where demonstrate. The capitalists, in free society, live in ten times the luxury and show that Southern masters do, because the slaves to capital work harder and cost less, than negro slaves.

The negro slaves of the South are the happiest, and, in some sense, the freest people in the world. The children and the aged and infirm work not at all, and yet have all the comforts and necessaries of life provided for them. They enjoy liberty, because they are oppressed neither by care nor labor. The women do little hard work, and are protected from the despotism of their husbands by their masters. The negro men and stout boys work, on the average, in good weather, not more than nine hours a day. The balance of their time is spent in perfect abandon Besides, they have their Sabbaths and holidays. White men, with so much of license and liberty, would die of ennui; but negroes luxuriate in corporeal and mental repose. With their faces upturned to the sun, they can sleep at any hour; and quiet sleep is the greatest of human enjoyments. "Blessed be the man who invented sleep." 'Tis happiness in itself—and results from contentment with the present, and confident assurance of the future. We do not know whether free laborers ever sleep. They are fools to do so; for, whilst they sleep, the wily and watchful capitalist is devising means to ensnare and exploit them. The free laborer must work or starve. He is more of a slave than the negro, because he works longer and harder for less allowance than the slave, and has no holiday, because the cares of life with him begin when its labors end. He has no liberty, and not a single right. We know, 'tis often said, air and water, are common property, which all have equal right to participate and enjoy; but this is utterly false. The appropriation of the lands carries with it the appropriation of all on or above the lands, *usque ad coelumm aut ad inferos.* A man cannot breathe the air, without a place to breathe it from, and all places are appropriated. All water is private property "to the middle of the stream," except the ocean, and that is not fit to drink.

Free laborers have not a thousandth part of the rights and liberties of negro slaves. Indeed, they have not a single right or a single liberty, unless it be the right or liberty to die. But the reader may think that he and other capitalists and employers are freer than negro slaves. Your capital would soon vanish, if you dared indulge in the liberty and abandon of negroes. You hold your wealth and position by the tenure of constant watchfulness, care and circumspection. You never labor; but you are never free.

Where a few own the soil, they have unlimited power over the balance of society, until domestic slavery comes in, to compel them to permit this balance of society to draw a sufficient and comfortable living from "terra mater." Free society, asserts the right of a few to the earth—slavery, maintains that it belongs, in different degrees, to all.

But, reader, well may you follow the slave trade. It is the only trade worth following, and slaves the only property worth owning. All other is worthless, a mere caput mortuum, except in so far as it vests the owner with the power to command the labors of others—to enslave them. Give you a palace, ten thousand acres of land, sumptuous clothes, equipage and every other luxury; and with your artificial wants, you are poorer than Robinson Crusoe, or the lowest working man, if you have no slaves to capital, or domestic slaves. Your capital will not bring you an income of a cent, nor supply one of your wants, without labor. Labor is indispensable to give value to property, and if you owned every thing else, and did not own labor, you would be poor. But fifty thousand dollars means, and is, fifty thousand dollars worth of slaves. You can command, without touching on that capital, three thousand dollars' worth of labor per annum. You could do no more were you to buy slaves with it, and then you would be cumbered with the cares of governing and providing for them. You are a slaveholder now, to the amount of fifty thousand dollars, with all the advantages, and none of the cares and responsibilities of a master.

"Property in man" is what all are struggling to obtain. Why should they not be obliged to take care of man, their property, as they do of their horses and their hounds, their cattle and their sheep. Now, under the delusive name of liberty, you work him, "from morn to dewy eve"—from infancy to old age—then turn him out to starve. You treat your horses and hounds better. Capital is a cruel master. The free slave trade, the commonest, yet the cruelest of trades.

DOCUMENT 7

William H. Seward Calls for Support of the New Republican Party

Context: William H. Seward was a Whig politician from New York who became one of the leaders of the new Republican party. Seward was favored to become the Republican nominee for president in 1860, but he lost the nomination to Abraham Lincoln because some Republicans feared he was too radical on the slavery issue. Seward would later become Lincoln's secretary of state. This speech, given in the aftermath of the Kansas-Nebraska controversy, was designed to attract antislavery Whigs and Democrats to the fledging Republican party.

Questions to Consider: What evidence did Seward present to bolster his claim that slaveholders were a threat to the political liberty of northerners? Compare Seward's speech to Andrew Jackson's veto message—are there any similarities in their rhetoric? Why did Seward invoke the Declaration of Independence and American Revolution? Did Seward show any sympathy for the slaves themselves?

William H. Seward
The Dangers of Extending Slavery, and the Contest and the Crisis. Delivered in Albany, October 12, 1855

The nation was founded on the simple and practically new principle of the equal and inalienable rights of all men, and therefore it necessarily became a republic. Other Governments, founded on the ancient principle of the inequality of men, are, by force of an equal necessity, monarchies or aristocracies. Whenever either of these kinds of Government loses by lapse of time and change of circumstances its elementary principle, whether of equality or inequality, thenceforward it takes a rapid and irresistible course toward a reorganization of the opposite kind. No one, here or elsewhere, is so disloyal to his country or to mankind as to be willing to see our republican system fail. All agree that in every case, and throughout all hazards, aristocracy must be abhorred and avoided, and republican institutions must be defended and preserved.

Think it not strange or extravagant when I say that an aristocracy has already arisen here, and that it is already undermining the Republic. An aristocracy could not arise in any country where there was no privileged class, and no special foundation on which such a class could permanently stand. On the contrary, every State, however republican its Constitution may be, is sure to become an aristocracy, sooner or later, if it has a privileged class standing firmly on an enduring special foundation; and if that class is continually growing stronger and stronger, and the unprivileged classes are continually growing weaker and weaker. It is not at all essential to a privileged class that it rest on feudal tenures, or on military command, or on ecclesiastical authority, or that its rights be hereditary, or even that it be distinguished by titles of honor. It may be even the more insidious and more dangerous for lacking all these things, because it will be less obnoxious to popular hostility.

A privileged class has existed in this country, from an early period of its settlement. Slaveholders constitute that class. They have a special foundation on which to stand—namely, personal dominion over slaves. Conscience and sound policy forbid all men alike from holding slaves, but some citizens disregard the injunction. Some of the States enforce the inhibition; other States neglect or refuse to enforce it. In all of the States, there are but three hundred and fifty thousand citizens who avail themselves of this peculiar indulgence; and those, protected by the laws of their States, constitute a privileged class. They confess themselves to be such a class, when they designate the system of Slavery as a "peculiar" institution.

The spirit of the revolutionary age was adverse to that privileged class. America and Europe were firmly engaged then in prosecuting what was expected to be a speedy, complete, and universal abolition of African Slavery. Nearly all of the privileged class admitted that Slavery as a permanent system was indefensible, and favored its removal. They asked only, what seemed by no means unreasonable, some securities against a sudden, rash, and violent removal of the evil. Under these circumstances, even the most decided opponents of Slavery consented to some provisions of the Federal Constitution which were inconsistent with the stern logic of equality that pervaded all its other parts, and pervaded the whole of the Declaration of American Independence, on which the Constitution itself was based. We are not to censure the fathers for these concessions; they had a union of the States to create, and to their ardent and generous minds the voluntary removal of Slavery, by the action of the several States themselves, without Federal interference, seemed not only certain, but close at hand.

These provisions of the Constitution were:

First: That the foreign slave trade should not be abolished before 1808.

Second: That any law or regulation which any State might establish in favor of Freedom, should not impair the legal remedy, then supposed to exist by common law, for the recapture, by legal process, in such State, of fugitives from labor or service, escaping from other States.

Third: That three-fifths of all slaves should be counted, in settling the basis of representation in the several States.

These three concessions, which in themselves seem very limited, and almost harmless are all that the fathers consciously made to the privileged class.

But privileged classes always know well how to improve even any indirect advantages which the Constitution or laws of a country afford. Such indirect advantages they acquired from two other provisions of the Constitution: 1st. That provision which makes the State authority independent and sovereign in municipal affairs, Slavery being understood to be purely municipal in its nature. 2d. That provision which, out of tenderness to the small States, gives them a representation in the Senate equal to that of the largest State. . . .

Thus we see that the American slaveholders are a privileged class, standing on a special and permanent foundation, and that they are protected in their advantages by the organic laws.

A privileged class, thus established on an exceptional principle, that is wrong in itself, and antagonistic to the fundamental principle of the Government, must necessarily be dangerous, if it be suffered to expand and aggrandize itself. . . . The invention of the cotton gin, which easily separates the seed from the fibre, has made cotton an almost exclusive agricultural staple in the States of the privileged class, and an eminent commercial staple of the whole country. The national territory has necessarily been enlarged, from time to time, to accommodate an overgrowing population and an ever-increasing commerce. Favored by these circumstances, the privileged class have at the same time found, in a home production of slaves in Maryland and Virginia and other States, a compensation for the loss of the African slave trade; and they have not been slothful in unlearning all the fears and dismissing all the timidity and conciliation which marked their conduct during and immediately after the revolutionary war. . . .

[In the 1830s] The privileged class . . . entered Texas, established Slavery there in violation of Mexican laws, detached that territory from Mexico, and organized it as an independent sovereign State. Texas, thus independent and sovereign, sought annexation to the United States. . . . A war [with Mexico] ensued, [which] transferred of the northern portion of Mexico to the United States. . . . [T]he privileged class demand either an equal partition, or that the whole should be opened to their colonization with slaves. The House of Representatives resisted these pretensions, as it had resisted similar ones before; but the Senate seconded the privileged class with its accustomed zeal. So Congress was divided, and failed to organize civil Governments for the newly acquired Mexican territories, and they were left under martial law.

You all know well the way of that memorable controversy. . . How the Missouri Compromise, which extended that Ordinance across the Mississippi, and over all Kansas and Nebraska, was made at once the authority, precedent, and formula, of the new compromise, and even declared to be an irrepealable law forever. How California, which refused to become a slave State, was admitted into the Union as a free one. How the hateful and detestable slave auctions were banished from under the eaves of the Capitol, quite across to the opposite banks of the Potomac river. And how, in consideration of these magnanimous and vast concessions made by the privileged class, it was stipulated that Slavery should be continued in the District of Columbia as long as the privileged class should require its continuance. . . .

You remember how it was solemnly stipulated that Utah and New Mexico, if the slaveholders could corrupt them, should come into the Union, in due time, as slaveholding States; and, finally, how the privileged class, so highly offended and exasperated, were brought to accept this compromise on their part, by a re-enactment of the then obsolete fugitive slave law of 1793, with the addition of the revolting features of an attempted suspension of the habeas corpus; an absolute prohibition of the trial by jury; and effective repeal of vital rules of procedure and evidence, and the substitution of commissioners in place of courts of justice, in derogation of the Constitution. . . .

Nevertheless, scarcely one year had elapsed, before the privileged class, using some of our own representatives as their instruments, broke up not only this Compromise of 1850, but even the Compromise of 1820 and the Ordinance of 1787, and obtained the declaration of Congress, that all these settlements, so far as they were adverse to the privileged class, were unconstitutional usurpations of legislative power.

I do not dwell, as others so often and so justly do, upon the atrocious usurpation of the government of Kansas by the slaveholders of Missouri, nor even on the barbarous and tyrannical code which they have established to stifle Freedom in that Territory, nor even yet on the fraudulent and nefarious connivance of the President with the usurpers. Nor will I draw into this picture, already too darkly shaded, the personal humiliations which daily come home to yourselves in the conduct of your own affairs. You are commanded by an unconstitutional law of Congress to seize and deliver up to the members of that privileged class their fugitive slaves, under pain of imprisonment and forfeiture of your estates. You may not interpose between the armed slaveholder and the wounded slave, to prevent his being murdered, without coming under arrest for treason, nor may you cover his naked and lacerated limbs except by stealth. You may not tell the freed slave who reaches your borders that he is free, without being seized by a Federal Court, and condemned, without a trial or even an accusation, to an imprisonment without bail. Your representatives in either House of Congress must speak with bated breath and humble countenance in presence of the representatives of the privileged class, lest justice be denied to your old soldiers when they claim their pensions, or to your laborers when they claim the performance of their contracts with the Government. The President of the United States is reduced to the position of a deputy of the privileged class, emptying the treasury and marshalling battalions and ships of war to dragoon you into the execution of the Fugitive Slave Law on the one hand, while he removes Governors and Judges, at their command, who attempt to maintain lawful and constitutional resistance against them in the Territory of Kansas. . . .

I will only ask, in concluding this humiliating rehearsal, whether there is not in this favored country a privileged class; whether it does not stand on an enduring foundation; whether it is not growing stronger and stronger, while the unprivileged class grows weaker and weaker; whether its further growth and extent would not be, not merely detrimental, but dangerous; and whether there is any hope to arrest that growth and extension hereafter, if the attempt shall not be made now?

The change, that has become at last so necessary, is as easy to be made as it is necessary. The whole number of slaveholders is only three hundred and fifty thousand, one-hundredth part of the entire population of the country. If you add their parents, children, immediate relatives and dependents, they are two millions— one-fifteenth part of the American people. Slavery is not, and never can be, perpetual. It will be overthrown either peacefully or lawfully under this Constitution, or it will work the subversion of the Constitution, together with its own overthrow. Then the slaveholders would perish in the struggle. The change can now be made without violence, and by the agency of the ballot-box. . . .

The will exists, because the evil has become intolerable, and the need of a remedy is universally acknowledged. What, then, is wanted? Organization. Organization! Nothing but organization. . .

How shall we organize? The evil is a national one. The power and the influence and the organization of the privileged class pervade all parts of the Union. It knows no North, no South, no East, no West. . . . Our organization, therefore, must be a national one. The means of success are national. We must restore the demoralized virtue of the nation. We must restore the principle of equality among the members of the State—the principle of the sacredness of the absolute and inherent rights of man. We want, then, an organization open to all classes of men, and that excludes none.

We want a bold, out-spoken, free-spoken organization—one that openly proclaims its principles, its purposes, and its objects—in fear of God, and not of man. . . .

It is best to take an existing organization that answers to these conditions, if we can find one; if we cannot find one such, we must create one. . . .

The Republican organization has sagaciously seen this, and magnanimously laid a new, sound, and liberal platform. . . . Its principles are equal and exact justice; its speech open, decided, and frank. Its banner is untorn in former battles, and unsullied by past errors. That is the party for us. I do not know that it will always, or even long, preserve its courage, its moderation, and its consistency. If it shall do so, it will rescue and save the country. If it, too, shall become unfaithful, as all preceding parties have done, it will, without sorrow or regret on my part, perish as they are perishing, and will give place to another truer and better one.

So long as the Republican party shall be firm and faithful to the Constitution, the Union, and the rights of Man, I shall serve it, with the reservation of that personal independence which is my birthright, but at the same time with the zeal and devotion that patriotism allows and enjoys.

DOCUMENT 8

Hinton Rowan Helper Attacks Slavery

Context: Hinton Rowan Helper was a small farmer from western North Carolina, a region of the South that had very few slaves. His economic critique of the South reflected the sentiments of northern free labor ideology. Helper's book—*The Impending Crisis* (1857)—was banned in some southern states, but was extremely popular in the North. The Republican party published an abridged edition that many congressmen endorsed.

Questions to Consider: What is the basis for Helper's critique of the slavery? Does Helper show any sympathy for the slaves themselves? Why did southern slaveholders find Helper's arguments particularly dangerous?

Hinton Rowan Helper, *The Impending Crisis* (1857)

Comparisons are at the bottom of all philosophy. It is by comparisons that we ascertain the difference which exists between things, and it is by comparisons, also, that we ascertain the general features of things, and it is by comparisons that we reach general propositions. Without comparisons we never can generalize. Without comparisons we never could go beyond the knowledge of isolated, disconnected facts. . . .

NEW YORK AND VIRGINIA

In 1790, when the first census was taken, New York contained 340,120 inhabitants; at the same time the population of Virginia was 748,308, being more than twice the number of New York. Just sixty years afterward, as we learn from the census of 1850, New York had a population of 3,097,394; while that of Virginia was only 1,421,661, being less than half the number of New York! In 1791, the exports of New York amounted to $2,505,465; the exports of Virginia amounted to $3,130,865. In 1852, the exports of New York amounted to $87,484,456; the exports of Virginia, during the same year, amounted to only $2,724,657. In 1790, the imports of New York and Virginia were about equal; in 1853, the imports of New York amounted to the enormous sum of $178,270,999: while those of Virginia, for the same period, amounted to the comparatively pitiful aggregate of only $399,004. In 1850, the products of manufactures, mining and the mechanics arts in New York amounted to $237,597,249; those of Virginia amounted to only $29,705,387. At the taking of the last census, the value of real and personal property in Virginia, including Negroes, was $391,646,438; that of New York, exclusive of any monetary valuation of human beings, was $1,080,309,216. In August, 1856, the real and personal estate assessed in the City of New York amounted in valuation to $511,740,491, showing that New York City alone is worth far more than the whole State of Virginia. . . .

The cash value of all the farms, farming implements and machinery in Virginia, in 1850, was $223,423,315; the value of the same in New York, in the same year, was $576,631,568. In about the same ratio does the value of the agricultural products and live stock of New York exceed the value of the agricultural products and live stock of Virginia. But we will pursue this humiliating comparison no further. With feelings mingled with indignation and disgust, we turn from the picture, and will now pay our respects to

Massachusetts and North Carolina

In 1790, Massachusetts contained 378,717 inhabitants; in the same year North Carolina contained 393,751; in 1850, the population of Massachusetts was 994,514, all freemen; while that of North Carolina was only 869,039, of whom 288,548 were slaves. Massachusetts has an area of only 7,800 square miles; the area of North Carolina is 50,704 square miles, which, though less than Virginia, is considerably larger than the State of New York. Massachusetts and North Carolina each have a harbor, Boston and Beaufort, which harbors, with the States that back them, are, by nature, possessed of about equal capacities and advantages for commercial and manufacturing enterprise. Boston has grown to be the second commercial city in the Union; her ships, freighted with the useful and unique inventions and manufactures of her ingenious artisans and mechanics, and bearing upon their stalwart arms the majestic flag of our country, glide triumphantly through the winds and over the waves of every ocean. She has done, and is now doing, great honor to herself, her State and the nation, and her name and fame are spoken with reverence in the remotest regions of the earth. How is it with Beaufort, in North Carolina, whose harbor is said to be the safest and most commodious anywhere to be found on the Atlantic coast south of the harbor of New York, and but little inferior to that? Has anybody ever heard of her? Do the masts of her ships ever cast a shadow on foreign waters? Upon what distant or benighted shore have her merchants and mariners ever hoisted our national ensign, or spread the arts of civilization and peaceful industry? What changes worthy of note have taken place in the physical features of her superficies since "the evening and the morning were the third day?" But we will make no further attempt to draw a comparison between the populous, wealthy, and renowned city of Boston and the obscure, despicable little village of Beaufort, which, notwithstanding "thee placid bosom of its deep and well-protected harbor," has no place in the annals or records of the country, and has scarcely ever been hear fifty miles from home?!

In 1856, the real and personal estate assessed in the city of Boston amounted in valuation to within a fraction of $250,000,000, showing conclusively that so far as dollars and cents are concerned, that single city could buy the whole State of North Carolina, and by right of purchase, if sanctioned by the Constitution of the United States, and by State Constitutions, hold her as a province. In 1850, there were in Massachusetts 1,861 native white and free colored persons over twenty years of age who could not read and write; in the same year, the same class of persons in North Carolina numbered 80,063; while her 288,548 slaves were, by legislative enactments, kept in a state of absolute ignorance and unconditional subordination.

Hoping, however, and believing, that a large majority of the most respectable and patriotic citizens of North Carolina have resolved, or will soon resolve, with unyielding purpose, to cast aside the great obstacle that impedes their progress, and bring into action a new policy which will lead them from poverty and ignorance to wealth and intellectual greatness, and which will shield them not only from the rebukes of their own consciences, but also from the just reproaches of the civilized world, we will, for the present, in deference to their feelings, forbear the further enumeration of these degrading disparities, and turn our attention to

PENNSYLVANIA AND SOUTH CAROLINA

An old gentleman, now residing in Charleston, told us, but a short while ago, that he had a distinct recollection of the time when Charleston imported foreign fabrics for the Philadelphia trade, and when, on a certain occasion, his mother went into a store on Market street to select a silk dress for herself, the merchant, unable to please her fancy, persuaded her to postpone the selection for a few days, or until the arrival of a new stock of superb styles and fashions which he had recently purchased in the metropolis of South Carolina. This was all very proper. Charleston had a spacious harbor, a central position, and a mild climate; and from priority of settlement and business connections, to say nothing of other advantages, she enjoyed greater facilities for commercial transactions than Philadelphia. She had a right to get custom wherever she could find it, and in securing so valuable a customer as the Quaker City, she exhibited no small degree of laudable enterprise. . . .

A most unfortunate day was that for the Palmetto State, and indeed for the whole South, when the course of trade was changed, and she found herself the retailer of foreign and domestic goods, imported and vended by wholesale merchants at the North. Philadelphia ladies no longer look to the South for late fashions, and fine silks and satins; no Quaker dame now wears drab apparel of Charleston importation. Like all other centres of trade in our disreputable part of the confederacy, the commercial emporium of South Carolina is sick and impoverished; her silver cord has been loosed; her golden bowl has been broken; and her unhappy people, without proper or profitable employment, poor in pocket, and few in number, go mourning or loafing about the streets. Her annual importations are actually less now than they were a century ago, when South Carolina was the second commercial province on the continent, Virginia being the first. . . .

In 1850, the products of manufactures, mining, and the mechanic arts, in Pennsylvania, amounted to $155,044,910; the products of the same in South Carolina, amounted to only $7,063,513. As shown by the census report of 1850, which was prepared under the superintendence of a native of South Carolina, who certainly will not be suspected of injustice to his own section—the cash value of all the farms, farming implements, and machinery in Pennsylvania, was $422,598,640; the value of the same in South Carolina, in the same year, was only $86,518,038. From a compendium of the same census, we learn that the value of all the real and personal property in Pennsylvania, actual property, no slaves, amounted to $729,144,998; the value of the same in South Carolina, including the estimated— we were about to say fictitious value of 384,925 Negroes, amounted to only $288,257,694. We have not been able to obtain the figures necessary to show the exact value of the real and personal estate in Philadelphia, but the amount is estimated to be not less than $300,000,000; and as, in 1859, there were 408,762 free inhabitants in the single city of Philadelphia, against 283,544 of the same class in the whole State of South Carolina, it is quite evident that the former is more powerful than the latter, and far ahead of her in all the elements of genuine and permanent superiority.

In Pennsylvania, in 1850, the annual income of public schools amounted to $1,348,249; the same in South Carolina, in the same year, amounted to only $200,600; in the former State there were 393 libraries other than private, in the latter only 26; in Pennsylvania 310 newspapers and periodicals were published, circulating 84,898,672 copies annually; in South Carolina only 46 newspapers and periodicals were published, circulating but 7,145,930 copies per annum.

The incontrovertible facts we have thus far presented are, we think, amply sufficient, both in number and magnitude, to bring conviction to the mind of every candid reader, that there is something wrong, socially, politically and morally wrong, in the policy under which the South has so long loitered and languished. Else, how is it that the North, under the operations of a policy directly the opposite of ours, has surpassed us in almost everything great and good, and left us standing before the world, an object of merited reprehension and derision? For one, we are heartily ashamed of the inexcusable weakness, inertia and dilapidation everywhere so manifest throughout our native section; but the blame properly attaches itself to an usurping minority of the people, and we are determined that it shall rest where it belongs. More on this subject, however, after a brief but general survey of the inequalities and disparities that exist between those two grand divisions of the country.

Why the North Has Surpassed the South

And now that we have come to the very heart and soul of our subject, we feel no disposition to mince matters, but mean to speak plainly and to the point, without any equivocation, mental reservation, or secret evasion whatever. The son of a venerated parent, who, while he lived, was a considerate and merciful slaveholder, a native of the South, born and bred in North Carolina, of a family whose home has been in the valley of the Yadkin for nearly a century and a Southerner by instinct and by all the influences of thought, habits and kindred, and with the desire and fixed purpose to reside permanently within the limits of the South, and with the expectation of dying there also—we feel that we have the right to express our opinion, however humble or unimportant it may be, on any and every question that affects the public good; and, so help us God, "sink or swim, live or die, survive or perish," we are determined to exercise that right with manly firmness, and without fear, favor or affection. And now to the point. In our opinion, an opinion which has been formed from data obtained by assiduous researches, and comparisons, from laborious investigation, logical reasoning, and earnest reflection, the causes which have impeded the progress and prosperity of the South, which have dwindled our commerce and other similar pursuits, into the most contemptible insignificance; sunk a large majority of our people in galling poverty and ignorance, rendered a small minority conceited and tyrannical, and driven the rest away from their homes; entailed upon us a humiliating dependence on the Free States; disgraced us in the recesses of our own souls and brought us under reproach in the eyes of all civilized and enlightened nations—may all be traced to one common source, and there find solution in the most hateful and horrible word, that was ever incorporated into the vocabulary of human economy—slavery.

Reared amidst the institution of slavery, believing it to be wrong both in principle and in practice, and having seen and felt its evil influences upon individuals, communities and states, we deem it a duty, no less than a privilege, to enter our protest against it, and, as a Southern man, to use all constitutional means and our most strenuous efforts to overturn and abolish it. Our repugnance to slavery springs from no one-sided idea, or sickly sentimentality. We have not been hasty in making up our mind on the subject; we have jumped at no conclusions; we have acted with perfect calmness and deliberation; we have carefully considered, and examined the reasons for and against the institution, and have also taken into account the probable consequences of our decision. The more we investigate the matter, the deeper becomes the conviction that we are right; and with this to impel and sustain us, we pursue our labor with love, with hope, and with constantly renewing vigor. That we shall encounter opposition we consider as certain; perhaps we may even be subjected to insult and violence. From the cruel and conceited defenders of slavery we could look for nothing less. But we shall shrink from no responsibility, and do nothing unbecoming a man; we know how to repel indignity, and if assaulted, shall not fail to make the blow recoil upon the aggressor's head. . . .

But, thanks to heaven, we have no ominous forebodings of the result of the contest now pending between Liberty and Slavery in this confederacy. Though neither a prophet nor the son of a prophet, our vision is sufficiently penetrative to divine the future so far as to be able to see that the "peculiar institution" has but a short and, as heretofore, inglorious existence before it. Time, the righter of every wrong, is ripening events for the desired consummation of our labors and the fulfillment of our cherished hopes. Each revolving year brings nearer the inevitable crisis. The sooner it comes the better; may heaven, through our humble efforts, hasten its advent. The first and most sacred duty of every Southerner, who has the honor and the interest of his country at heart, is to declare himself an unqualified and uncompromising opponent of slavery. No conditional or half-way declaration will avail; no mere threatening demonstration will succeed. With those who desire to be instrumental in bringing about the triumph of liberty over slavery, there should be neither evasion, vacillation, nor equivocation. We should listen to no modifying terms or compromises that may be proposed by the proprietors of the unprofitable and ungodly institution. Nothing short of the complete abolition of slavery can save the South from falling into the vortex of utter ruin. Too long have we yielded a submissive obedience to the tyrannical domination of an inflated oligarchy; too long have we tolerated their arrogance and self-conceit; too long have we submitted to their unjust and savage exactions. Let us now wrest from them the sceptre of power, establish liberty and equal rights throughout the land, and henceforth and forever guard our legislative halls from the pollutions and usurpations of pro-slavery demagogues.

DOCUMENT 9

Republicans Adopt a Strong Anti-Slavery Platform

Context: When the Republican Party met in 1860, it faced the difficult task of satisfying its abolitionist wing while avoiding positions that would alienate more conservative voters. The resulting platform attempted to walk that fine line. Supporting this platform, Republican nominee Abraham Lincoln carried every northern state except New Jersey.

Questions to Consider: Did the Republican party endorse the abolition of slavery or repeal of the Fugitive Slave Act? Can you locate the veiled references to the Dred Scott Case and John Brown's Raid? What was ultimately more important to the Republican Party: economic issues such as the tariff and internal improvements, or preventing the expansion of slavery?

Republican National Platform, Adopted at Chicago, 1860

Resolved, That we, the delegated representatives of the Republican electors of the United States, in Convention assembled, in discharge of the duty we owe to our constituents and our country, unite in the following declarations:

That the history of the nation, during the last four years, has fully established the propriety and necessity of the organization and perpetuation of the Republican party, and that the causes which called it into existence are permanent in their nature, and now, more than ever before, demand its peaceful and constitutional triumph.

That the maintenance of the principles promulgated in the Declaration of Independence and embodied in the Federal Constitution, "That all men are created equal; that they are endowed by their Creator with certain inalienable rights; that

49

among these are life, liberty, and the pursuit of happiness; that to secure these rights, governments are instituted among men, deriving their just powers from the consent of the governed," is essential to the preservation of our Republican institutions; and that the Federal Constitution, the Rights of the States, and the Union of the States, must and shall be preserved.

That to the Union of the States this nation owes its unprecedented increase in population, its surprising development of material resources, its rapid augmentation of wealth, its happiness at home and its honor abroad; and we hold in abhorrence all schemes for Disunion, come from whatever source they may: And we congratulate the country that no Republican member of Congress has uttered or countenanced the threats of Disunion so often made by Democratic members without rebuke and with applause from their political associates; and we denounce those threats of Disunion, in case of a popular overthrow of their ascendancy, as denying the vital principles of a free government, and as an avowal of contemplated treason, which it is the imperative duty of an indignant People sternly to rebuke and forever silence.

That the maintenance inviolate of the rights of the States, and especially the right of each State to order and control its own domestic institutions according to its own judgment exclusively, is essential to that balance of powers on which the perfection and endurance of our political fabric depends; and we denounce the lawless invasion by armed force of the soil of any State or Territory, no matter under what pretext, as among the gravest of crimes.

That the present Democratic Administration has far exceeded our worst apprehensions, in its measureless subservience to the exactions of a sectional interest, as especially evinced in its desperate exertions to force the infamous Lecompton Constitution upon the protesting people of Kansas; in construing the personal relation between master and servant to involve an unqualified property in persons; in its attempted enforcement, everywhere, on land and sea, through the intervention of Congress and of the Federal Courts of the extreme pretensions of a purely local interest; and in its general and unvarying abuse of the power entrusted to it by a confiding people.

That the people justly view with alarm the reckless extravagance which pervades every department of the Federal Government; that a return to rigid economy and accountability is indispensable to arrest the systematic plunder of the public treasury by favored partisans, while the recent startling developments of frauds and corruptions at the Federal metropolis, show that an entire change of administration is imperatively demanded.

That the new dogma, that the Constitution, of its own force, carries Slavery into any or all of the Territories of the United States, is a dangerous political heresy, at variance with the explicit provisions of that instrument itself, with contemporaneous exposition, and with legislative and judicial precedent; is revolutionary in its tendency, and subversive of the peace and harmony of the country. . . .

That in the recent vetoes, by their Federal Governors, of the acts of the Legislatures of Kansas and Nebraska, prohibiting Slavery in those Territories, we find a practical illustration of the boasted Democratic principle of Non- Intervention and Popular Sovereignty, embodied in the Kansas-Nebraska bill, and a demonstration of the deception and fraud involved therein.

That Kansas should, of right, be immediately admitted as a State under the Constitution recently formed and adopted by her people, and accepted by the House of Representatives.

That, while providing revenue for the support of the General Government by duties upon imports, sound policy requires such an adjustment of these imposts as to encourage the development of the industrial interest of the whole country; and we commend that policy of national exchanges which secures to the working men liberal wages, to agriculture remunerative prices, to mechanics and manufactures an adequate reward for their skill, labor, and enterprise, and to the nation commercial prosperity and independence.

That we protest against any sale or alienation to others of the Public Lands held by actual settlers, and against any view of the Homestead policy which regards the settlers as paupers or suppliants for public bounty; and we demand the passage by Congress of the complete and satisfactory Homestead measure which has already passed the House. . . .

That appropriations by Congress for River and Harbor improvements of a National character, required for the accommodation and security of an existing commerce, are authorized by the Constitution, and justified by the obligations of Government to protect the lives and property of its citizens.

That a Railroad to the Pacific Ocean is imperatively demanded by the interest of the whole country; that the Federal Government ought to render immediate and efficient aid in its construction; and that, as preliminary thereto, a daily Overland Mail should be promptly established. . . .

DOCUMENT 10

South Carolinians Justify Secession

Context: With the election of Abraham Lincoln in November of 1860, South Carolinians moved quickly to leave the Union. The secession movement had overwhelming support in South Carolina, which had traditionally been the most radical of the southern states. This address solicited the support of other southern states. By February of 1861, all of the "cotton" states (South Carolina, Georgia, Florida, Alabama, Mississippi, Louisiana, and Texas) had left the Union.

Questions to Consider: What parallels did South Carolinians draw between the American Revolution and their own cause? What view of democracy is embedded in this address? In what ways did this document highlight the profound mistrust between northerners and southerners?

"The Address of the People of South Carolina, Assembled in Convention, to the People of the Slaveholding States of the United States" (December 1860)

It is seventy-three years since the Union between the United States was made by the Constitution of the United States. During this time, their advance in wealth, prosperity and power has been with scarcely a parallel in the history of the world. The great object of their Union was defense against external aggression of more powerful nations; which object is now attained, from their mere progress in power. Thirty-one millions of people, with a commerce and navigation which explore every sea, and with agricultural productions which are necessary to every civilized people, command the friendship of the world. But unfortunately, our internal peace has not grown with our external prosperity. Discontent and contention have moved in the bosom of the Confederacy for the last thirty-five years. . . .

The one great evil, from which all other evils have flowed, is the overthrow of the Constitution of the United States. The Government of the United States is no longer the Government of Confederated Republics, but of a consolidated Democracy. It is no longer a free government, but a Despotism. It is, in fact, such a Government as Great Britain attempted to set over our fathers; and which was resisted and defeated by a seven years' struggle for independence.

The Revolution of 1776 turned upon one great principle of self-government and self-taxation; the criterion of self-government. Where the interests of two people united together under one Government, are different, each must have the power to protect its interests by the organization of the Government, or they cannot be free. The interests of Great Britain and of the Colonies were different and antagonistic. Great Britain was desirous of carrying out the policy of all nations towards their Colonies, of making them tributary to her wealth and power. She had vast and complicated relations with the whole world. Her policy towards her North American Colonies was to identify them with her in all these complicated relations; and to make them bear, in common with the rest of the Empire, the full burden of her obligations and necessities. She had a vast public debt; she had an European policy and an Asiatic policy, which had occasioned the accumulation of her public debt; and which kept her in continual wars. The North American Colonies saw their interests, political and commercial, sacrificed by such a policy. Their interests required that they should not be identified with the burdens and wars of the mother country. They had been settled under Charters, which gave them self-government; at least so far as their property was concerned. They had taxed themselves, and had never been taxed by the Government of Great Britain. To make them a part of a consolidated Empire, the Parliament of Great Britain determined to assume the power of legislating for the Colonies in all cases whatsoever. Our ancestors resisted the pretension. They refused to be a part of the consolidated Government of Great Britain.

The Southern States now stand exactly in the same position towards the Northern States that the Colonies did towards Great Britain. The Northern States, having the majority in Congress, claim the same power of omnipotence in legislation as the British Parliament. "The General Welfare," is the only limit to the legislation of either; and the majority in Congress, as in the British Parliament, are the sole judges of the expediency of the legislation this "General Welfare" requires. Thus, the Government of the United States has become a consolidated Government; and the people of the Southern States are compelled to meet the very despotism their fathers threw off in the Revolution of 1776.

The consolidation of the Government of Great Britain over the Colonies, was attempted to be carried out by the taxes. The British Parliament undertook to tax the Colonies, to promote British interests. Our fathers resisted this pretension. They claimed the right of self-taxation through their Colonial Legislatures. They were not represented in the British Parliament, and, therefore, could not rightly be taxed by its Legislation. The British Government, however, offered them a representation in Parliament; but it was not sufficient to enable them to protect themselves from the majority, and they refused it. Between taxation without any representation, and taxation without a representation adequate to protection, there was no difference. In neither case would the Colonies tax themselves. Hence, they refused to pay the taxes laid by the British Parliament.

And so with the Southern States, towards the Northern States, in the vital matter of taxation. They are in a minority in Congress. Their representation in Congress is useless to protect them against unjust taxation; and they are taxed by the people of the North for their benefit, exactly as the people of Great Britain taxed our ancestors in the British Parliament for their benefit. For the last forty years, the taxes laid by the Congress of the United States, have been laid with a view of subserving the interests of the North. The people of the South have been taxed by duties on imports, not for revenue, but for an object inconsistent with revenue—to promote, by prohibitions, Northern interests in the productions of their mines and manufactures.

There is another evil, in the condition of the Southern towards the Northern States, which our ancestors refused to bear towards Great Britain. Our ancestors not only taxed themselves, but all the taxes collected from them, were expended amongst them. Had they submitted to the pretensions of the British Government, the taxes collected from them would have been expended in other parts of the British Empire. They were fully aware of the effect of such a policy in impoverishing the people from whom taxes are collected, and in enriching those who receive the benefit of their expenditure. To prevent the evils of such a policy was one of the motives which drove them on to revolution. Yet this British policy has been fully realized towards the Southern States by the Northern States. The people of the Southern States are not only taxed for the benefit of the Northern States, but after the taxes are collected, three-fourths of them are expended at the North. This cause, with others, connected with the operation of the General Government, has made the cities of the South provincial. Their growth is paralyzed; they are mere suburbs of Northern cities. The agricultural productions of the South are the basis of the foreign commerce of the United States; yet Southern cities do not carry it on. Our foreign trade is almost annihilated.

No man can, for a moment, believe that our ancestors intended to establish over their posterity, exactly the same sort of Government they had overthrown. The great object of the Constitution of the United States, in its internal operation, was, doubtless, to secure the great end of the Revolution—a limited free Government—a Government limited to those matters only, which were general and common to all portions of the United States. All sectional or local interests were to be left to the States. By no other arrangement would they obtain free Government, by a Constitution common to so vast a Confederacy. Yet, by gradual and steady encroachments on the part of the people of the North, and acquiescence on the part of the South, the limitations in the Constitution have been swept away; and the Government of the United States has become consolidated, with a claim of limitless powers in its operations.

It is not at all surprising, whilst such is the character of the Government of the United States, that it should assume to possess power over all the institutions of the country. The agitations on the subject of slavery are the natural results of the consolidation of the Government. Responsibility follows power; and if the people of the North have the power by Congress "to promote the general welfare of the United States," by any means they deem expedient—why should they not assail and overthrow the institution of slavery in the South? They are responsible for its continuance or existence, in proportion to their power. A majority in Congress, according to their interested and perverted views, is omnipotent. The inducements to act upon the subject of slavery, under such circumstances, were so imperious, as to amount almost to a moral necessity. To make, however, their numerical power available to rule the Union, the North must consolidate their power. It would not be united, on any matter common to the whole Union—in other words, on any constitutional subject—for on such subjects divisions are as likely to exist in the North as in the South. Slavery was strictly a sectional interest. If this could be made the criterion of parties at the North, the North could be united in its power; and thus carry out its measures of sectional ambition, encroachment and aggrandizement. To build up their sectional predominance in the Union, the Constitution must first be abolished by constructions; but that being done, the consolidation of the North, to rule the South, by the tariff and slavery issues, was in the obvious course of things.

The Constitution of the United States was an experiment. The experiment consisted in uniting under one Government, different peoples living in different climates, and having different pursuits of industry and institutions. It matters not how carefully the limitations of such a Government be laid down in the Constitution—its success must, at least, depend upon the good faith of the parties to the constitutional compact, in enforcing them. It is not in the power of human language to exclude false inferences, constructions and perversions, in any Constitution; and when vast sectional interests are to be subserved, involving the appropriation of countless millions of money, it has not been the usual experience of mankind, that words on parchments can arrest power. The Constitution of the United States, irrespective of the interposition of the States, rested on the assumption that power would yield to faith—that integrity would be stronger than interest; and that thus, the limitations of the Constitution would be observed. The experiment has been fairly made. The Southern States, from the commencement of the Government, have striven to keep it within the orbit prescribed by the Constitution. The experiment has failed. The whole Constitution, by the constructions of the Northern people, has been absorbed by its preamble. . . . [t]he General Government [thus] must necessarily be a despotism, because all sectional or local interests must ever be represented by a minority in the councils of the General Government, having no power to protect itself against the rule of the majority. The majority, constituted from those who do not represent these sectional or local interests, will control and govern them. A free people cannot submit to such a Government. . . .

Under such a Government, there must, of course, be many and endless "irrepressible conflicts," between the two great sections of the Union. The same faithlessness which has abolished the Constitution of the United States, will not fail to carry out the sectional purposes for which it has been abolished. There must be conflict; and the weaker section of the Union can only find peace and liberty in an independence of the North. The repeated efforts made by South Carolina, in a wise conservatism, to arrest the progress of the General Government in its fatal progress to consolidation, have been unsupported, and she has been denounced as faithless to the obligations of the Constitution, by the very men and States, who were destroying it by their usurpations. It is now too late to reform or restore the Government of the United States. All confidence in the North is lost by the South. The faithlessness of the North for half a century has opened a gulf of separation between the North and the South which no promises nor engagements can fill. . . .

The Union of the Constitution was a Union of slaveholding States. It rests on slavery, by prescribing a representation in Congress for three-fifths of our slaves. There is nothing in the proceedings of the Convention which framed the Constitution, to show that the Southern States would have formed any other Union; and still less, that they would have formed a Union with more powerful non-slaveholding States, having majority in both branches of the Legislature of the Government. They were guilty of no such folly. Time and the progress of things have totally altered the relations between the Northern and Southern States, since the Union was established. That identity of feelings, interests and institutions which once existed, is gone. They are now divided, between agricultural and manufacturing, and commercial States; between slaveholding and non-slaveholding States. Their institutions and industrial pursuits have made them totally different peoples. That equality in the Government between the two sections of the Union which once existed, no longer exists. We but imitate the policy of our fathers in dissolving a union with non-slaveholding confederates, and seeking a confederation with slaveholding States.

Experience has proved that slaveholding States cannot be safe in subjection to non-slaveholding States. Indeed, no people can ever expect to preserve its rights and liberties, unless these be in its own custody. To plunder and oppress, where plunder and oppression can be practiced with impunity, seems to be the natural order of things. The fairest portions of the world elsewhere, have been turned into wildernesses, and the most civilized and prosperous communities have been impoverished and ruined by anti-slavery fanaticism. The people of the North have not left us in doubt as to their designs and policy. United as a section in the late Presidential election, they have elected as the exponent of their policy, one who has openly declared that all the States of the United States must be made free States or slave States. It is true, that amongst those who aided in his election, there are various shades of anti-slavery hostility. But if African slavery in the Southern States be the evil their political combination affirms it to be, the requisitions of an inexorable logic must lead them to emancipation. If it is right to preclude or abolish slavery in a Territory, why should it be allowed to remain in the States? The one is not at all more unconstitutional than the other, according to the decisions of the Supreme Court of the United States. And when it is considered that the Northern States will soon have the power to make that Court what they please, and that the Constitution never has been any barrier whatever to their exercise of power, what check can there be, in the unrestrained counsels of the North, to emancipation? There is sympathy in association, which carries men along without principle; but when there is principle, and that principle is fortified by long existing prejudices and feelings, association is omnipotent in party influences. In spite of all disclaimers and professions, there can be but one end by the submission of the South to the rule of a sectional anti-slavery government at Washington; and that end, directly or indirectly, must be—the emancipation of the slaves of the South. The hypocrisy of thirty years—the faithlessness of their whole course from the commencement of our union with them, show that the people of the non-slaveholding North are not, and cannot be safe associates of the slaveholding South, under a common Government.

Not only their fanaticism, but their erroneous views of the principles of free Governments, render it doubtful whether, if separated from the South, they can maintain a free Government amongst themselves. Numbers, with them, is the great element of free Government. A majority is infallible and omnipotent. "The right divine to rule in Kings," is only transferred to their majority. The very object of all Constitutions, in free popular Government, is to restrain the majority. Constitutions, therefore, according to their theory, must be most unrighteous inventions, restricting liberty. None ought to exist; but the body politic ought simply to have a political organization, to bring out and enforce the will of the majority. This theory may be harmless in a small community, having identity of interests and pursuits; but over a vast State—still more, over a vast Confederacy, having various and conflicting interests and pursuits, it is a remorseless despotism. In resisting it, as applicable to ourselves, we are vindicating the great cause of free Government, more important, perhaps, to the world, than the existence of all the United States. Nor in resisting it, do we intend to depart from the safe instrumentality, the system of Government we have established with them, requires. In separating from them, we invade no rights—no interest of theirs. We violate not obligation or duty to them. As separate, independent States in Convention, we made the Constitutions of the United States with them; and as separate independent States, each State acting for itself, we adopted it.

South Carolina, acting in her sovereign capacity, now thinks proper to secede from the Union. She did not part with her Sovereignty in adopting the Constitution. The last thing a State can be presumed to have surrendered, is her Sovereignty. Her Sovereignty is her life. Nothing but a clear express grant can alienate it. Inference has no place. Yet it is not at all surprising that those who have construed away all the limitations of the Constitution, should also by construction, claim the annihilation of the Sovereignty of the States. Having abolished all barriers to their omnipotence, by their faithless constructions in the operations of the General Government, it is most natural that they should endeavor to do the same towards us in the States. The truth is, they having violated the express provisions of the Constitution, it is at an end, as a compact. It is morally obligatory only on those who choose to accept its perverted terms. South Carolina, deeming the compact not only violated in particular features, but virtually abolished by her Northern confederates, withdraws herself as a party from its obligations. The right to do so is denied by her Northern confederates. They desire to establish a sectional despotism, not only omnipotent in Congress, but omnipotent over the States; and as if to manifest the imperious necessity of our secession, they threaten us with the sword, to coerce submission to their rule.

Citizens of the slaveholding States of the United States! Circumstances beyond our control have placed us in the van of the great controversy between the Northern and Southern States. We would have preferred that other States should have assumed the position we now occupy. Independent ourselves, we disclaim any design or desire to lead the counsels of the other Southern States. Providence has cast our lot together, by extending over us an identity of pursuits, interests, and institutions. South Carolina desires no destiny separated from yours. To be one of a great Slaveholding Confederacy, stretching its arms over a territory larger than any power in Europe possesses—with a population four times greater than that of the whole United States when they achieved their independence of the British Empire—with productions which make our existence more important to the world than that of any other people inhabiting it—with common institutions to defend, and common dangers to encounter—we ask your sympathy and confederation. Whilst constituting a portion of the United States, it has been your statesmanship which has guided it, in its mighty strides to power and expansion. In the field, as in the cabinet, you have led the way to its renown and grandeur. You have loved the Union, in whose service your great statesmen have labored, and your great soldiers have fought and conquered—not for the material benefits it conferred, but with the faith of a generous and devoted chivalry. You have long lingered in hope over the shattered remains of a broken Constitution. Compromise after compromise, formed by your concessions, has been trampled under foot by your Northern confederates. All fraternity of feeling between the North and the South is lost, or has been converted into hate; and we, of the South, are at last driven together by the stern destiny which controls the existence of nations.

Your bitter experience of the faithlessness and rapacity of your Northern confederates may have been necessary to evolve those great principles of free Government, upon which the liberties of the world depend, and to prepare you for the grand mission of vindicating and reestablishing them. We rejoice that other nations should be satisfied with their institutions. Contentment is a great element of happiness, with nations as with individuals. We are satisfied with ours. If they prefer a system of industry, in which capital and labor are in perpetual conflict— and chronic starvation keeps down the natural increase of population—and a man is worked out in eight years—and the law ordains that children shall be worked only ten hours a day—and the sabre and the bayonet are the instruments of order—be it so. It is their affair, not ours. We prefer, however, our system of industry, by which labor and capital are identified in interest, and capital, therefore, protects labor—by which our population doubles every twenty years—which starvation is unknown, and abundance crowns the land—by which order is preserved by an unpaid police, and many fertile regions of the world, where the Caucasian cannot labor, are brought into usefulness by the labor of the African, and the whole world is blessed by our productions. All we demand of other peoples is to be left alone, to work out our own high destinies. United together, and we must be the most independent, as we are among the most important, of the nations of the world. United together, and we require no other instrument to conquer peace, than our beneficent productions. United together, and we must be a great, free and prosperous people, whose renown must spread throughout the civilized world, and pass down, we trust, to the remotest ages. We ask you to join us in forming a Confederacy of Slaveholding States.

DOCUMENT 11

Refugees from Slavery Flood Northern Lines

Context: During the Civil War, tens of thousands of escaped or liberated slaves headed for northern lines. These refugees presented political questions that northerners had not anticipated. What was the legal status of these escaped slaves? Should the Union army provide them with rations and material aid? Should they be allowed to serve the Union's military forces? The following report, issued in December of 1862 by the Society of Friends (the Quakers), outlines the extent of the problem. The Quakers, it should be noted, were staunch abolitionists.

Questions to Consider: According to the report, what motivated slaves to escape to Union lines? What conditions did the ex-slaves face when in northern camps? Speculate on the political impact of refugees. In what ways did they encourage Lincoln and other northern politicians to abolish slavery?

Report of a Committee of Representatives of New York Yearly Meeting of Friends Upon the Condition and Wants of the Colored Refugees (December 1862)

Pursuant to appointment, the committee have visited . . . several thousand of the [black] refugees, of all ages and conditions. We received polite attention from all the officers of government upon whom we called, and every facility to accomplish the desired investigation.

During this engagement, we have met with much to interest us and excite our sympathy in behalf of multitudes of our fellow-men, now passing through painful vicissitudes, in their transition from a state of bondage and degradation to an unknown future, which, though enveloped in present darkness, and filled with trial and sorrow, is yet lighted by hope, and cheered and comforted by faith and trust in the wisdom and mercy of the Almighty. . . .

The present shelter of the refugees in Washington is called Camp Barker. We visited it on the 25th of 11th month. It consists of a large oblong square, surrounded on three sides by huts or barracks, and other buildings, all opening within the square; and by a high fence on the west side. The entrance is under a military guard. The huts, about forty-eight in number, are about twelve feet square, and each have from ten to twelve inmates. There are also several large tents, occupied by old or infirm men, and two buildings called hospitals—one for men, and one for women. The residence of the superintendent is within the enclosure. . . .

The superintendent reported as follows: There were 400 in camp, on the 16th of June (when he came). Since then there have come in 3,350—making a total of 3,750. Of these 280 have died. The present number is from 600 to 650, of whom 231 are children. The rest have found employment about Washington in various service—excepting about 20 who have gone North. They generally object to go there on account of the cold. There are 125 sick, all of whom have been sent in from other places, except about 25 who have sickened in the camp. This place is the general receptacle for the sick of about 6,000 refugees in and around Washington. The superintendent did not report the number of births, but they are not equal to the deaths.

The government gives employment to all the able-bodied men, at wages according to their service, from $12 to $25 per month, and all have rations except the teamsters, at the latter rate. There are about 100 women, who go out to day's work, returning at night to camp. They are said to earn fifty cents per day.

Apart from the crowded condition of these people, and their deficiency of clothing, those who were well appeared tolerably comfortable. The sick in hospital were in a miserable condition. In consequence of necessary repairs to the men's hospital, all the sick were crowded in the women's hospital. This was ill-ventilated, and disgusting in the extreme. Those with whom we spoke complained of cold; but the state of the air was such that we could not remain in it long enough for intelligent inquiry. Some were reported to be in a dying condition; and all the circumstances of the hospital seemed to us inexcusably bad. The north side of the camp was not weather-proof—some of the women remarked that "the rain came in like a spring" and wet their beds. . . .

The neighborhood of the camp was not properly drained. There were ponds of water that could easily be removed; and it appeared to be wanting in many accommodations necessary to the health and convenience of its inmates. Upon the whole, we thought the camp sadly deficient in almost every respect. The chief wants were a good hospital, properly warmed and ventilated, and a supply of hot and cold water, with conveniences for washing and bathing, so that the sick might be kept clean and comfortable. A sympathizing and competent doctor, and a sufficient number of nurses, could easily accomplish this result so necessary to the restoration of health. A superintendent who would enforce order and cleanliness, and the faithful performance of duties, could remedy much existing evil.*

We went to Alexandria on the 26th, and called on the acting superintendent of the colored refugees there, under the Provost Marshal. He informed us there were, on the 12th of October, 1,230 refugees of all ages and conditions, quartered in twenty-five houses. We visited a considerable number of them. One had been formerly used as a slave-pen by a trader. Although the poor people were unreasonably crowded in the two wings, it was interesting to contemplate the difference between its present and former uses. Then it was the entrance into the darkness of hopeless bondage; now the vestibule of hoped-for freedom! . . .

They are quartered in small rooms, about 12 feet square, and average from 10 to 12 persons in each They were generally associated together in families, and several families occasionally in one room. We were told that about two thirds are married.

All the able-bodied men and women, not obliged to take care of the children, are at work. The men earn about $20 per month, and the women from $2 to $6 per month, with rations. . . .

One man in the same house, seemed anxious for us to visit his family, in an upper room. In silence he led the way up the dilapidated staircase, and into the room. The poor man's heart seemed full; and words were not needed to understand and sympathize. The first object that attracted attention, was the corpse of a youth, laid out near the door, and covered with a white cloth. In reply, he said it was that of his son, who had died last night. Had been sick about ten days with pains in the head and back—suffered from cold—and gradually became worse, until he died. Another son was lying sick upon the floor, wrapped in coarse clothing and suffering from similar disease, but knew not what it was. The wife was engaged with the younger children near some smoking embers, which yielded but little of the needful warmth. The scene was impressive and touching in the extreme.

There was here an interesting school for boys and girls, taught by two colored teachers who had been educated in the North, and who were intelligent and efficient. The number of scholars was 160—half taught in the daytime and half in the evening. There were two rooms occupied by these schools—one about 12 by 15, and the other 10 by 12. The scholars paid 50 cents to $1 dollar per month each, and the school is self-sustaining. The pupils appeared to be well taught, and very promising. They read well, and apparently understood figures on the black board, although the school had been in operation only a few weeks.

Upon the whole, we regarded the condition of the refugees about Alexandria as very far from what it ought to be. In some respects it was not unfavorable; but in others it showed a want of attention to the ordinary requirements of tolerable existence. They expressed almost without exception, a preference for their present condition with freedom, to a more favorable one in slavery; because, as they said, they would have at least what they earned, and enjoy the fruits of their own labor; while in slavery, their masters took all and returned them but little. . . .

[After our visit] we called on the Attorney-General, at his own residence, in company with two friends, by whom we were introduced; and the next day on the President, and the Secretary of War. We explained to them the objects of our visit, and also reported what we had seen in Washington and Alexandria, believing that, in the multiplicity of their engagements, they were uninformed of the facts, and urging the importance of prompt measures to remedy existing evils. We were received with great kindness; and full approbation was expressed of the motives and action of Friends in this matter. The President was glad that Friends were ready to aid in the relief of these people. We assured him he had our full sympathy, and that of our Friends, in the cares and responsibilities which devolved upon him; that our object was not to add to those cares, but to do what little we could towards relieving them. We had an interesting interview, and took leave of him with renewed interest in his behalf.

We left Washington on the 28th, and reached Baltimore in time to take the evening boat, for Fort Monroe, where we arrived in the morning of the 29th. The number of refugees in this vicinity were reported to us as follows: We were informed that there were considerable numbers at Yorktown, Suffolk, and Portsmouth, but could not learn how many were there. The government gives employment to all the able-bodied men. Some of the women are employed also, but most of the women and children are without employment. The rate of wages, as we understood, was, at Fort Monroe, $10 per month, and rations. But little of the wages had been paid. The women and children have no rations here, and depend upon occasional employment and charity for subsistence. . . .

The men are said to work well. They are kept at work all day, and sometimes called upon to work at nights, and on the first day of the week, in cases of emergency. We were informed that they were treated very roughly; sometimes abused and maimed, by the brutality of those under whom they work. We were witness of one case of abuse on our arrival at Fort Monroe, by a white man, who appeared to have the superintendence of discharging the freight of the steamboat, in which we came from Norfolk; but, whether he was a government employee, or connected with the boat, we did not learn. . . .

We attended the first part of a meeting for worship of the colored refugees, held at three o'clock, on the afternoon of the 30th. When we entered, they were all kneeling, at prayer; and one of them, in simple eloquence, was pleading at the throne of Infinite Mercy, for aid to overcome the evil of their hearts, and live in obedience to His law; that they might be enabled to bear with patience all the troubles of life, and when all was over, be received in mansions of eternal rest! They then united in singing. The air was plaintive, but the words were not understood by us. At its conclusion, they again knelt in prayer. After acknowledging the evil of their past lives, the speaker pleaded for mercy and forgiveness, and for help in the future. He remembered the strangers now with them, for whom he asked the blessing of Most High. Then he prayed for the President of the United States; that he might be preserved, comforted, and strengthened by Almighty power; that he might be endowed with wisdom, and enabled to perform the will of Heaven; also, for the Union and the rulers of the nation, and its armies; that the Lord would be with them, and strengthen them to overcome all enemies, and re-establish the laws, and maintain the rights of all. Our hearts were touched by these simple, but fervent petitions, and we realized afresh the assurance: "Of a truth I perceive that God is no respecter of persons, but in every nation, he that feareth him, and worketh righteousness, is accepted with him."

We inquired of many where they came from, and why they left their masters. Generally the latter question seemed to excite surprise or incredulity, but the answer was nearly the same in all cases: they came away for their freedom, so that they might enjoy the reward of their own labor; but that if they could have this at home they would rather go back and live where they had lived. Not one of all the multitude, whom we saw, was desirous of going North. . . .

The poor people appeared to think that our visit was designed for their benefit, in some way; and when informed of its objects, they were wild in their expressions of joy and thanks. One old woman said she had been praying for us to come, and had full faith that we would come. That when she saw us land, she blessed God that her prayer had been heard and answered. They said in substance: "We will endure this suffering in patience, for the sake of the prospect of freedom. We are patient through all, because we see a good time coming. We pray the good Lord for all Union-men constantly." When we came away they followed us in a crowd to the end of the pier, and as the steamboat moved off, raised their hands, and waived us adieu. . . .

On our way from Washington, we learned from a gentleman well acquainted with North Carolina, that there is now a great scarcity of laborers in the northeastern part, in consequence of the escape of the slaves; and that many people there are suffering serious inconvenience and loss for want of their services.

We feel the vast importance of a correct and clear conclusion upon this branch of our inquiry, because it must have a controlling influence upon every honest man, whose opinion or action may affect the condition and welfare of millions of the human family. "To him who knoweth to do good, and doeth it not, to him it is sin." Therefore, lest some of our readers may doubt the facts we have reported, or our judgment upon them, and in view of the request before mentioned, that we should look beyond the present wants of these people, we will adduce the testimony of other witnesses respecting the same race in different localities, and various periods. The following are extracts from a letter published in the Alton Telegraph, and dated October 13th, 1862. Speaking of the refugees whom he had lately seen at Lawrence (Kansas), the writer says:

"As I learned that all the children of this school, had, within a few months, been rescued from Slavery, I expected to see a motley, lawless group of little, ragged, dirty children, something like those gathered up at the Five Points, in New York. But not a bit of it! Not a bit of it! For cleanliness, neatness, order, general good behavior, and apparent comfort, I have seldom seen a Sunday School that excelled it. Many of the little girls had neat straw bonnets, of the latest fashion, ornamented with a profusion of flowers and ribbons and with such regard to colors, too, as might repulse every suspicion of disloyalty. 'Why,' said I to the Superintendent, 'it must have cost the citizens a good deal of money to dress up all these children in this style.' 'Not a cent, not a cent, sir!' said he. 'Every one of these is dressed at the expense of their parents, from the proceeds of their own earnings since they have been here.'

"Most of them (the Negroes), in and about this town and vicinity, have emigrated from Missouri and Arkansas within a few months. Although they amount to many hundreds, not one, that I could learn of, has been a public expense. They readily get employment, and fair wages, which enables them at once to make themselves and families comfortable. A benevolent gentleman, on whom they are accustomed to call on their first entry into the place, usually tells them where they can get employment, and further inquires into their circumstances; and if he finds they need a shovel, an axe, or a pair of shoes he gives them an order on a store for such articles, and states, in the order, that if the bearer does not pay for them, in a reasonable length of time, he will. This gentleman told me, that he had recently called at the store, to learn the state of his account, and he found of five or six hundred dollars charged to him on these orders within a few months, all but eight dollars had been paid by the contrabands themselves."

We could adduce the testimony of many other witnesses to show the industry of these people, and the value of their labor, but it is deemed unnecessary. . . . When these people enjoy the rights and privileges of freemen, they are not only able to take care of themselves, but that they have, in some instances, by their industry, accomplished what few other men, under like circumstances, could equal, and perhaps none surpass. . . .

There will doubtless be a constant accession to the number of refugees, and a consequent necessity for help. They reach the Federal lines in various numbers, and of all ages, and mostly in great destitution. Then it is that relief is greatly needed. And when at length the weary stranger is enabled to reach a place of refuge, under the care of a kind superintendent, he appreciates the relief provided by his friends in the North. The extent of this depends upon the supplies on hand.

In reflecting upon the condition of the refugees, with a view of relieving their present wants and providing for their future support, it is evident that the chief reliance must be upon themselves. It is well that they have, in this respect, been cared for by their Maker, for vain would be the attempt of any government to provide for such a multitude! But so far as others are concerned, we have arrived at a simple conclusion. It is briefly comprehended in the command which is binding alike upon all Christians, whether Rulers, Statesmen, or People: "All things whatsoever ye would that men should do to you, do ye even so to them."

DOCUMENT 12

Lincoln's Position on Slavery Gradually Changes

Context: The following documents chart Lincoln's evolving views on the relationship between slavery and the Civil War. Keep in mind that South Carolina and six other cotton states had already left the Union when he gave his first inaugural speech. Four years later, when he delivered his second inaugural speech, northerners could sense that the war was nearing the end.

Questions to Consider: What was Lincoln's primary concern during the first two years of the War? Why did Lincoln issue the emancipation proclamation? Compare Lincoln's second inaugural with his first. How had his views about the War changed?

Lincoln's First Inaugural Address (March 1861)

Fellow-Citizens of the United States:

In compliance with a custom as old as the Government itself, I appear before you to address you briefly and to take in your presence the oath prescribed by the Constitution of the United States to be taken by the President "before he enters on the execution of this office." I do not consider it necessary at present for me to discuss those matters of administration about which there is no special anxiety or excitement.

Apprehension seems to exist among the people of the Southern States that by the accession of a Republican Administration their property and their peace and personal security are to be endangered. There has never been any reasonable cause for such apprehension. Indeed, the most ample evidence to the contrary has all the while existed and been open to their inspection. It is found in nearly all the published speeches of him who now addresses you. I do but quote from one of those speeches when I declare that:

I have no purpose, directly or indirectly, to interfere with the institution of slavery in the States where it exists. I believe I have no lawful right to do so, and I have no inclination to do so.

Those who nominated and elected me did so with full knowledge that I had made this and many similar declarations and had never recanted them; and more than this, they placed in the platform for my acceptance, and as a law to themselves and to me, the clear and emphatic resolution which I now read:

Resolved, That the maintenance inviolate of the rights of the States, and especially the right of each State to order and control its own domestic institutions according to its own judgment exclusively, is essential to that balance of power on which the perfection and endurance of our political fabric depend; and we denounce the lawless invasion by armed force of the soil of any State or Territory, no matter what pretext, as among the gravest of crimes.

I now reiterate these sentiments, and in doing so I only press upon the public attention the most conclusive evidence of which the case is susceptible that the property, peace, and security of no section are to be in any wise endangered by the now incoming Administration. I add, too, that all the protection which, consistently with the Constitution and the laws, can be given will be cheerfully given to all the States when lawfully demanded, for whatever cause—as cheerfully to one section as to another.

There is much controversy about the delivering up of fugitives from service or labor. The clause I now read is as plainly written in the Constitution as any other of its provisions:

No person held to service or labor in one State, under the laws thereof, escaping into another, shall in consequence of any law or regulation therein be discharged from such service or labor, but shall be delivered up on claim of the party to whom such service or labor may be due.

It is scarcely questioned that this provision was intended by those who made it for the reclaiming of what we call fugitive slaves; and the intention of the lawgiver is the law. All members of Congress swear their support to the whole Constitution—to this provision as much as to any other. To the proposition, then, that slaves whose cases come within the terms of this clause "shall be delivered up" their oaths are unanimous. Now, if they would make the effort in good temper, could they not with nearly equal unanimity frame and pass a law by means of which to keep good that unanimous oath?

There is some difference of opinion whether this clause should be enforced by national or by State authority, but surely that difference is not a very material one. If the slave is to be surrendered, it can be of but little consequence to him or to others by which authority it is done. And should anyone in any case be content that his oath shall go unkept on a merely unsubstantial controversy as to how it shall be kept?

Again: In any law upon this subject ought not all the safeguards of liberty known in civilized and humane jurisprudence to be introduced, so that a free man be not in any case surrendered as a slave? And might it not be well at the same time to provide by law for the enforcement of that clause in the Constitution which guarantees that "the citizens of each State shall be entitled to all privileges and immunities of citizens in the several States"?

I take the official oath today with no mental reservations and with no purpose to construe the Constitution or laws by any hypercritical rules; and while I do not choose now to specify particular acts of Congress as proper to be enforced, I do suggest that it will be much safer for all, both in official and private stations, to conform to and abide by all those acts which stand unrepealed than to violate any of them trusting to find impunity in having them held to be unconstitutional.

It is seventy-two years since the first inauguration of a President under our National Constitution. During that period fifteen different and greatly distinguished citizens have in succession administered the executive branch of the Government. They have conducted it through many perils, and generally with great success. Yet, with all this scope of precedent, I now enter upon the same task for the brief constitutional term of four years under great and peculiar difficulty. A disruption of the Federal Union, heretofore only menaced, is now formidably attempted.

I hold that in contemplation of universal law and of the Constitution the Union of these States is perpetual. Perpetuity is implied, if not expressed, in the fundamental law of all national governments. It is safe to assert that no government proper ever had a provision in its organic law for its own termination. Continue to execute all the express provisions of our National Constitution, and the Union will endure forever, it being impossible to destroy it except by some action not provided for in the instrument itself.

Again: If the United States be not a government proper, but an association of States in the nature of contract merely, can it, as a contract, be peaceably unmade by less than all the parties who made it? One party to a contract may violate it—break it, so to speak—but does it not require all to lawfully rescind it?

Descending from these general principles, we find the proposition that in legal contemplation the Union is perpetual confirmed by the history of the Union itself. The Union is much older than the Constitution. It was formed, in fact, by the Articles of Association in 1774. It was matured and continued by the Declaration of Independence in 1776. It was further matured, and the faith of all the then thirteen States expressly plighted and engaged that it should be perpetual, by the Articles of Confederation in 1778. And finally, in 1787, one of the declared objects for ordaining and establishing the Constitution was "to form a more perfect Union."

But if destruction of the Union by one or by a part only of the States be lawfully possible, the Union is less perfect than before the Constitution, having lost the vital element of perpetuity.

It follows from these views that no State upon its own mere motion can lawfully get out of the Union; that resolves and ordinances to that effect are legally void, and that acts of violence within any State or States against the authority of the United States are insurrectionary or revolutionary, according to circumstances.

I therefore consider that in view of the Constitution and the laws the Union is unbroken, and to the extent of my ability, I shall take care, as the Constitution itself expressly enjoins upon me, that the laws of the Union be faithfully executed in all the States. Doing this I deem to be only a simple duty on my part, and I shall perform it so far as practicable unless my rightful masters, the American people, shall withhold the requisite means or in some authoritative manner direct the contrary. I trust this will not be regarded as a menace, but only as the declared purpose of the Union that it will constitutionally defend and maintain itself.

In doing this there needs to be no bloodshed or violence, and there shall be none unless it be forced upon the national authority. The power confided to me will be used to hold, occupy, and possess the property and places belonging to the Government and to collect the duties and imposts; but beyond what may be necessary for these objects, there will be no invasion, no using of force against or among the people anywhere. Where hostility to the United States in any interior locality shall be so great and universal as to prevent competent resident citizens from holding the Federal offices, there will be no attempt to force obnoxious strangers among the people for that object. While the strict legal right may exist in the Government to enforce the exercise of these offices, the attempt to do so would be so irritating and so nearly impracticable withal that I deem it better to forego for the time the uses of such offices.

The mails, unless repelled, will continue to be furnished in all parts of the Union. So far as possible the people everywhere shall have that sense of perfect security which is most favorable to calm thought and reflection. The course here indicated will be followed unless current events and experience shall show a modification or change to be proper, and in every case and exigency my best discretion will be exercised, according to circumstances actually existing and with a view and a hope of a peaceful solution of the national troubles and the restoration of fraternal sympathies and affections.

That there are persons in one section or another who seek to destroy the Union at all events and are glad of any pretext to do it I will neither affirm nor deny; but if there be such, I need address no word to them. To those, however, who really love the Union may I not speak?

Before entering upon so grave a matter as the destruction of our national fabric, with all its benefits, its memories, and its hopes, would it not be wise to ascertain precisely why we do it? Will you hazard so desperate a step while there is any possibility that any portion of the ills you fly from have no real existence? Will you, while the certain ills you fly to are greater than all the real ones you fly from, will you risk the commission of so fearful a mistake?

All profess to be content in the Union if all constitutional rights can be maintained. Is it true, then, that any right plainly written in the Constitution has been denied? I think not. Happily, the human mind is so constituted that no party can reach to the audacity of doing this. Think, if you can, of a single instance in which a plainly written provision of the Constitution has ever been denied. If by the mere force of numbers a majority should deprive a minority of any clearly written constitutional right, it might in a moral point of view justify revolution; certainly would if such right were a vital one. But such is not our case. All the vital rights of minorities and of individuals are so plainly assured to them by affirmations and negations, guaranties and prohibitions, in the Constitution that controversies never arise concerning them. But no organic law can ever be framed with a provision specifically applicable to every question which may occur in practical administration. No foresight can anticipate nor any document of reasonable length contain express provisions for all possible questions. Shall fugitives from labor be surrendered by national or by State authority? The Constitution does not expressly say. May Congress prohibit slavery in the Territories? The Constitution does not expressly say. Must Congress protect slavery in the Territories? The Constitution does not expressly say.

From questions of this class spring all our constitutional controversies, and we divide upon them into majorities and minorities. If the minority will not acquiesce, the majority must, or the Government must cease. There is no other alternative, for continuing the Government is acquiescence on one side or the other. If a minority in such case will secede rather than acquiesce, they make a precedent which in turn will divide and ruin them, for a minority of their own will secede from them whenever a majority refuses to be controlled by such minority. For instance, why may not any portion of a new confederacy a year or two hence arbitrarily secede again, precisely as portions of the present Union now claim to secede from it? All who cherish disunion sentiments are now being educated to the exact temper of doing this.

Is there such perfect identity of interests among the States to compose a new union as to produce harmony only and prevent renewed secession?

Plainly the central idea of secession is the essence of anarchy. A majority held in restraint by constitutional checks and limitations, and always changing easily with deliberate changes of popular opinions and sentiments, is the only true sovereign of a free people. Whoever rejects it does of necessity fly to anarchy or to despotism. Unanimity is impossible. The rule of a minority, as a permanent arrangement, is wholly inadmissible; so that, rejecting the majority principle, anarchy or despotism in some form is all that is left.

I do not forget the position assumed by some that constitutional questions are to be decided by the Supreme Court, nor do I deny that such decisions must be binding in any case upon the parties to a suit as to the object of that suit, while they are also entitled to very high respect and consideration in all parallel cases by all other departments of the Government. And while it is obviously possible that such decision may be erroneous in any given case, still the evil effect following it, being limited to that particular case, with the chance that it may be overruled and never become a precedent for other cases, can better be borne than could the evils of a different practice. At the same time, the candid citizen must confess that if the policy of the Government upon vital questions affecting the whole people is to be irrevocably fixed by decisions of the Supreme Court, the instant they are made in ordinary litigation between parties in personal actions the people will have ceased to be their own rulers, having to that extent practically resigned their Government into the hands of that eminent tribunal. Nor is there in this view any assault upon the court or the judges. It is a duty from which they may not shrink to decide cases properly brought before them, and it is no fault of theirs if others seek to turn their decisions to political purposes.

One section of our country believes slavery is right and ought to be extended, while the other believes it is wrong and ought not to be extended. This is the only substantial dispute. The fugitive-slave clause of the Constitution and the law for the suppression of the foreign slave trade are each as well enforced, perhaps, as any law can ever be in a community where the moral sense of the people imperfectly supports the law itself. The great body of the people abide by the dry legal obligation in both cases, and a few break over in each. This, I think, can not be perfectly cured, and it would be worse in both cases after the separation of the sections than before. The foreign slave trade, now imperfectly suppressed, would be ultimately revived without restriction in one section, while fugitive slaves, now only partially surrendered, would not be surrendered at all by the other.

Physically speaking, we can not separate. We can not remove our respective sections from each other nor build an impassable wall between them. A husband and wife may be divorced and go out of the presence and beyond the reach of each other, but the different parts of our country can not do this. They can not but remain face to face, and intercourse, either amicable or hostile, must continue between them. Is it possible, then, to make that intercourse more advantageous or more satisfactory after separation than before? Can aliens make treaties easier than friends can make laws? Can treaties be more faithfully enforced between aliens than laws can among friends? Suppose you go to war, you can not fight always; and when, after much loss on both sides and no gain on either, you cease fighting, the identical old questions, as to terms of intercourse, are again upon you.

This country, with its institutions, belongs to the people who inhabit it. Whenever they shall grow weary of the existing Government, they can exercise their constitutional right of amending it or their revolutionary right to dismember or overthrow it. I can not be ignorant of the fact that many worthy and patriotic citizens are desirous of having the National Constitution amended. While I make no recommendation of amendments, I fully recognize the rightful authority of the people over the whole subject, to be exercised in either of the modes prescribed in the instrument itself; and I should, under existing circumstances, favor rather than oppose a fair opportunity being afforded the people to act upon it. I will venture to add that to me the convention mode seems preferable, in that it allows amendments to originate with the people themselves, instead of only permitting them to take or reject propositions originated by others, not especially chosen for the purpose, and which might not be precisely such as they would wish to either accept or refuse. I understand a proposed amendment to the Constitution—which amendment, however, I have not seen—has passed Congress, to the effect that the Federal Government shall never interfere with the domestic institutions of the States, including that of persons held to service. To avoid misconstruction of what I have said, I depart from my purpose not to speak of particular amendments so far as to say that, holding such a provision to now be implied constitutional law, I have no objection to its being made express and irrevocable.

The Chief Magistrate derives all his authority from the people, and they have referred none upon him to fix terms for the separation of the States. The people themselves can do this if also they choose, but the Executive as such has nothing to do with it. His duty is to administer the present Government as it came to his hands and to transmit it unimpaired by him to his successor.

Why should there not be a patient confidence in the ultimate justice of the people? Is there any better or equal hope in the world? In our present differences, is either party without faith of being in the right? If the Almighty Ruler of Nations, with His eternal truth and justice, be on your side of the North, or on yours of the South, that truth and that justice will surely prevail by the judgment of this great tribunal of the American people.

By the frame of the Government under which we live this same people have wisely given their public servants but little power for mischief, and have with equal wisdom provided for the return of that little to their own hands at very short intervals. While the people retain their virtue and vigilance no Administration by any extreme of wickedness or folly can very seriously injure the Government in the short space of four years.

My countrymen, one and all, think calmly and well upon this whole subject. Nothing valuable can be lost by taking time. If there be an object to hurry any of you in hot haste to a step which you would never take deliberately, that object will be frustrated by taking time; but no good object can be frustrated by it. Such of you as are now dissatisfied still have the old Constitution unimpaired, and, on the sensitive point, the laws of your own framing under it; while the new Administration will have no immediate power, if it would, to change either. If it were admitted that you who are dissatisfied hold the right side in the dispute, there still is no single good reason for precipitate action. Intelligence, patriotism, Christianity, and a firm reliance on Him who has never yet forsaken this favored land are still competent to adjust in the best way all our present difficulty.

In your hands, my dissatisfied fellow-countrymen, and not in mine, is the momentous issue of civil war. The Government will not assail you. You can have no conflict without being yourselves the aggressors. You have no oath registered in heaven to destroy the Government, while I shall have the most solemn one to "preserve, protect, and defend it."

I am loath to close. We are not enemies, but friends. We must not be enemies. Though passion may have strained it must not break our bonds of affection. The mystic chords of memory, stretching from every battlefield and patriot grave to every living heart and hearthstone all over this broad land, will yet swell the chorus of the Union, when again touched, as surely they will be, by the better angels of our nature.

Letter to Horace Greeley (August 1862)

Executive Mansion,

Washington, August 22, 1862.

Hon. Horace Greeley:

Dear Sir:

I have just read yours of the 19th. addressed to myself through the *New-York Tribune*. If there be in it any statements, or assumptions of fact, which I may know to be erroneous, I do not, now and here, controvert them. If there be in it any inferences which I may believe to be falsely drawn, I do not now and here, argue against them. If there be perceptable [sic] in it an impatient and dictatorial tone, I waive it in deference to an old friend, whose heart I have always supposed to be right.

As to the policy I "seem to be pursuing" as you say, I have not meant to leave any one in doubt.

I would save the Union. I would save it the shortest way under the Constitution. The sooner the national authority can be restored; the nearer the Union will be "the Union as it was." If there be those who would not save the Union, unless they could at the same time save slavery, I do not agree with them. If there be those who would not save the Union unless they could at the same time destroy slavery, I do not agree with them. My paramount object in this struggle is to save the Union, and is not either to save or to destroy slavery. If I could save the Union without freeing any slave I would do it, and if I could save it by freeing all the slaves I would do it; and if I could save it by freeing some and leaving others alone I would also do that. What I do about slavery, and the colored race, I do because I believe it helps to save the Union; and what I forbear, I forbear because I do not believe it would help to save the Union. I shall do less whenever I shall believe what I am doing hurts the cause, and I shall do more whenever I shall believe doing more will help the cause. I shall try to correct errors when shown to be errors; and I shall adopt new views so fast as they shall appear to be true views.

I have here stated my purpose according to my view of official duty; and I intend no modification of my oft-expressed personal wish that all men everywhere could be free.

Yours,

A. Lincoln.

Emancipation Proclamation (January 1863)

By the President of the United States of America:

A Proclamation.

Whereas, on the twenty second day of September, in the year of our Lord one thousand eight hundred and sixty two, a proclamation was issued by the President of the United States, containing, among other things, the following, to wit:

"That on the first day of January, in the year of our Lord one thousand eight hundred and sixty-three, all persons held as slaves within any State or designated part of a State, the people whereof shall then be in rebellion against the United States, shall be then, thenceforward, and forever free; and the Executive Government of the United States, including the military and naval authority thereof, will recognize and maintain the freedom of such persons, and will do no act or acts to repress such persons, or any of them, in any efforts they may make for their actual freedom.

"That the Executive will, on the first day of January aforesaid, by proclamation, designate the States and parts of States, if any, in which the people thereof, respectively, shall then be in rebellion against the United States; and the fact that any State, or the people thereof, shall on that day be, in good faith, represented in the Congress of the United States by members chosen thereto at elections wherein a majority of the qualified voters of such State shall have participated, shall, in the absence of strong countervailing testimony, be deemed conclusive evidence that such State, and the people thereof, are not then in rebellion against the United States."

Now, therefore I, Abraham Lincoln, President of the United States, by virtue of the power in me vested as Commander-in-Chief, of the Army and Navy of the United States in time of actual armed rebellion against the authority and government of the United States, and as a fit and necessary war measure for suppressing said rebellion, do, on this first day of January, in the year of our Lord one thousand eight hundred and sixty three, and in accordance with my purpose so to do publicly proclaimed for the full period of one hundred days, from the day first above mentioned, order and designate as the States and parts of States wherein the people thereof respectively, are this day in rebellion against the United States, the following, to wit:

Arkansas, Texas, Louisiana, (except the Parishes of St. Bernard, Plaquemines, Jefferson, St. Johns, St. Charles, St. James Ascension, Assumption, Terrebonne, Lafourche, St. Mary, St. Martin, and Orleans, including the City of New Orleans) Mississippi, Alabama, Florida, Georgia, South-Carolina, North-Carolina, and Virginia, (except the forty eight counties designated as West Virginia, and also the counties of Berkley, Accomac, Northampton, Elizabeth-City, York, Princess Ann, and Norfolk, including the cities of Norfolk and Portsmouth), and which excepted parts, are for the present, left precisely as if this proclamation were not issued.

And by virtue of the power, and for the purpose aforesaid, I do order and declare that all persons held as slaves within said designated States, and parts of States, are, and henceforward shall be free; and that the Executive government of the United States, including the military and naval authorities thereof, will recognize and maintain the freedom of said persons.

And I hereby enjoin upon the people so declared to be free to abstain from all violence, unless in necessary self-defense; and I recommend to them that, in all cases when allowed, they labor faithfully for reasonable wages.

And I further declare and make known, that such persons of suitable condition, will be received into the armed service of the United States to garrison forts, positions, stations, and other places, and to man vessels of all sorts in said service.

And upon this act, sincerely believed to be an act of justice, warranted by the Constitution, upon military necessity, I invoke the considerate judgment of mankind, and the gracious favor of Almighty God.

In witness whereof, I have hereunto set my hand and caused the seal of the United States to be affixed. Done at the City of Washington, this first day of January, in the year of our Lord one thousand eight hundred and sixty three, and of the Independence of the United States of America the eighty-seventh.

Letter to James C. Conkling (August 1863)

Executive Mansion,

Washington, August 26, 1863.

Hon. James C. Conkling

My Dear Sir.

Your letter inviting me to attend a mass-meeting of unconditional Union-men, to be held at the Capitol of Illinois, on the 3d day of September, has been received.

It would be very agreeable to me, to thus meet my old friends, at my own home; but I cannot, just now, be absent from here, so long as a visit there, would require.

The meeting is to be of all those who maintain unconditional devotion to the Union; and I am sure my old political friends will thank me for tendering, as I do, the nation's gratitude to those other noble men, whom no partizan malice, or partizan hope, can make false to the nation's life.

There are those who are dissatisfied with me. To such I would say: You desire peace; and you blame me that we do not have it. But how can we attain it? There are but three conceivable ways. First, to suppress the rebellion by force of arms. This I am trying to do. Are you for it? If you are, so far we are agreed. If you are not for it, a second way is to give up the Union. I am against this. Are you for it? If you are, you should say so plainly. If you are not for force, nor yet for dissolution, there only remains some imaginable compromise. I do not believe any compromise, embracing the maintenance of the Union, is now possible. All I learn, leads to a directly opposite belief. The strength of the rebellion, is its military—its army. That army dominates all the country, and all the people, within its range. Any offer of terms made by any man or men within that range, in opposition to that army, is simply nothing for the present; because such man or men, have no power whatever to enforce their side of a compromise, if one were made with them. . . .

But to be plain, you are dissatisfied with me about the negro. Quite likely there is a difference of opinion between you and myself upon that subject. I certainly wish that all men could be free, while I suppose you do not. Yet I have neither adopted, nor proposed any measure, which is not consistent with even your view, provided you are for the Union. I suggested compensated emancipation; to which you replied you wished not to be taxed to buy negroes. But I had not asked you to be taxed to buy negroes, except in such way, as to save you from greater taxation to save the Union exclusively by other means.

You dislike the emancipation proclamation; and, perhaps, would have it retracted. You say it is unconstitutional—I think differently. I think the constitution invests its Commander-in-chief, with the law of war, in time of war. The most that can be said, if so much, is, that slaves are property. Is there—has there ever been—any question that by the law of war, property, both of enemies and friends, may be taken when needed? And is it not needed whenever taking it, helps us, or hurts the enemy? Armies, the world over, destroy enemy's property when they can not use it; and even destroy their own to keep it from the enemy. Civilized belligerents do all in their power to help themselves, or hurt the enemy, except a few things regarded as barbarous or cruel. Among the exceptions are the massacre of vanquished foes, and non-combatants, male and female.

But the proclamation, as law, either is valid, or is not valid. If it is not valid, it needs no retraction. If it is valid, it cannot be retracted, any more than the dead can be brought to life. Some of you profess to think its retraction would operate favorably for the Union. Why better after the retraction, than before the issue? There was more than a year and a half of trial to suppress the rebellion before the proclamation issued, the last one hundred days of which passed under an explicit notice that it was coming, unless averted by those in revolt, returning to their allegiance. The war has certainly progressed as favorably for us, since the issue of proclamation as before. I know, as fully as one can know the opinions of others, that some of the commanders of our armies in the field who have given us our most important successes believe the emancipation policy and the use of the colored troops constitute the heaviest blow yet dealt to the Rebellion, and that at least one of these important successes could not have been achieved when it was but for the aid of black soldiers. Among the commanders holding these views are some who have never had any affinity with what is called abolitionism or with the Republican party policies but who held them purely as military opinions. I submit these opinions as being entitled to some weight against the objections often urged that emancipation and arming the blacks are unwise as military measures and were not adopted as such in good faith.

You say you will not fight to free negroes. Some of them seem willing to fight for you; but, no matter. Fight you, then exclusively to save the Union. I issued the proclamation on purpose to aid you in saving the Union. Whenever you shall have conquered all resistence to the Union, if I shall urge you to continue fighting, it will be an apt time, then, for you to declare you will not fight to free negroes.

I thought that in your struggle for the Union, to whatever extent the negroes should cease helping the enemy, to that extent it weakened the enemy in his resistance to you. Do you think differently? I thought that whatever negroes can be got to do as soldiers, leaves just so much less for white soldiers to do, in saving the Union. Does it appear otherwise to you? But negroes, like other people, act upon motives. Why should they do any thing for us, if we will do nothing for them? If they stake their lives for us, they must be prompted by the strongest motive—even the promise of freedom. And the promise being made, must be kept.

The signs look better. The Father of Waters again goes unvexed to the sea. Thanks to the great Northwest for it. Nor yet wholly to them. Three hundred miles up, they met New England, Empire, Keystone, and Jersey, hewing their way right and left. The Sunny South too, in more colors than one, also lent a hand. On the spot, their part of the history was jotted down in black and white. The job was a great national one; and let none be banned who bore an honorable part in it. And while those who have cleared the great river may well be proud, even that is not all. It is hard to say that anything has been more bravely, and well done, than at Antietam, Murfreesboro, Gettysburg, and on many fields of lesser note. Nor must Uncle Sam's web-feet be forgotten. At all the watery margins they have been present. Not only on the deep sea, the broad bay, and the rapid river, but also up the narrow muddy bayou, and wherever the ground was a little damp, they have been, and made their tracks. Thanks to all. For the great republic—for the principle it lives by, and keeps alive—for man's vast future—thanks to all.

Peace does not appear so distant as it did. I hope it will come soon, and come to stay; and so come as to be worth the keeping in all future time. It will then have been proved that, among free men, there can be no successful appeal from the ballot to the bullet; and that they who take such appeal are sure to lose their case, and pay the cost. And then, there will be some black men who can remember that, with silent tongue, and clenched teeth, and steady eye, and well-poised bayonet, they have helped mankind on to this great consummation; while, I fear, there will be some white ones, unable to forget that, with malignant heart, and deceitful speech, they strove to hinder it.

Still, let us not be over-sanguine of a speedy final triumph. Let us be quite sober. Let us diligently apply the means, never doubting that a just God, in his own good time, will give us the rightful result.

Second Inaugural Address (March 1865)

Fellow-Countrymen:

At this second appearing to take the oath of the Presidential office there is less occasion for an extended address than there was at the first. Then a statement somewhat in detail of a course to be pursued seemed fitting and proper. Now, at the expiration of four years, during which public declarations have been constantly called forth on every point and phase of the great contest which still absorbs the attention and engrosses the energies of the nation, little that is new could be presented. The progress of our arms, upon which all else chiefly depends, is as well known to the public as to myself, and it is, I trust, reasonably satisfactory and encouraging to all. With high hope for the future, no prediction in regard to it is ventured.

On the occasion corresponding to this four years ago all thoughts were anxiously directed to an impending civil war. All dreaded it, all sought to avert it. While the inaugural address was being delivered from this place, devoted altogether to saving the Union without war, urgent agents were in the city seeking to destroy it without war—seeking to dissolve the Union and divide effects by negotiation. Both parties deprecated war, but one of them would make war rather than let the nation survive, and the other would accept war rather than let it perish, and the war came.

One-eighth of the whole population were colored slaves, not distributed generally over the Union, but localized in the southern part of it. These slaves constituted a peculiar and powerful interest. All knew that this interest was somehow the cause of the war. To strengthen, perpetuate, and extend this interest was the object for which the insurgents would rend the Union even by war, while the Government claimed no right to do more than to restrict the territorial enlargement of it. Neither party expected for the war the magnitude or the duration which it has already attained. Neither anticipated that the cause of the conflict might cease with or even before the conflict itself should cease. Each looked for an easier triumph, and a result less fundamental and astounding. Both read the same Bible and pray to the same God, and each invokes His aid against the other. It may seem strange that any men should dare to ask a just God's assistance in wringing their bread from the sweat of other men's faces, but let us judge not, that we be not judged. The prayers of both could not be answered. That of neither has been answered fully. The Almighty has His own purposes. "Woe unto the world because of offenses; for it must needs be that offenses come, but woe to that man by whom the offense cometh." If we shall suppose that American slavery is one of those offenses which, in the providence of God, must needs come, but which, having continued through His appointed time, He now wills to remove, and that He gives to both North and South this terrible war as the woe due to those by whom the offense came, shall we discern therein any departure from those divine attributes which the believers in a living God always ascribe to Him? Fondly do we hope, fervently do we pray, that this mighty scourge of war may speedily pass away. Yet, if God wills that it continue until all the wealth piled by the bondsman's two hundred and fifty years of unrequited toil shall be sunk, and until every drop of blood drawn with the lash shall be paid by another drawn with the sword, as was said three thousand years ago, so still it must be said "the judgments of the Lord are true and righteous altogether."

With malice toward none, with charity for all, with firmness in the right as God gives us to see the right, let us strive on to finish the work we are in, to bind up the nation's wounds, to care for him who shall have borne the battle and for his widow and his orphan, to do all which may achieve and cherish a just and lasting peace among ourselves and with all nations.

DOCUMENT 13

Frederick Douglass Advocates Suffrage for African Americans

Context: As one of America's foremost abolitionists, Frederick Douglass hoped to turn the Civil War into a civil rights crusade. This speech was given in Boston before a largely sympathetic crowd. Keep in mind that Douglass was also a delegate at the Seneca Falls convention, where he had forcefully advocated women's suffrage.

Questions to Consider: According to Douglass, how did the slaves respond to the Civil War? Why did that response justify voting rights for blacks? What pragmatic arguments for black suffrage did Douglass make for his primarily white audience?

Frederick Douglass, "What the Black Man Wants" (1864)

I have had but one idea for the last three years, to present to the American people, and the phraseology in which I clothe it is the old abolition phraseology. I am for the "immediate, unconditional, and universal" enfranchisement of the black man, in every State in the Union. (Loud applause.) Without this, his liberty is a mockery; without this, you might as well almost retain the old name of slavery for his condition; for, in fact, if he is not the slave of the individual master, he is the slave of society, and holds his liberty as a privilege, not as a right. He is at the mercy of the mob, and has no means of protecting himself.

It may be objected, however, that this pressing of the negro's right to suffrage is premature. Let us have slavery abolished, it may be said, let us have labor organized, and then, in the natural course of events, the right of suffrage will be extended to the negro. I do not agree with this. The constitution of the human mind is such, that if it once disregards the conviction forced upon it by a revelation of truth, it requires the exercise of a higher power to produce the same conviction afterwards. The American people are now in tears. The Shenandoah has run blood—the best blood of the North. All around Richmond, the blood of New England and of the North has been shed—of your sons, your brothers and your fathers. We all feel, in the existence of this Rebellion, that judgments terrible, widespread, far-reaching, overwhelming, are abroad in the land; and we feel, in view of these judgments, just now, a disposition to learn righteousness. This is the hour. Our streets are in mourning, tears are falling at every fireside, and under the chastisement of this Rebellion we have almost come up to the point of conceding this great, this all-important right of suffrage. I fear that if we fail to do it now, if abolitionists fail to press it now, we may not see, for centuries to come, the same disposition that exists at this moment. (Applause.) Hence, I say, now is the time to press this right.

It may be asked, "Why do you want it? Some men have got along very well without it. Women have not this right." Shall we justify one wrong by another? That is a sufficient answer. Shall we at this moment justify the deprivation of the negro of the right to vote, because some one else is deprived of that privilege? I hold that women, as well as men, have the right to vote (applause), and my heart and my voice go with the movement to extend suffrage to woman; but that question rests upon another basis than that on which our right rests. We may be asked, I say, why we want it. I will tell you why we want it. We want it because it is our right, first of all. (Applause.) No class of men can, without insulting their own nature, be content with any deprivation of their rights. We want it, again, as a means for educating our race. Men are so constituted that they derive their conviction of their own possibilities largely from the estimate formed of them by others. If nothing is expected of a people, that people will find it difficult to contradict that expectation. By depriving us of suffrage, you affirm our incapacity to form an intelligent judgment respecting public men and public measures; you declare before the world that we are unfit to exercise the elective franchise, and by this means lead us to undervalue ourselves, to put a low estimate upon ourselves, and to feel that we have no possibilities like other men. Again, I want the elective franchise, for one, as a colored man, because ours is a peculiar government, based upon a peculiar idea, and that idea is universal suffrage. . . . [W]here universal suffrage is the rule, where that is the fundamental idea of the Government, to rule us out is to make us an exception, to brand us with the stigma of inferiority, and to invite to our heads the missiles of those about us; therefore, I want the franchise for the black man.

There are, however, other reasons, not derived from any consideration merely of our rights, but arising out of the condition of the South, and of the country— considerations which have already been referred to by Mr. Phillips—considerations which must arrest the attention of statesmen. I believe that when the tall heads of this Rebellion shall have been swept down, as they will be swept down, when the Davises and Toombses and Stephenses, and others who are leading in this Rebellion shall have been blotted out, there will be this rank undergrowth of treason, to which reference has been made, growing up there, and interfering with, and thwarting the quiet operation of the Federal Government in those States. You will see those traitors handing down, from sire to son, the same malignant spirit which they have manifested, and which they are now exhibiting, with malicious hearts, broad blades, and bloody hands in the field, against our sons and brothers. That spirit will still remain; and whoever sees the Federal Government extended over those Southern States will see that Government in a strange land, and not only in a strange land, but in an enemy's land. A post-master of the United States in the South will find himself surrounded by a hostile spirit; a collector in a Southern port will find himself surrounded by a hostile spirit; a United States marshal or United States judge will be surrounded there by a hostile element. That enmity will not die out in a year, will not die out in an age. . . . They will endeavor to circumvent, they will endeavor to destroy, the peaceful operation of this Government. Now, where will you find the strength to counterbalance this spirit, if you do not find it in the negroes of the South? They are your friends, and have always been your friends. They were your friends even when the Government did not regard them as such. They comprehended the genius of this war before you did. It is a significant fact, it is a marvellous fact, it seems almost to imply a direct interposition of Providence, that this war, which began in the interest of slavery on both sides, bids fair to end in the interest of liberty on both sides. (Applause.) It was begun, I say, in the interest of slavery on both sides. The South was fighting to take slavery out of the Union, and the North fighting to keep it in the Union; the South fighting to get it beyond the limits of the United-States Constitution, and the North fighting to retain it within those limits; the South fighting for new guarantees, and the North fighting for the old guarantees—both despising the negro, both insulting the negro. Yet, the negro, apparently endowed with wisdom from on high, saw more clearly the end from the beginning than we did. When Seward said the status of no man in the country would be changed by the war, the negro did not believe him. (Applause.) When our generals sent their underlings in shoulder-straps to hunt the flying negro back from our lines into the jaws of slavery, from which he had escaped, the negroes thought that a mistake had been made, and that the intentions of the Government had not been rightly understood by our officers in shoulder-straps, and they continued to come into our lines, threading their way through bogs and fens, over briers and thorns, fording streams, swimming rivers, bringing us tidings as to the safe path to march, and pointing out the dangers that threatened us. They are our only friends in the South, and we should be true to them in this their trial hour, and see to it that they have the elective franchise.

I know that we are inferior to you in some things—virtually inferior. We walk about among you like dwarfs among giants. Our heads are scarcely seen above the great sea of humanity. The Germans are superior to us; the Irish are superior to us; the Yankees are superior to us (laughter); they can do what we cannot, that is, what we have not hitherto been allowed to do. But while I make this admission, I utterly deny that we are originally, or naturally, or practically, or in any way, or in any important sense, inferior to anybody on this globe. (Loud applause.) This charge of inferiority is an old dodge. It has been made available for oppression on many occasions. It is only about six centuries since the blue-eyed and fair-haired Anglo-Saxons were considered inferior by the haughty Normans, who once trampled upon them. If you read the history of the Norman Conquest, you will find that this proud Anglo-Saxon was once looked upon as of coarser clay than his Norman master, and might be found in the highways and byways of old England laboring with a brass collar on his neck, and the name of his master marked upon it. You were down then! (Laughter and applause.) You are up now. I am glad you are up, and I want you to be glad to help us up also. (Applause.)

The story of our inferiority is an old dodge, as I have said; for wherever men oppress their fellows, wherever they enslave them, they will endeavor to find the needed apology for such enslavement and oppression in the character of the people oppressed and enslaved. When we wanted, a few years ago, a slice of Mexico, it was hinted that the Mexicans were an inferior race, that the old Castilian blood had become so weak that it would scarcely run down hill, and that Mexico needed the long, strong and beneficent arm of the Anglo-Saxon care extended over it. We said that it was necessary to its salvation, and a part of the "manifest destiny" of this Republic, to extend our arm over that dilapidated government. So, too, when Russia wanted to take possession of a part of the Ottoman Empire, the Turks were "an inferior race." So, too, when England wants to set the heel of her power more firmly in the quivering heart of old Ireland, the Celts are an "inferior race." So, too, the negro, when he is to be robbed of any right which is justly his, is an "inferior man." It is said that we are ignorant; I admit it. But if we know enough to be hung, we know enough to vote. If the negro knows enough to pay taxes to support the government, he knows enough to vote; taxation and representation should go together. If he knows enough to shoulder a musket and fight for the flag, fight for the government, he knows enough to vote. If he knows as much when he is sober as an Irishman knows when drunk, he knows enough to vote, on good American principles. (Laughter and applause.)

But I was saying that you needed a counterpoise in the persons of the slaves to the enmity that would exist at the South after the Rebellion is put down. I hold that the American people are bound, not only in self-defense, to extend this right to the freedmen of the South, but they are bound by their love of country, and by all their regard for the future safety of those Southern States, to do this—to do it as a measure essential to the preservation of peace there. But I will not dwell upon this. I put it to the American sense of honor. The honor of a nation is an important thing. It is said in the Scriptures, "What doth it profit a man if he gain the whole world, and lose his own soul?" It may be said, also, What doth it profit a nation if it gain the whole world, but lose its honor? I hold that the American government has taken upon itself a solemn obligation of honor, to see that this war—let it be long or let it be short, let it cost much or let it cost little—that this war shall not cease until every freedman at the South has the right to vote. (Applause.) It has bound itself to it. What have you asked the black men of the South, the black men of the whole country, to do? Why, you have asked them to incur the deadly enmity of their masters, in order to befriend you and to befriend this Government. You have asked us to call down, not only upon ourselves, but upon our children's children, the deadly hate of the entire Southern people. You have called upon us to turn our backs upon our masters, to abandon their cause and espouse yours; to turn against the South and in favor of the North; to shoot down the Confederacy and uphold the flag—the American flag. You have called upon us to expose ourselves to all the subtle machinations of their malignity for all time. And now, what do you propose to do when you come to make peace? To reward your enemies, and trample in the dust your friends? Do you intend to sacrifice the very men who have come to the rescue of your banner in the South, and incurred the lasting displeasure of their masters thereby? Do you intend to sacrifice them and reward your enemies? Do you mean to give your enemies the right to vote, and take it away from your friends? Is that wise policy? Is that honorable? Could American honor withstand such a blow? I do not believe you will do it. I think you will see to it that we have the right to vote. There is something too mean in looking upon the negro, when you are in trouble, as a citizen, and when you are free from trouble, as an alien. When this nation was in trouble, in its early struggles, it looked upon the negro as a citizen. In 1776 he was a citizen. At the time of the formation of the Constitution the negro had the right to vote in eleven States out of the old thirteen. In your trouble you have made us citizens. In 1812 Gen. Jackson addressed us as citizens—"fellow-citizens." He wanted us to fight. We were citizens then! And now, when you come to frame a conscription bill, the negro is a citizen again. He has been a citizen just three times in the history of this government, and it has always been in time of trouble. In time of trouble we are citizens. Shall we be citizens in war, and aliens in peace? Would that be just?

I ask my friends who are apologizing for not insisting upon this right, where can the black man look, in this country, for the assertion of this right, if he may not look to the Massachusetts Anti-Slavery Society? Where under the whole heavens can he look for sympathy, in asserting this right, if he may not look to this platform? Have you lifted us up to a certain height to see that we are men, and then are any disposed to leave us there, without seeing that we are put in possession of all our rights? We look naturally to this platform for the assertion of all our rights, and for this one especially. I understand the anti-slavery societies of this country to be based on two principles—first the freedom of the blacks of this country; and, second, the elevation of them. Let me not be misunderstood here. I am not asking for sympathy at the hands of abolitionists, sympathy at the hands of any. I think the American people are disposed often to be generous rather than just. I look over this country at the present time, and I see Educational Societies, Sanitary Commissions, Freedmen's Associations, and the like, all very good: but in regard to the colored people there is always more that is benevolent, I perceive, than just, manifested towards us. What I ask for the negro is not benevolence, not pity, not sympathy, but simply justice. . . . Let him live or die by that. If you will only untie his hands, and give him a chance, I think he will live. He will work as readily for himself as the white man. A great many delusions have been swept away by this war. One was, that the negro would not work; he has proved his ability to work. Another was, that the negro would not fight; that he possessed only the most sheepish attributes of humanity; was a perfect lamb, or an "Uncle Tom;" disposed to take off his coat whenever required, fold his hands, and be whipped by anybody who wanted to whip him. But the war has proved that there is a great deal of human nature in the negro, and that "he will fight," as Mr. Quincy, our President, said, in earlier days than these, "when there is a reasonable probability of his whipping anybody." (Laughter and applause.)

Part III:
The Rise of Big Business
and the
Settlement of the West

DOCUMENT 14

William Graham Sumner
Opposes Reform

Context: A sociologist and economist, William Graham Sumner was an influential professor at Yale University. Sumner was a champion of free trade and free markets who criticized government intervention as ineffectual and downright counterproductive. Sumner equated the laws of economic competition with Darwin's theory of evolution. Just as evolution led to the survival of the fittest species, so, too, would free markets lead to the survival of the most productive and efficient capitalists and workers. Sumner's unflinching free-market philosophy sometimes made him a critic of big business. He railed against protective tariffs that the iron and steel business often favored, and also opposed land grants to powerful railroad corporations. Sumner, like Andrew Carnegie, also wrote against imperialism.

Questions to Consider: Why did Sumner oppose reform? Who did Sumner blame for poverty? In Sumner's view, how do individuals relate to each other in modern society? What basic values did Sumner extol? What values did he criticize?

William Graham Sumner, *What Social Classes Owe Each Other* (1907)

It is commonly asserted that there are in the United States no classes, and any allusion to classes is resented. On the other hand, we constantly read and hear discussions of social topics in which the existence of social classes is assumed as a simple fact. "The poor," "the weak," "the laborers," are expressions which are used as if they had exact and well- understood definition. Discussions are made to bear upon the assumed rights, wrongs, and misfortunes of certain social classes;

and all public speaking and writing consists, in a large measure, of the discussion of general plans for meeting the wishes of classes of people who have not been able to satisfy their own desires. These classes are sometimes discontented, and sometimes not. Sometimes they do not know that anything is amiss with them until the "friends of humanity" come to them with offers of aid. Sometimes they are discontented and envious. They do not take their achievements as a fair measure of their rights. They do not blame themselves or their parents for their lot, as compared with that of other people. Sometimes they claim that they have a right to everything of which they feel the need for their happiness on earth. To make such a claim against God or Nature would, of course, be only to say that we claim a right to live on earth if we can. But God and Nature have ordained the chances and conditions of life on earth once for all. The case cannot be re-opened. We cannot get a revision of the laws of human life. We are absolutely shut up to the need and duty, if we would learn how to live happily, of investigating the laws of Nature, and deducing the rules of right living in the world as it is. These are very wearisome and commonplace tasks. They consist in labor and self-denial repeated over and over again in learning and doing. When the people whose claims we are considering are told to apply themselves to these tasks they become irritated and feel almost insulted. They formulate their claims as rights against society-that is, against some other men. In their view they have a right, not only to *pursue* happiness, but to *get* it; and if they fail to get it, they think they have a claim to the aid of other men -that is, to the labor and self-denial of other men-to get it for them. They find orators and poets who tell them that they have grievances, so long as they have unsatisfied desires.

Now, if there are groups of people who have a claim to other people's labor and self-denial, and if there are other people whose labor and self-denial are liable to be claimed by the first groups, then there certainly are "classes," and classes of the oldest and most vicious type. For a man who can command another man's labor and self-denial for the support of his own existence is a privileged person of the highest species conceivable on earth. Princes and paupers meet on this plane, and no other men are on it at all. On the other hand, a man whose labor and self-denial may be diverted from his maintenance to that of some other man is not a free man, and approaches more or less toward the position of a slave. ... We shall find that all the schemes for producing equality and obliterating the organization of society produce a new differentiation based on the worst possible distinction—the right to claim and the duty to give one man's effort for another man's satisfaction. We shall find that every effort to realize equality necessitates a sacrifice of liberty. ...

Certain ills belong to the hardships of human life. They are natural. They are part of the struggle with Nature for existence. We cannot blame our fellow-men for our share of these. My neighbor and I are both struggling to free ourselves from these ills. The fact that my neighbor has succeeded in this struggle better than I constitutes no grievance for me. Certain other ills are due to the malice of men, and to the imperfections or errors of civil institutions. These ills are an object of agitation, and a subject of discussion. The former class of ills is to be met only by manly effort and energy; the latter may be corrected by associated effort. The former class of ills is constantly grouped and generalized, and made the object of social schemes. We shall see, as we go on, what that means. The second class of ills may fall on certain social classes, and reform will take the form of interference by other classes in favor of that one. The last fact is, no doubt, the reason why people have been led, not noticing distinctions, to believe that the same method was applicable to the other class of ills. The distinction here made between the ills which belong to the struggle for existence and those which are due to the faults of human institutions is of prime importance. ...

There is no possible definition of "a poor man." A pauper is a person who cannot earn his living; whose producing powers have fallen positively below his necessary consumption; who cannot, therefore, pay his way. A human society needs the active co-operation and productive energy of every person in it. A man who is present as a consumer, yet who does not contribute either by land, labor, or capital to the work of society, is a burden. On no sound political theory ought such a person to share in the political power of the State. He drops out of the ranks of workers and producers. Society must support him. It accepts the burden, but he must be cancelled from the ranks of the rulers likewise. So much for the pauper. About him no more need be said. But he is not the "poor man." The " poor man" is an elastic term, under which any number of social fallacies may be hidden.

Neither is there any possible definition of "the weak." Some are weak in one way, and some in another; and those who are weak in one sense are strong in another. In general, however, it may be said that those whom humanitarians and philanthropists call the weak are the ones through whom the productive and conservative forces of society are wasted. They constantly neutralize and destroy the finest efforts of the wise and industrious, and are a dead-weight on the society in all its struggles to realize any better things. Whether the people who mean no harm, but are weak in the essential powers necessary to the performance of one's duties in life, or those who are malicious and vicious, do the more mischief, is a question not easy to answer.

Under the names of the poor and the weak the negligent, shiftless, inefficient, silly, and imprudent are fastened upon the industrious and prudent as a responsibility and a duty. On the one side, the terms are extended to cover the idle, intemperate, and vicious, who, by the combination, gain credit which they do not deserve, and which they could not get if they stood alone. On the other hand, the terms are extended to include wage-receivers of the humblest rank, who are degraded by the combination. The reader who desires to guard himself against fallacies should always scrutinize the terms "poor" and "weak" as used, so as to see which or how many of these classes they are made to cover.

The humanitarians, philanthropists, and reformers, looking at the facts of life as they present themselves, find enough which is sad and unpromising in the condition of many members of society. They see wealth and poverty side by side. They note great inequality of social position and social chances. They eagerly set about the attempt to account for what they see, and to devise schemes for remedying what they do not like. In their eagerness to recommend the less fortunate classes to pity and consideration they forget all about the rights of other classes; they gloss over all the faults of the classes in question and they exaggerate their misfortunes and their virtues. They invent new theories of property, distorting rights and perpetrating injustice, as any one is sure to do who sets about the readjustment of social relations with the interests of one group distinctly before his mind, and the interests of all other groups thrown into the background. When I have read certain of these discussions I have thought that it must be quite disreputable to be respectable, quite dishonest to own property, quite unjust to go one's own way and earn one's own living, and that the only really admirable person was the good-for-nothing. The man who by his own effort raises himself above poverty appears, in these discussions, to be of no account. The man who has done nothing to raise himself above poverty finds that the social doctors flock about him, bringing the capital which they have collected from the other class, and promising him the aid of the State to give him what the other had to work for. In all these schemes and projects the organized intervention of society through the State is either planned or hoped for, and the State is thus made to become the protector and guardian of certain classes.

The agents who are to direct the State action are, of course, the reformers and philanthropists. Their schemes, therefore, may always be reduced to this type-that A and B decide what C shall do for D. It will be interesting to inquire, at a later period of our discussion, who C is, and what the effect is upon him of all these arrangements. In all the discussions attention is concentrated on A and B, the noble social reformers, and on D, the " poor man." I call C the Forgotten Man, because I have never seen that any notice was taken of him in any of the discussions. When we have disposed of A, B, and D we can better appreciate the case of C, and I think that we shall find that he deserves our attention, for the worth of his character and the magnitude of his unmerited burdens. Here it may suffice to observe that, on the theories of the social philosophers to whom I have referred, we should get a new maxim of judicious living: Poverty is the best policy. If you get wealth, you will have to support other people; if you do not get wealth, it will be the duty of other people to support you.

No doubt one chief reason for the unclear and contradictory theories of class relations lies in the fact that our society, largely controlled in all its organization by one set of doctrines, still contains survivals of old social theories. In the Middle Ages men were united by custom and prescription into associations, ranks, guilds, and communities of various kinds. These ties endured as long as life lasted. Consequently society was dependent, throughout all its details, on status, and the tie, or bond, was sentimental. In our modern state, and in the United States more than anywhere else, the social structure is based on contract, and status is of the least importance. Contract, however, is rational-even rationalistic. It is also realistic, cold, and matter-of-fact. A contract relation is based on a sufficient reason, not on custom or prescription. It is not permanent. It endures only so long as the reason for it endures. In a state based on contract sentiment is out of place in any public or common affairs. It is relegated to the sphere of private and personal relations, where it depends not at all on class types, but on personal acquaintance and personal estimates. The sentimentalists among us always seize upon the survivals of the old order. They want to save them and restore them.

Whether social philosophers think it desirable or not, it is out of the question to go back to status or to the sentimental relations which once united baron and retainer, master and servant, teacher and pupil, comrade and comrade. That we have lost some grace and elegance is undeniable. That life once held more poetry and romance is true enough. But it seems impossible that any one who has studied the matter should doubt that we have gained immeasurably, and that our farther gains lie in going forward, not in going backward. The feudal ties can never be restored. If they could be restored they would bring back personal caprice, favoritism, sycophancy, and intrigue. A society based on contract is a society of free and independent men, who form ties without favor or obligation, and cooperate without cringing or intrigue. A society based on contract, therefore, gives the utmost room and chance for individual development, and for all the self-reliance and dignity of a free man. ... a society of free men, co-operating under contract, is by far the strongest society which has ever yet existed; that no such society has ever yet developed the full measure of strength of which it is capable; and that the only social improvements which are now conceivable lie in the direction of more complete realization of a society of free men united by contract, are points which cannot be controverted. It follows, however, that one man, in a free state, cannot claim help from, and cannot be charged to give help to, another. ...

DOCUMENT 15

Andrew Carnegie Defends the Accumulation of Wealth

Context: The son of poor Scottish immigrants, Andrew Carnegie began his business career as a telegraph operator for the Pennsylvania Railroad. After rapidly rising through the ranks of the railroad company and acquiring a substantial fortune, he next turned to the business of making steel. Technological and managerial innovations allowed Carnegie to dominate the market. When Carnegie sold his steel interests in 1901, he became one of the richest men in the world. Carnegie donated most of his vast fortune to various philanthropic causes, including the pursuit of world peace. Carnegie published this essay in 1889.

Questions to Consider: How did Carnegie defend the rise of big business and the inequality that accompanied it? What, in Carnegie's view, did the rich and the government owe the poor? What did Carnegie support some types of charities and oppose others? Why did Carnegie believe that individual businessmen should exert tight control over their philanthropic endeavors? How might Abraham Lincoln and other supporters of free-labor ideology have reacted to this document?

Andrew Carnegie, "Wealth" (1889)

The problem of our age is the proper administration of wealth, so that the ties of brotherhood may still bind together the rich and poor in harmonious relationship. The conditions of human life have not only been changed, but revolutionized, within the past few hundred years. In former days there was little difference between the swelling, dress, food, and environment of the chief and those of his retainers. ... The contrast between the palace of the millionaire and the cottage of the laborer with us to-day measures the change which has come with civilization.

This change, however, is not to be deplored, but welcomed as highly beneficial. It is well, nay, essential for the progress of the race, that the houses of some should be homes for all that is highest and best in literature and the arts, and for all the refinements of civilization, rather than that none should be so. Much better this great irregularity than universal squalor. ... The "good old times" were not good old times. Neither master nor servant was as well situated then as to-day. A relapse to old conditions would be disastrous to both — not the least so to him who serves — and would sweep away civilization with it. But whether the change be for good or ill, it is upon us, beyond our power to alter, and therefore to be accepted and made the best of. It is waste of time to criticize the inevitable.

It is easy to see how the change has come. One illustration will serve for almost every phase of the cause. In the manufacture of products we have the whole story. It applies to all combinations of human industry, as stimulated and enlarged by the inventions of this scientific age. Formerly articles were manufactured at the domestic hearth or in small shops which formed part of the household. The master and his apprentices worked side by side, the latter living with the master, and therefore subject to the same conditions. When these apprentices rose to be masters, there was little or no change in their mode of life, and they, in turn, educated in the same routine succeeding apprentices. There was, substantially, social equality, and even political equality, for those engaged in industrial pursuits had then little or no political voice in the State.

But the inevitable result of such a mode of manufacture was crude articles at high prices. Today the world obtains commodities of excellent quality at prices which even the generation preceding this would have deemed incredible. In the commercial world similar causes have produced similar results, and the race is benefited thereby. The poor enjoy what the rich could not before afford. What were the luxuries have become the necessaries of life. The laborer has now more comforts than the farmer had a few generations ago. The farmer has more luxuries than the landlord had, and is more richly clad and better housed. The landlord has books and pictures rarer, and appointments more artistic, than the King could then obtain.

The price we pay for this salutary change is, no doubt, great. We assemble thousands of operatives in the factory, in the mine, and in the counting-house, of whom the employer can know little or nothing, and to whom the employer is little better than a myth. All intercourse between them is at an end. Rigid Castes are formed, and, as, usual, mutual ignorance breeds mutual distrust. Each Caste is without sympathy for the other, and ready to credit anything disparaging in regard to it. Under the law of competition, the employer of thousands is forced into the strictest economies, among which the rates paid to labor figure prominently, and often there is friction between the employer and the employed, between capital and labor, between rich and poor. Human society loses homogeneity.

The price which society pays for the law of competition, like the price it pays for cheap comforts and luxuries, is also great; but the advantages of this law are also greater still, for it is to this law that we owe our wonderful material development, which brings improved conditions in its train. But, whether the law be benign or not, we must say of it, as we say of the change in the conditions of men to which we have referred: It is here; we cannot evade it; no substitutes for it have been found; and while the law may be sometimes hard for the individual, it is best for the race, because it insures the survival of the fittest in every department. We accept and welcome, therefore, as conditions to which we must accommodate ourselves, great inequality of environment, the concentration of business, industrial and commercial, in the hands of a few, and the law of competition between these, as being not only beneficial, but essential for the future progress of the race. Having accepted these, it follows that there must be great scope for the exercise of special ability in the merchant and in the manufacturer who has to conduct affairs upon a great scale, That this talent for organization and management is rare among men is proved by the fact that it invariably secures for its possessor enormous rewards, no matter where or under what laws or conditions. ... It is a law, as certain as any of the others named, that men possessed of this peculiar talent for affairs, under the free play of economic forces, must, of necessity, soon be in receipt of more revenue than can be judiciously expended upon themselves; and this law is as beneficial for the race as the others.

Objections to the foundations upon which society is based are not in order, because the condition of the race is better with these than it has been with any others which have been tried. Of the effect of any new substitutes proposed we cannot be sure. The Socialist or Anarchist who seeks to overturn present conditions is to be regarded as attacking the foundation upon which civilization itself rests, for civilization took its start from the day that the capable, industrious workman said to his incompetent and lazy fellow, "If thou dost not sow, thou shalt no reap," and thus ended primitive Communism by separating the drones from the bees. One who studies this subject will soon be brought face to face with the conclusion that upon the sacredness of property civilization itself depends — the right of the laborer to his hundred dollars in the savings bank, and equally the legal right of the millionaire to his millions. To those who propose to substitute Communism for this intense Individualism the answer, therefore, is: The race has tried that. All progress from that barbarous day to the present time has resulted from its displacement. Not evil, but good, has come to the race from the accumulation of wealth by those who have the ability and energy that produce it. ... Individualism, Private Property, the Law of Accumulation of Wealth, and the Law of Competition; these are the highest results of human experience, the soil in which society so far has produced the best fruit. Unequally or unjustly, perhaps, as these laws sometimes operate, and imperfect as they appear to the Idealist, they are, nevertheless, like the highest type of man, the best and most valuable of all that humanity has yet accomplished.

We start, then, with a condition of affairs under which the best interests of the race are promoted, but which inevitably gives wealth to the few. Thus far, accepting conditions as they exist, the situation can be surveyed and pronounced good. The question then arises, — and, if the foregoing be correct, it is the only question with which we have to deal, — What is the proper mode of administering wealth after the laws upon which civilization is founded have thrown it into the hands of the few? And it is of this great question that I believe I offer the true solution. It will be understood that *fortunes* are here spoken of, not moderate sums saved by many years of effort, the returns from which are required for the comfortable maintenance and education of families. This is not *wealth*, but only *competence*, which it should be the aim of all to acquire.

There are but three modes in which surplus wealth can be disposed of. It can be left to the families of the decedents; or it can be bequeathed for public purposes; or, finally, it can be administered during their lives by its possessors. Under the first and second modes most of the wealth of the world that has reached the few has hitherto been applied. Let us in turn consider each of these modes. The first is the most injudicious. In monarchical countries, the estates and the greatest portion of the wealth are left to the first son, that the vanity of the parent may be gratified by the thought that his name and title are to descend to succeeding generations unimpaired. The condition of this class in Europe to-day teaches the futility of such hopes or ambitions. The successors have become impoverished through their follies or from the fall in the value of land. Even in Great Britain the strict law of entail has been found inadequate to maintain the status of an hereditary class. Its soil is rapidly passing into the hands of the stranger. Under republican institutions the division of property among the children is much fairer, but the question which forces itself upon thoughtful men in all lands is: Why should men leave great fortunes to their children? If this is done from affection, is it not misguided affection? Observation teaches that, generally speaking, it is not well for the children that they should be so burdened. Neither is it well for the state. Beyond providing for the wife and daughters moderate sources of income, and very moderate allowances indeed, if any, for the sons, men may well hesitate, for it is no longer questionable that great sums bequeathed oftener work more for the injury than for the good of the recipients. Wise men will soon conclude that, for the best interests of the members of their families and of the state, such bequests are an improper use of their means. ...

As to the second mode, that of leaving wealth at death for public uses, it may be said that this is only a means for the disposal of wealth, provided a man is content to wait until he is dead before it becomes of much good in the world. Knowledge of the results of legacies bequeathed is not calculated to inspire the brightest hopes of much posthumous good being accomplished. The cases are not few in which the real object sought by the testator is not attained, nor are they few in which his real wishes are thwarted. In many cases the bequests are so used as to become only monuments of his folly. It is well to remember that it requires the exercise of not less ability than that which acquired the wealth to use it so as to be really beneficial to the community. Besides this, it may fairly be said that no man is to be extolled for doing what he cannot help doing, nor is he to be thanked by the community to which he only leaves wealth at death. Men who leave vast sums in this way may fairly be thought men who would not have left it at all, had they been able to take it with them. The memories of such cannot be held in grateful remembrance, for there is not grace in their gifts. It is not to be wondered at that such bequests seems so generally to lack the blessing.

The growing disposition to tax more and more heavily large estates left at death is a cheering indication of the growth of a salutary change in public opinion. . . . Men who continue hoarding great sums all their lives, the proper use of which for the public ends would work good to the community, should be made to feel that the community, in the form of the state, cannot thus be deprived of its proper share. By taxing estates heavily at death the state marks its condemnation of the selfish millionaire's unworthy life. ...

There remains, then, only one mode of using great fortunes; but in this we have the true antidote for the temporary unequal distribution of wealth, the reconciliation of the rich and the poor — a reign of harmony — another ideal, differing, indeed, from that of the Communist in requiring only the further evolution of existing conditions, not the total overthrow of our civilization. It is founded upon the present most intense individualism, and the race is prepared to put it in practice by degrees whenever it pleases. Under its sway we shall have an ideal state, in which the surplus wealth of the few will become, in the best sense, the property of the many, because administered for the common good, and this wealth, passing through the hands of the few, can be made a much more potent force for the elevation of our race than if it had been distributed in small sums to the people themselves. Even the poorest can be made to see this, and to agree that great sums gathered by some of their fellow-citizens and spent for public purposes, from which the masses reap the principal benefit, are more valuable to them than if scattered among them through the course of many years in trifling amounts. ...

Poor and restricted are our opportunities in this life; narrow our horizon; our best work most imperfect; but rich men should be thankful for one inestimable boon. They have it in their power during their lives to busy themselves in organizing benefactions from which the masses of their fellows will derive lasting advantage, and thus dignify their own lives. ...

This, then, is held to be the duty of the man of Wealth: First, to set an example of modest, unostentatious living, shunning display or extravagance; to provide moderately for the legitimate wants of those dependent upon him; and after doing so to consider all surplus revenues which come to him simply as trust funds, which he is called upon to administer, and strictly bound as a matter of duty to administer in the manner which, in his judgment, is best calculated to produce the most beneficial results for the community — the man of wealth thus becoming the mere agent and trustee for his poorer brethren, bringing to their service his superior wisdom, experience, and ability to administer, doing for them better than they would or could do for themselves. ...

The best uses to which surplus wealth can be put have already been indicated. Those who would administer wisely must, indeed, be wise, for one of the serious obstacles to the improvement of our race is indiscriminate charity. It were better for mankind that the millions of the rich were thrown into the sea than so spent as to encourage the slothful, the drunken, the unworthy. Of every thousand dollars spent in so called charity to-day, it is probable that $950 is unwisely spent; so spent, indeed, as to produce the very evils which it proposes to mitigate or cure. A well-known writer of philosophic books admitted the other day that he had given a quarter of a dollar to a man who approached him as he was coming to visit the house of his friend. He knew nothing of the habits of this beggar; knew not the use that would be made of this money, although he had every reason to suspect that it would be spent improperly. This man professed to be a disciple of Herbert Spencer; yet the quarter-dollar given that night will probably work more injury than all the money which its thoughtless donor will ever be able to give in true charity will do good. He only gratified his own feelings, saved himself from annoyance, — and this was probably one of the most selfish and very worst actions of his life, for in all respects he is most worthy.

In bestowing charity, the main consideration should be to help those who will help themselves; to provide part of the means by which those who desire to improve may do so; to give those who desire to rise the aids by which they may rise; to assist, but rarely or never to do all. ... Every one has, of course, cases of individuals brought to his own knowledge where temporary assistance can do genuine good, and these he will not overlook. But the amount which can be wisely given by the individual for individuals is necessarily limited by his lack of knowledge of the circumstances connected with each. He is the only true reformer who is as careful and as anxious not to aid the unworthy as he is to aid the worthy, and, perhaps, even more so, for in aims-giving more injury is probably done by rewarding vice than by relieving virtue. ...

Thus is the problem of Rich and Poor to be solved. The laws of accumulation will be left free; the laws of distribution free. Individualism will continue, but the millionaire will be but a trustee for the poor; intrusted for a season with a great part of the increased wealth of the community, but administering it for the community far better than it could or would have done for itself. The best minds will thus have reached a stage in the development of the race in which it is clearly seen that there is no mode of disposing of surplus wealth creditable to thoughtful and earnest men into whose hands it flows save by using it year by year for the general good. This day already dawns. But a little while, and although, without incurring the pity of their fellows, men may die sharers in great business enterprises from which their capital cannot be or has not been withdrawn, and is left chiefly at death for public uses, yet the man who dies leaving behind him millions of available wealth, which was his to administer during life, will pass away "unwept, unhonored, and unsung," no matter to what uses he leaves the dross which he cannot take with him. Of such as these the public verdict will then be: "The man who dies thus rich dies disgraced."

Such, in my opinion, is the true Gospel concerning Wealth, obedience to which is destined some day to solve the problem of the Rich and the Poor, and to bring "Peace on earth, among men Good Will."

DOCUMENT 16

Union Leaders Debate
"Pure and Simple" Unionism

Context: In the late nineteenth and early twentieth century, union leaders and grassroots organizers heatedly debated how workers could best respond to the growing power of corporations. Many workers belonged to the Knights of Labor, an inclusive organization that sought to abolish the "wage system." When the Knights of Labor collapsed, Samuel Gompers and the American Federation of Labor became the most influential voice of the labor movement. Focusing on pragmatic demands for higher wages and an eight-hour day, the AFL organized mostly skilled and craft workers. The AFL strategy upset many socialists, who believed that a more inclusive political approach was needed. In the first document, Adolph Strasser, a long-time ally of Gompers, defines what would become known as "Pure and Simple" unionism. In the second document, socialist Mahlon Barnes criticizes this approach as "pure and simpledom."

Questions to Consider: What were the ultimate goals of Strasser and his trade union? Why did Strasser stress the negative consequences of overproduction and how did he propose to combat them? In what ways, according to Strasser, were trade unions actually conservative institutions? Were there any radical elements to Strasser's political program? What, according to Barnes, were the weaknesses of the AFL? What political program did Barnes support? What type of worker was more likely to support Barnes instead of Strasser?

Adolph Strasser, Congressional Testimony (1883)

Question. Please state your residence and occupation.—Answer. I reside in New York. At present I am acting president and secretary of the Cigarmakers' International Union of America, and editor of the journal of the organization. I do not work at my trade now, but am simply acting as an officer of the Cigarmakers' International Union. ...

Q. I see you recognize the idea of overproduction and of the necessity of obtaining outlets for our products in order that panics may be avoided. In that line it occurs to me to ask you whether it is in contemplation, as one of the ultimate purposes of the trades unions, that their funds shall be accumulated so that if, in order to prevent a panic by the excess of products being thrown upon the market, they can in future lessen production by suspending labor for a time, and maintain the laborers meanwhile out of the accumulated fund. Have your trades organizations any such idea as that?—A. The trades unions try to prevent panics, but in fact they cannot prevent them, because panics are governed by influences beyond their control.

Q. Panics result, do they not, largely from overproduction?—A. The trades unions try to make their members better consumers, thereby enlarging the home market, and at the same time to make them better producers. If we can make the working people generally better consumers we shall have no panics.

Q. But if the increase of the power of production goes on by the improvement of machinery and all that, will no your efforts be counteracted in that way?—A. Then we propose a reduction of the hours of labor. That will decrease production and will increase consumption. We hold that a man who works but eight hours a day will demand a better home than a man who works longer hours; he will not be willing to live in one or two squalid rooms; he will demand better clothes, better food, more books, more newspapers, more education; more of the commodities that labor provides, more of the world's wealth, and that will bring about a better distribution of wealth and will consequently check panics to a certain extent. I do not believe that it is possible for the trades unions to do away with panics altogether, because panics depend not merely upon the condition of the industries of the United States, but upon the condition of the industries of the whole civilized world.

Q. Do you not contemplate, in the end, the participation of all labor and of all men in the benefits of the trades unions?—A. Of course we try to extend the good of the trades unions as well as we can and as far as we can.

By Mr. Pugh:

Q. You are seeking to improve home matters first?—A. Yes, sir; I look first to the trade I represent; I look first to cigars, to the interests of men who employ me to represent their interests.

The CHAIRMAN. I was only asking you in regard to your ultimate ends.

The WITNESS. We have no ultimate ends. We are going on from day to day. We are fighting only for immediate objects—objects that can be realized in a few years.

By Mr. Call:

Q. You want something better to eat and to wear, and better houses to live in?—A. Yes; we want to dress better and to live better, and become better off and better citizens generally.

The CHAIRMAN. I see that you are a little sensitive lest it should be thought that you are a mere theorizer. I do not look upon you in that light at all.

The WITNESS. Well, we say in our constitution that we are opposed to theorists, and I have to represent the organization here. We are all practical men.

By The Chairman:

Q. Have you not a theory upon which you have organized?—A. Yes, sir; our theory is the experience of the past in the United States and in Great Britain. That is our theory, based upon actual facts. Our organization has been experimenting for the last twenty years until we have arrived at a solid footing resting on experience.

Q. In other words you have arrived at the theory which you are trying to apply?—A. We have arrived at a practical result.

Q. But a practical result is the application of a theory, is it not?—A. Well, certainly there is no practical result without some theory.

Q. I agree to that. The difference is between good theories and bad ones, between false theories and true ones.—A. Yes; that is all.

By Mr. Pugh:

Q. You have furnished us with a very valuable fund of information. Have you any further statement to make of any other facts connected with this labor question?—A. Well, I have not yet proposed any remedies.

Q. We shall be glad to hear your views on that subject.

A. Well, we propose—

1. That trades unions shall be incorporated. At present there are a great many of the States that do not protect our funds. It is simply a breach of trust to use our funds improperly and we have lost considerable money in that way. There was one case where the president of an organization ran away with $327 and it cost us over $1,000 to bring him to justice, and if it had not been in the State of Illinois, we probably could not have done anything with him. In the State of Michigan we have no protection for our funds. Being, as we are, a benevolent organization, we desire some protection from the Government, that is, a legal recognition and protection for the property we hold. The money we hold today is invested in savings

banks, in probably 145 different banks, and there may be an opportunity to invest it in some safer institutions or in something else; but at present we have no right to invest our money except in Government bonds or in savings banks, and we claim the same right as the banks and other corporations have to be incorporated. ...

2. The next demand we make, one which we think will benefit labor, is the enforcement of the eight-hour law and its extension to the operation of all patents granted by the, Government. By that I mean that if the Government grants a patent to anybody for any kind of invention, it shall be with the stipulation that the labor performed under that patent shall not be more than eight hours a day.

3. Our third demand is this: We claim that it is necessary to obtain information in regard to such questions as those which this committee is now investigating, and to that end we believe there is a necessity for a national bureau of labor statistics. That was attempted by the organized workingmen of the United States in 1866, and we hold that it is time to provide for it by law. To-day there are very few trades in the United States which have the means of getting such information in regard to their own members as I am able to give in regard to the members of our organization, as to wages, cost of living, and so on. We hold that such a national bureau of labor statistics would give our legislators a great deal of information which will be very valuable to them as legislators, and we hold further that it would be a benefit, not only to labor, but, also, even greater benefit to capital, to have all this information compiled annually and distributed generally.

4. Our fourth demand is what I have already stated, that the Senate Committee on Finance shall report an amendment to the revenue laws, prohibiting the granting of licenses after May 4, 1884, to prisons, penitentiaries, and other such places for the manufacture of cigars. This demand is made, of course, simply in the interest of my own trade.

These are all the demands which we think it necessary to make now, and we believe that if these are granted, they will tend to relieve labor, to prevent strikes, and to accomplish the results formulated in the resolution of the Senate under which you are acting.

Q. Is the tendency of the trades unions on the whole to increase or to lessen strikes, as an ultimate result?—A. Our organization has prevented within the last three years over 200 strikes. No strike for an increase of wages can be approved under our constitution unless by a two-thirds vote of all the unions, and if a union makes an unreasonable demand it is voted down. For instance, within three years, Rochester has made three applications, and they have all been voted down. And so it is with other cities.

Q. Do you not believe that is the tendency of trades organizations generally?— A. Yes; there is a tendency in old organizations to avoid strikes; new organizations are generally formed for the purpose of jumping into a strike. ...

Q. What is the feeling on the part of wage receivers generally towards their employers; is it a feeling of amity and confidence or is it a feeling of distrust?—A.

In places where men receive good wages there is a general good feeling; where they receive poor wages—starvation wages—there is generally bad feeling. The feeling between labor and capital depends largely on the employers. If they treat their men well and pay them fair wages, there is generally good feeling. If the employers treat their men badly and pay starvation wages, there is generally bad feeling. It depends wholly upon the employer. He has the power to encourage good feeling or the reverse.

Q. Mr. Lenz, the editor of a paper called Capital and Labor, expressed an opinion here that there was a growing socialistic feeling among the members of the trades unions; what is your observation in regard to that?—A. It is not so in the Cigar-makers' International Union. That organization does not inquire into the private opinions of a member; it takes in Democrats and Republicans, or anybody else so long as they are workers at the trade; that organization aims at practical measures, and will not allow any vague theories to be foisted upon it.

Q. Then you deny Mr. Lenz's statement so far as it relates to your organization?—A. As regards the Cigar-makers' International Union, I positively deny it. The members of that organization are simply practical men, going for practical objects that can be accomplished in a few years; they are no "trimmers."

Mahlon Barnes, "Pure and Simpledom" (1896)

And what is pure and simpledom doing to meet the changed conditions which confront us? . . . You can just about as much batter down monopoly with the boycott and wring material concessions from organized capital through strikes, with the law, the machinery of the State, and the power and armament of government on land and sea against you, as you can batter down the great granite shaft on Bunker Hill with a battering ram pointed with a pumpkin ...

Mind you, we do not undervalue the potency of strikes nor ignore the necessity of boycotts. We Socialists are the best, the most persistent and the most uncompromising strikers and boycotters on earth. ... But we Socialists desire to extend the power of trades unions and of the working class by uniting political action with economic resistance. We propose to use the highest intellectual weapon known to man; that which has come to us through 600 years of struggle in which the brain and brawn of Roman, Dane, Celt and Saxon and Norman was commingled, and we propose to unite the ballot with the strike and boycott.

In England and the United States trades unions preceded Socialism. Our spirit is now slowly but persistently, and I believe triumphantly, entering the body of the rank and file of organized labor. It has already done so to considerable extent in the large cities, and is gradually permeating the most alert and intelligent men and women in the ranks of labor. ...

What is all this, let me ask you in all seriousness, but the broader and more-intelligent application of trades union methods? To strike down the representatives of capitalism in the supreme law-making bodies of the world, and placing therein the representatives of organized labor is the kind of a strike that ever can be engaged in.

To refuse to vote money out of the pockets of the people to be expended for powder, bullets and guns, to make your sons bayonet-bearers and cannon-fodder, to orphan your brother and widow your sisters, to break mothers' hearts and fill the land with tears and blood so that plutocracy may survive and barbarism perpetuate itself—that is the most sublime boycott conceivable to the mind of man.

But at the exact point where old trades unionism raises the white flag, Socialism raises the red flag, and insists that there is a class struggle and that capitalism can and must be disarmed at the ballot box, where the workers outnumber its cohorts a thousand to one.

Let me point out to you the fundamental difference between this—the method of Socialism, and the methods of pure and simpledom.

We have had, upon the economic field, such reverses as came to us from Homestead, Chicago, Philadelphia, Brooklyn, Milwaukee, etc , from which even the most fossilized trades unionist cannot possibly draw more than the "sweet use of adversity." If concentration of wealth into the hands of the few necessitates the pauperization of the masses proportioned to the perfection of machinery, the reduction of wages and increased precariousness of the position of the wage earners, then it follows that the power of resistance on the part of the worker becomes constantly more feeble—defeats more certain and frequent, and victories like angel's visits, fewer and farther between. The result is the logical and necessary outcome of conditions—is certain, absolute and inevitable—and it is discouraging and disheartening to trades unionists and all who sympathize with labor.

Mark now the difference. With honest leaders who will preach the truth and labor for class-consciousness, the great lessons taught by the failures will intensify class feeling, rending more and more clearly apparent the necessity of political action, and as every election, municipal, state and national, registers the growth of class-consciousness, we shall go, instead of from defeat to defeat, like scourged hounds, from triumph to victory as our growing numbers pass in review, and as the unconquerable hosts of labor, armed with the freeman's ballot, come nearer and nearer possessing themselves of the functions of governmental power, legislative, judicial and executive.

I know very well the pure and simple leaders call us dreamers; but are you [not] quite sure that they themselves are either asleep, or blind, or both?

Dreamers! Indeed? So was Moses, marching out of plague-smitten Egypt with hope-uplifted Israel. So was Luther of Worms defying Rome in her pride of power—the noblest of all the noble there. ... And so was [William Lloyd] Garrison, the iron-hearted, whom you have placed in magnificent bronze overlooking the Commons.

Darkness or light, justice or might, slavery or freedom, Socialism or capitalism, that is the real issue which confronts the world to-day ...

DOCUMENT 17

The AFL Supports Chinese Exclusion

Context: Between 1851 and 1882, approximately 300,000 Chinese settled in the United States, often working as railroads laborers, miners, and agricultural workers. Fearing a huge influx of Chinese workers, Congress passed the Chinese Exclusion Act in 1882, which was vigorously supported by trade unions. Twenty years later, the AFL published a pamphlet entitled Some Reasons for Chinese Exclusion: Meat vs. Rice, which called for an extension of the Chinese Exclusion Act. Samuel Gompers and the AFL argued that large numbers of immigrants allowed big business to ruthlessly exploit their workers. Congress extended the Chinese Exclusion Act in 1902.

Questions to Consider: How did this pamphlet use racism and gender ideology to make its case? Why had U. S. foreign policy made Chinese exclusion a particularly important goal of organized labor? To what extent could the general arguments here, whether economic or social, also be applied to immigrants from Eastern Europe? What does this pamphlet tell us about the strengths and weaknesses of the early twentieth-century labor movement?

Some Reasons for Chinese Exclusion: Meat vs. Rice (1901)

In view of the near expiration of the present law excluding Chinese laborers from coming to the United States and the recognized necessity of either reenacting the present or adopting a similar law, the American Federation of Labor has determined to present its reasons and solicit the cooperation of not only all of its affiliated organizations, but also of all citizens who may consider the preservation of American institutions and the welfare of a majority of our people of sufficient importance to assist in this work.

To those anxious or willing to familiarize themselves with the actual conditions and with the causes which prompt us at this time to present our case, a careful perusal of this little pamphlet is recommended.

We have been to some trouble in obtaining the data herein contained, but were extremely careful in presenting only such as is entirely reliable and obtained through official sources. We furthermore desire to assure our readers that in maintaining our position we are not inspired by a scintilla of prejudice of any kind, but with the best interests of our country uppermost in our mind simply request fair consideration.

HISTORICAL

Beginning with the most menial avocations they gradually invaded our industry they gradually invaded one industry after another until they not merely took the places of our girls as domestics and cooks, the laundry of our poorer white women, but the places of the men and boys, as boot and shoemakers, cigarmakers, bagmakers, miners, farm laborers, brickmakers, tailors, slippermakers, etc. In the ladies' furnishing line they have absolute control, displacing hundreds of our girls, who would otherwise find profitable employment. Whatever business or trade they enter is doomed for the white laborer, as competition is surely impossible. Not that the Chinese would not rather work for high wages than low, but in order to gain control he will work so cheaply as to bar all efforts of his competitor. But not only has the workingman gained this bitter experience, but the manufacturers and merchants have equally been the sufferers. The Chinese laborer will work cheaper for a Chinese employer than he will for a white man, as has been invariably proven, and, as a rule, he boards with his Chinese employer. The Chinese merchant or manufacturer will undersell his white competitor, and if uninterrupted will finally gain possession of the entire field. Such is the history of the race wherever they have come in contact with other peoples. None can understand their silent and irresistible flow, and their millions already populate and command labor and the trade of the islands and nations of the Pacific. ...

DOES HISTORY REPEAT ITSELF?

The people of the Pacific coast, who by reason of their long enforced contact and bitter experience ought to be credited with some knowledge on the subject, almost unanimously declare that it does.

It is a most serious mistake for the citizens of the Eastern States to believe that anti-Chinese sentiment is limited to any particular class or faction, creed or nationality.

The sentiment is general; there is practically no division of opinion on that subject. At an election held in 1879 the question of Chinese immigration was submitted to the voters of the State of California as a test of sentiment, and resulted in 154,638 votes being cast against immigration and only 883 votes in favor. In other words, the people of California in proportion of 175 to 1 voted for the protection of the Federal Government from Chinese immigration. Surely it can not be held that this almost unanimous vote of the electors of an entire State was cast without good and sufficient cause, and not as a result of demagogic or irresponsible agitation.

There is no good reason to believe that this sentiment has undergone the slightest change. On the contrary, there is a great cause for stricter exclusion. Our recently acquired possessions of the Hawaiian and Philippine Islands have added hundreds of thousands of Asiatic coolies to our population, the correct disposal of which already causes serious apprehension to our American statesmen. ...

The reports of the bureau of labor statistics of California of the years 1883–4, 1886, 1890, and 1900 furnish ample proof of the utter impossibility of our race to compete with the Mongolian. Their ability to subsist and thrive under conditions which would mean starvation and suicide to the cheapest laborer of Europe secures to them an advantage which baffles the statesman and economist to overcome, how much less the chances of the laborers pitted in competition against them.

For many years it was impossible to get white persons to do the menial labor usually performed by Chinese. It was Chinaman's labor, and not fit for white. In the agricultural districts a species of tramp has been created, known as the blanket man. White agricultural laborers seldom find permanent employment; the Chinese are preferred. During harvest time the white man is forced to wander from ranch to ranch and find employment here and there for short periods of time, with the privilege of sleeping in barns or haystacks. He is looked upon as a vagabond, unfit to associate with his employer of to eat from the same table with him. The negro slave of the South was housed and fed, but the white trash of California is placed beneath the Chinese.

The white domestic servant was expected to live in the room originally built for John, generally situated in the cellar and void of all comforts, frequently unpainted or unpapered, containing a bedstead and a chair. Anything was good enough for John, and the white girl had to be satisfied as well. Is it any wonder that self-respecting girls refused to take service under those conditions? And what is true of agricultural laborers and domestics equally applies to the trades in which Chinese were largely employed. Absolute servility was expected from those who took the place of the Chinaman, and it will take years to obliterate these traces of inferiority and reestablish the proper relations of employer and employee. ...

Social Habits

Of their social habits, none can form a proper conception unless personally familiar therewith.

In a sanitary point of view Chinatown presents a singular anomaly. With the habits, manners, customs, and whole economy of life violating every accepted rule of hygiene; with open cesspools, exhalations from water-closets, sinks, urinals, and sewers tainting the atmosphere with noxious vapors and stifling odors;

with people herded and packed in damp cellars, living literally the life of vermin, badly fed and clothed, addicted to the daily use of opium to the extent that many hours of each day or night are passed in the delirious stupefaction of its influence, it is not to be denied that, as a whole, the general health of this locality compares more than favorably with other sections of the city which are surrounded by far more favorable conditions. ...

The frequent custom with these people is to have the brick and mortar bench where cooking is carried on, the sink, always more or less filthy, and an open, filthy, bad-smelling water-closet, all adjoining each other in the same room, or under the same cover. Frequently a space at the end of this cooking range—if we may call it so—is used as a urinal, the only outlet from which is the absorption of and seepage through some earth placed there for that purpose, while the intermingling odors of cooking, sink, water-closet, and urinal added to fumes of opium and tobacco smoke, and indescribable, unknowable, all pervading atmosphere of the Chinese quarter, make up a perfume which can neither be imagined nor described. This is no exaggeration, nor is it a fancy sketch. It is one of the common features of life in Chinatown.

The Federation of Chinese Exclusion 1881

As an evidence that the American Federation of Labor is by no means a latter-day convert to Chinese exclusion, we herewith present the following preamble and resolution, adopted at the convention of the Federation in 1881:

Whereas the experience of the last thirty years in California and on the Pacific coast having proved conclusively that the presence of Chinese and their competition with free white labor is one of the greatest evils with which any country can be afflicted: Therefore be it

Resolved, That we use our best efforts to get rid of this monstrous evil (which threatens, unless checked, to extend to other parts of the Union) by the dissemination of information respecting its true character, and by urging upon our Representatives in the United States Congress the absolute necessity of passing laws entirely prohibiting the immigration of Chinese into the United States.

1900

The position then taken by the American Federation of Labor has been constantly maintained, and at the convention of Louisville, Kentucky, December, 1900, the following preamble and resolutions were adopted:

Whereas recent events have increased the danger threatening the American workers from Mongolian labor; and

Whereas the Chinese-exclusion law expires in 1902; and

Whereas the Pacific Coast and intermountain States are suffering severely from Chinese and Japanese cheap coolie labor:

Therefore be it

Resolved, That Congress strengthen and reenact the Chinese exclusion law, including in its provisions all Mongolian labor.

Frederick Jackson Turner
Outlines the "Frontier Thesis"

Context: In 1893 Frederick Jackson Turner was a young historian when he delivered this paper in Chicago, which was the site of a huge world's fair commemorating the 400th anniversary of Christopher Columbus and the "discovery" of the Americas. Turner's paper gradually gained renown as one of the most influential arguments in U. S. history. Keep in mind that Turner was writing in a time of tremendous economic and social change, which included mass immigration and the dramatic growth of large cities. Many of Turner's specific arguments are now dated, but his broader thesis continues to generate debate among U. S. historians.

Questions to Consider: What is Turner's basic argument? How does Turner define the frontier—is it a place, a process, or something altogether different? What groups did Turner ignore? Why would Turner's contemporaries find "The Significance of the Frontier" alternatively reaffirming and disturbing?

Frederick Jackson Turner, "The Significance of the Frontier in American History" (1893)

In a recent bulletin of the Superintendent of the Census for 1890 appear these significant words: "Up to and including 1880 the country had a frontier of settlement, but at present the unsettled area has been so broken into by isolated bodies of settlement that there can hardly be said to be a frontier line. In the discussion of its extent, its westward movement, etc., it can not, therefore, any longer have a place in the census reports." This brief official statement marks the closing of a great historic movement. Up to our own day American history has been in a large degree the history of the colonization of the Great West. The existence of an area of free land, its continuous recession, and the advance of American settlement westward, explain American development.

Behind institutions, behind constitutional forms and modifications, lie the vital forces that call these organs into life and shape them to meet changing conditions. The peculiarity of American institutions is, the fact that they have been compelled to adapt themselves to the changes of an expanding people—to the changes involved in crossing a continent, in winning a wilderness, and in developing at each area of this progress out of the primitive economic and political conditions of the frontier into the complexity of city life. . . . American development has exhibited not merely advance along a single line, but a return to primitive conditions on a continually advancing frontier line, and a new development for that area. American social development has been continually beginning over again on the frontier. This perennial rebirth, this fluidity of American life, this expansion westward with its new opportunities, its continuous touch with the simplicity of primitive society, furnish the forces dominating American character. The true point of view in the history of this nation is not the Atlantic coast, it is the Great West. . . .

The American frontier is sharply distinguished from the European frontier—a fortified boundary line running through dense populations. The most significant thing about the American frontier is, that it lies at the hither edge of free land. In the census reports it is treated as the margin of that settlement which has a density of two or more to the square mile. The term is an elastic one, and for our purposes does not need sharp definition. We shall consider the whole frontier belt including the Indian country and the outer margin of the "settled area " of the census reports. This paper will make no attempt to treat the subject exhaustively; its aim is simply to call attention to the frontier as a fertile field for investigation, and to suggest some of the problems which arise in connection with it.

In the settlement of America we have to observe how European life entered the continent, and how America modified and developed that life and reacted on Europe. Our early history is the study of European germs developing in an American environment . . . The frontier is the line of most rapid and effective Americanization. The wilderness masters the colonist. It finds him a European in dress, industries, tools, modes of travel, and thought. It takes him from the railroad car and puts him in the birch canoe. It strips off the garments of civilization and arrays him in the hunting shirt and the moccasin. It puts him in the log cabin of the Cherokee and Iroquois and runs an Indian palisade around him. Before long he has gone to planting Indian corn and plowing with a sharp stick, he shouts the war cry and takes the scalp in orthodox Indian fashion. In short, at the frontier the environment is at first too strong for the man. He must accept the conditions which it furnishes, or perish, and so he fits himself into the Indian clearings and follows the Indian trails. Little by little he transforms the wilderness, but the outcome is not the old Europe, . . . [but] a new product that is American.

At first, the frontier was the Atlantic coast. It was the frontier of Europe in a very real sense. Moving westward, the frontier became more and more American. ... From decade to decade distinct advances of the frontier occurred. By the census of 1820 the settled area included Ohio, southern Indiana and Illinois, southeastern Missouri, and about one-half of Louisiana. This settled area had surrounded Indian areas, and the management of these tribes became an object of political concern. The frontier region of the time lay along the Great Lakes, where Astor's American Fur Company operated in the Indian trade, and beyond the Mississippi, where Indian traders extended their activity even to the Rocky Mountains; Florida also furnished frontier conditions. The Mississippi River region was the scene of typical frontier settlements. The rising steam navigation on western waters, the opening of the Erie Canal, and the westward extension of cotton culture added five frontier states to the Union in this period. ...

In the middle of this century the line indicated by the present eastern boundary of Indian Territory, Nebraska, and Kansas marked the frontier. Minnesota and Wisconsin still exhibited frontier conditions, but the distinctive frontier of the period is found in California, where the gold discoveries had sent a sudden tide of adventurous miners, and in Oregon, and the settlements in Utah. Railroads, fostered by land grants, sent an increasing tide of immigrants into the Far West. The United States Army fought a series of Indian wars in Minnesota, Dakota, and the Indian Territory. By 1880 the settled area had been pushed into northern Michigan, Wisconsin, and Minnesota, along Dakota rivers, and in the Black Hills region, and was ascending the rivers of Kansas and Nebraska. The development of mines in Colorado had drawn isolated frontier settlements into that region, and Montana and Idaho were receiving settlers. The frontier was found in these mining camps and the ranches of the Great Plains. The superintendent of the census for 1890 reports, as previously stated, that the settlements of the West lie so scattered over the region that there can no longer be said to be a frontier line. ...

At the Atlantic frontier one can study the germs of processes repeated at each successive frontier. We have the complex European life sharply precipitated by the wilderness into the simplicity of primitive conditions. The first frontier had to meet its Indian question, its question of the disposition of the public domain, of the means of intercourse with older settlements, of the extension of political organization, of religious and educational activity. And the settlement of these and similar questions for one frontier served as a guide for the next. ... But with all these similarities there are essential differences, due to the place element and the time element. It is evident that the farming frontier of the Mississippi Valley presents different conditions from the mining frontier of the Rocky Mountains. The frontier reached by the Pacific Railroad, surveyed into rectangles, guarded by the United States Army, and recruited by the daily immigrant ship, moves forward at a swifter pace and in a different way than the frontier reached by the birch canoe or the pack horse. The geologist traces patiently the shores of ancient seas, maps their areas, and compares the older and the newer. It would be a work worth the historian's labors to mark these various frontiers and in detail compare one with another. ...

We may next inquire what were the influences on the East and on the Old World. ... The most important effect of the frontier has been in the promotion of democracy here and in Europe. As has been indicated, the frontier is productive of individualism. Complex society is precipitated by the wilderness into a kind of primitive organization based on the family. The tendency is anti-social. It produces antipathy to control, and particularly to any direct control. ... The frontier individualism has from the beginning promoted democracy. The frontier States that came into the Union in the first quarter of a century of its existence came in with democratic suffrage provisions, and had reactive effects of the highest importance upon the older States whose peoples were being attracted there. An extension of the franchise became essential. ... The rise of democracy as an effective force in the nation came in with western preponderance under Jackson and William Henry Harrison, and it meant the triumph of the frontier— with all of its good and with all of its evil elements.

So long as free land exists, the opportunity for a competency exists, and economic power secures political power. But the democracy born of free land, strong in selfishness and individualism, intolerant of administrative experience and education, and pressing individual liberty beyond its proper bounds, has its dangers as well as its benefits. Individualism in America has allowed a laxity in regard to governmental affairs which has rendered possible the spoils system and all the manifest evils that follow from the lack of a highly developed civic spirit. In this connection may be noted also the influence of frontier conditions in permitting lax business honor, inflated paper currency and wild-cat banking. ...

The East has always feared the result of an unregulated advance of the frontier, and has tried to check and guide it. Even Thomas Benton, the man of widest views of the destiny of the West, ... declared [in 1825] that along the ridge of the Rocky mountains "the western limits of the Republic should be drawn, and the statue of the fabled god Terminus should be raised upon its highest peak, never to be thrown down." But the attempts to limit the boundaries, to restrict land sales and settlement, and to deprive the West of its share of political power were all in vain. Steadily the frontier of settlement advanced and carried with it individualism, democracy, and nationalism, and powerfully affected the East and the Old World.

From the conditions of frontier life came intellectual traits of profound importance. The works of travelers along each frontier from colonial days onward describe certain common traits, and these traits have, while softening down, still persisted as survivals in the place of their origin, even when a higher social organization succeeded. The result is that to the frontier the American intellect owes its striking characteristics. That coarseness and strength combined with acuteness and inquisitiveness; that practical, inventive turn of mind, quick to find expedients; that masterful grasp of material things, lacking in the artistic but powerful to effect great ends; that restless, nervous energy; that dominant individualism, working for good and for evil, and withal that buoyancy and exuberance which comes with freedom-these are traits of the frontier, or traits called out elsewhere because of the existence of the frontier. Since the days when the fleet of Columbus sailed into the waters of the New World, America has been another name for opportunity, and the people of the United States have taken their tone from the incessant expansion which has not only been open but has even been forced upon them. ... [E]ach frontier did indeed furnish a new field of opportunity, a gate of escape from the bondage of the past; and freshness, and confidence, and scorn of older society, impatience of its restraints and its ideas, and indifference to its lessons, have accompanied the frontier. ... And now, four centuries from the discovery of America, at the end of a hundred years of life under the Constitution, the frontier has gone, and with its going has closed the first period of American history.

DOCUMENT 19

J. Q. Smith Proposes
New Indian Policy

Context: J. Q. Smith was Indian Commissioner in 1876, when he wrote this report to the Secretary of the Interior. In 1877, federal troops under Philip Sheridan crushed a Sioux-Cheyenne uprising in the Dakotas, which spelled the end of Indian military resistance throughout much of the West. After the military subjugation of the western Indians, a reform movement to "civilize" Native Americans gained momentum among some white, middle-class Protestants. A major goal of the reform movement was to give land to individual families and end tribal ownership. In 1887 the Dawes Act allotted land directly to Indian families—just as Smith proposed in this plan—but much of the land ended up in the hands of white settlers.

Questions to Consider: What problems did Smith see in Indian policy as it stood in 1876? How does he defines "civilization"? Did Smith genuinely care for the welfare of Native Americans? In what ways were his proposals constructive? In what ways were they misguided? How did Smith characterize previous Indian Removals? Why did Smith refer to Reconstruction policies in the South?

"Report of J. Q. Smith to the Secretary of Interior" (1876)

From the first settlement of the country by white men until a comparatively recent period, the Indians have been constantly driven westward from the Atlantic. A zigzag, ever-varying line, more or less definitely marked, extending from Canada to the Gulf of Mexico, and always slowly moving west, has been known as the "frontier" or "border." Along this border has been an almost incessant struggle, the Indians to retain and the whites to get possession; the war being broken by periods of occasional and temporary peace, which usually followed treaties whereby the Indians agreed to surrender large tracts of their lands. This peace would continue until the lands surrendered had been occupied by whites, when the pressure of emigration would again break over the border, and the Indian, by force or treaty, be compelled to surrender another portion of his cherished hunting-grounds.

So long as the illimitable West offered to the Indian fresh hunting-grounds, he was unwilling to exchange his wild freedom and indolent existence for the restraints and toil of the rude and imperfect civilization to which it was possible for him in only one life-time to attain. If any tribe of Indians in this country had made the effort to abandon their savage mode of life, and undertake self-support by labor, it is at least doubtful whether for many years the change would not have rendered them more miserable and wretched. Their lack of means, of knowledge, and of previous training would, in all probability, have made such an attempt a conspicuous failure. If individual Indians had succeeded in acquiring property, they would probably have been swindled out of it by unscrupulous white men. The natural and the easiest course was to remove west and continue to hunt.

Toward the close of the first half of this century the tide of emigration and adventure swept even the frontier away and rushed across the continent. Throughout the vast regions of the West the adventurous, grasping Anglo-Saxon race is dominant and in possession of the fairest and richest portions of the land. Except in the Indian Territory and perhaps Dakota, the white exceeds the Indian population. No new hunting-grounds remain, and the civilization or the utter destruction of the Indians is inevitable. The next twenty-five years are to determine the fate of a race. If they cannot be taught, and taught very soon, to accept the necessities of their situation and begin in earnest to provide for their own wants by labor in civilized pursuits, they are destined to speedy extinction. From the fact that for so long a period Indian civilization has been retarded, it must not be concluded that some inherent characteristic in the race disqualifies it for civilized life. It may well be doubted whether this be true of any race of men. Surely it cannot be true of a race, any portion of which has made the actual progress realized by some of our Indians. They can and do learn to labor; they can and do learn to read. Many thousands today are engaged in civilized occupations. But the road out of barbarism is a long and difficult one. Even in enlightened Europe there are millions of people whose ancestors a few generations ago were as ignorant and poor and degraded as our most advanced Indian tribes now are. Civilization is a vague, indefinite, comparative term. Our children's grandchildren may look upon our civilization as very rude and imperfect. It is not my wish to give any rose-colored view of the present condition of our Indians. Many of them are as miserable and degraded as men can be; but it cannot be denied that others are making reasonably satisfactory progress.

Within a few years the Government has undertaken somewhat systematically to bring them into civilized life. The "peace policy" has sought to throw around them healthful associations; to place at the several agencies agents and employees of good moral and Christian character and of active sympathies; and an earnest effort has been made to teach Indians to labor and to read. It is too soon, perhaps, to assert that this effort has proved a success, but the accompanying reports of agents abundantly show that notwithstanding all surrounding difficulties, much has been accomplished toward establishing and maintaining peace, toward protecting Indians from evil influences, and toward awakening in them the desire for a better mode of life. The success of some of our agents, who have labored under reasonably favorable circumstances, deserves all praise, and has fully equaled the fondest hopes of the friends of the peace policy. Certainly enough improvement has been made to justify the continuance of the present benevolent efforts.

In considering whether modifications of existing methods may not be desirable, I have arrived at the conviction that the welfare and progress of the Indians require the adoption of three principles of policy:

First. Concentration of all Indians on a few reservations.

Second. Allotment to them of lands in severalty.

Third. Extension over them of United States law and the jurisdiction of United States courts.

CONSOLIDATION OF RESERVATIONS

The reservations upon which, in my opinion, the Indians should be, consolidated, are the Indian Territory (in Oklahoma), the White Earth reservation in Northern Minnesota, and a reservation in the southern part of Washington Territory, probably the Yakama reservation. If it should be found impracticable to remove the Indians of Colorado, Utah, New Mexico, and Arizona, to the Indian Territory, they might be concentrated on some suitable reservation either in Colorado or Arizona.

I am well aware that it will take a long time, much patient effort, and considerable expense, to effect this proposed consolidation; but after consulting with many gentlemen thoroughly acquainted with Indian questions and Indian character, I am satisfied that the undertaking can be accomplished. If legislation were secured giving the President authority to remove any tribe or band, or any portion of a tribe or band, whenever in his judgment it was practicable, to any one of the reservations named, and if Congress would appropriate, from year to year, a sum sufficient to enable him to take advantage of every favorable opportunity to make such removals, I am confident that a few years' trial would conclusively demonstrate the entire feasibility of the plan. I believe that all the Indians in Kansas, Nebraska, and Dakota, and a part at least of those in Wyoming and Montana, could be induced to remove to Indian Territory. There is also ground for the belief that the Colorado, Arizona, and New Mexico Indians, and a part if not all of those in Nevada, could also be taken to that Territory.

Many of these Indians are now located on lands utterly unfit for cultivation, where starvation or perpetual support by the Government are the only alternatives. It is doubtful whether even white people could cultivate profitably the greater part of the Sioux reservation in Dakota. In the Indian Territory, on the other hand, are fertile land, a genial climate, and room for more Indians than there are in the whole Union.

That the Indian sentiment is opposed to such removal is true. Difficulties were experienced in bringing to the Territory its present inhabitants from east of the Mississippi; but the obstacles were overcome, and experience shows that there the race can thrive. With a fair degree of persistence the removal thither of other Indians can also be secured. The Pawnees have recently gone there, and seem content with their new home. The Poncas, and even the Red Cloud and Spotted Tail Sioux, give evidence that they are ready for the change; and if Congress will make a liberal appropriation to effect the removal of these Sioux, it is quite likely that within a year or two, other bands now on the Missouri River may also be induced to remove. If the Sioux are given a suitable reservation in that Territory for a permanent home, and are aided by the Government for a few years in their efforts at agriculture and stock raising, I know of no reason why they may not, in one generation, become as far advanced as are the Cherokees and Choctaws now.

The importance of reducing the number of reservations is shown by the following considerations. Many of the present reserves are almost worthless for agricultural purposes; others are rich in soil, mineral wealth, and timber. Nearly all are too small to subsist the Indians by hunting, and too large for them to occupy in agricultural and civilized pursuits. Many are so remote and difficult of access, that needed supplies can be furnished only at great expense. Nearly all are surrounded by white settlers, more or less numerous. Wherever an Indian reservation has on it good land, or timber, or minerals, the cupidity of the white man is excited, and a constant struggle is inaugurated to dispossess the Indian, in which the avarice and determination of the white man usually prevails. The length of the boundary-line between the reservations and the contiguous white settlements amounts in the aggregate to thousands of miles, every mile being a point of contact and difficulty. This aggregate boundary is so extensive as to render almost impossible the prevention of illicit trade in arms and whisky. As now constituted, these reservations are a refuge to the most lawless and desperate white men in America. There the vagabonds, the outcasts, the criminals, the most immoral and licentious of the population of the western portion of the country take up their abode, because there they are practically beyond the reach and operation of law, and can live lives of crime and debauchery with impunity and without reproach. Such men seriously obstruct, if they do not render nugatory, every effort to give assistance to the Indians.

By the concentration of Indians on a few reservations, it is obvious that much of the difficulty now surrounding the Indian question will vanish. Many agencies now conducted at large expense could be abolished. The aggregate boundary-lines between the reservations and country occupied by white people would be greatly reduced, and the danger of violence, bloodshed, and mutual wrong materially lessened. The sale of liquors and arms could be more effectually prevented; bad white men could more easily be kept out of the Indian country; necessary supplies could be more cheaply furnished; a far smaller military force would be required to keep the peace; and generally, the Indians, being more compact, could be more efficiently aided and controlled by the officers of the Government. Moreover, large bodies of land would be thrown open to settlement, proceeds of whose sale would be ample to defray all expense of the removals.

ALLOTMENTS IN SEVERALTY

It is doubtful whether any high degree of civilization is possible without individual ownership of land. The records of the past and the experience of the present testify that the soil should be made secure to the individual by all the guarantees which law can devise, and that nothing less will induce men to put forth their best exertions. No general law exists which provides that Indians shall select allotments in severalty, and it seems to me a matter of great moment that provision should be made not only permitting, but requiring, the head of each Indian family, to accept the allotment of a reasonable amount of land, to be the property of himself and his lawful heirs, in lieu of any interest in any common tribal possession. Such allotments should be inalienable for at least twenty, perhaps fifty years, and if situated in a permanent Indian reservation, should be transferable only among Indians.

I am not unaware that this proposition will meet with strenuous opposition from the Indians themselves. Like the whites, they have ambitious men, who will resist to the utmost of their power any change tending to reduce the authority which they have acquired by personal effort or by inheritance; but it is essential that these men and their claims should be pushed aside and that each individual should feel that his home is his own; that he owes no allegiance to any great man or to any faction; that he has a direct personal interest in the soil on which he lives, and that that interest will be faithfully protected for him and for his children by the Government.

LAW FOR INDIANS

My predecessors have frequently called attention to the startling fact that we have within our midst 275,000 people, the least intelligent portion of our population, for whom we provide no law, either for their protection or for the punishment of crime committed among themselves. Civilization even among white men could not long exist without the guarantees which law alone affords; yet our Indians are remitted by a great civilized government to the control, if control it can be called, of the rude regulations of petty, ignorant tribes. Year after year we expend millions of dollars for these people in the faint hope that, without law, we can civilize them. That hope has been, to a great degree, a long disappointment; and year after year we repeat the folly of the past. That the benevolent efforts and purposes of the Government have proved so largely fruitless, is, in my judgment, due more to its failure to make these people amenable to our laws than to any other cause, or to all other causes combined.

I believe it to be the duty of Congress at once to extend over Indian reservations the jurisdiction of United States courts, and to declare that each Indian in the United States shall occupy the same relation to law that a white man does. An Indian should be given to understand that no ancient custom, no tribal regulation, will shield him from just punishment for crime; and also that he will be effectually protected, by the authority and power of the Government, in his life, liberty, property, and character, as certainly as if he were a white man. There can be no doubt of the power of Congress to do this, and surely the intelligent Committees on Indian Affairs of the Senate and House can readily propose legislation which will accomplish this most desirable result. I regard this suggestion as by far the most important which I have to make in this report.

Since our Government was organized two questions, or rather two classes of questions, have transcended all others in importance and difficulty, viz, the relations of the Government and the white people to the negroes and to the Indians. The negro question has doubtless absorbed more of public attention, aroused more intense feeling, and cost our people more blood and treasure than any other question, if not all others combined. That question, it is to be hoped, is settled forever in the only way in which its settlement was possible – by the full admission of the negro to all the rights and privileges of citizenship. Next in importance comes the Indian question, and there can be no doubt that our Indian wars have cost us more than all the foreign wars in which our Government has been engaged. It is time that some solution of this whole Indian problem, decisive, satisfactory, just, and final, should be found. In my judgment it can be reached only by a process similar to that pursued with the negroes.

In the three propositions above stated, will, I believe, be found the true and final settlement of this perplexing subject. However efficient may be the administration of the Indian Office, and however faithful the labors of its agents and their subordinates, I have little hope of any marked degree of success until the above suggestions are substantially adopted as a permanent Indian policy. If Congress concludes to act on these suggestions, laws should be passed at the coming session to extend the jurisdiction of the courts over all Indians, and to provide for the allotment of lands in severalty in the Indian Territory, and on such other reservations as may be selected as permanent; and an appropriation should be made with which to begin the removal of Indians to their permanent homes.

I trust I may be pardoned for stating that it appears to me that the fundamental difficulty in our relations hitherto with Indians has been the want of a well-defined, clearly-understood, persistent purpose on the part of the Government. Indians affairs have heretofore been managed largely by the application of mere temporary expedients in a fragmentary and disjointed manner. For a hundred years the United States has been wrestling with the "Indian question," but has never had an Indian policy. The only thing yet done by the Government in regard to the Indians which seems to have been permanent and far-reaching in its scope and purpose, is the dedication of the Indian Territory as the final home for the race. Surely it is time that a policy should be determined on, which shall be fully understood by the Government, the people, and the Indians. We cannot afford to allow this race to perish without making an honest effort to save it. We cannot afford to keep them in our midst as vagabonds and paupers.

I appeal to the statesmen of the country to give to this subject their earnest attention; the sooner it is settled on some wise and comprehensive principle the better for all concerned. We have despoiled the Indians of their rich hunting-grounds, thereby depriving them of their ancient means of support. Ought we not and shall we not give them at least a secure home, and the cheap but priceless benefit of just and equitable laws?

DOCUMENT 20

Chief Joseph Speaks for His People

Context: Much like the Cherokees, the Nez Percé tribe of eastern Oregon had cultivated good relations with white settlers. In 1855, the Nez Percé agreed to live on a large reservation that stretched from western Idaho to eastern Oregon. When gold was discovered on their lands in 1863, government officials tried to remove the Nez Percé to a far smaller reservation. The tribe resisted, and in 1877 Chief Joseph and his band of 700 (including many women and children) held off some 2,000 soldiers for months during a 1,400 mile march through Oregon, Idaho, Wyoming, and Montana. Although finally captured in October 1877, the exploits of the Nez Percé made Chief Joseph famous. His fame, though, did little good for his tribe. The Nez Percé were eventually forced to move to Indian Territory (present-day Oklahoma), where many died of disease.

Questions to Consider: What were the problems that the Nez Percé faced when trying to live peacefully with whites? What conditions eventually forced Chief Joseph to surrender in 1877? What are the major cultural differences, according to Chief Joseph, between whites and Indians? In what ways did Chief Joseph disagree with J. Q. Smith? In what ways did the two agree?

The Writings of Chief Joseph

I

The first white men of your people who came to our country were named Lewis and Clark. They brought many things which our people had never seen. They talked straight and our people gave them a great feast as proof that their hearts were friendly. They made presents to our chiefs and our people made presents to them. We had a great many horses of which we gave them what they needed, and they gave us guns and tobacco in return. All the Nez Perce made friends with Lewis and Clark and agreed to let them pass through their country and never to make war on white men. This promise the Nez Perce have never broken.

II

For a short time we lived quietly. But this could not last. White men had found gold in the mountains around the land of the Winding Water. They stole a great many horses from us and we could not get them back because we were Indians. The white men told lies for each other. They drove off a great many of our cattle. Some white men branded our young cattle so they could claim them. We had no friends who would plead our cause before the law councils. It seemed to me that some of the white men in Wallowa were doing these things on purpose to get up a war. They knew we were not strong enough to fight them. I labored hard to avoid trouble and bloodshed. We gave up some of our country to the white men, thinking that then we could have peace. We were mistaken. The white men would not let us alone. We could have avenged our wrongs many times, but we did not. Whenever the Government has asked for help against other Indians we have never refused. When the white men were few and we were strong we could have killed them off, but the Nez Perce wishes to live at peace.

On account of the treaty made by the other bands of the Nez Perce the white man claimed my lands. We were troubled with white men crowding over the line. Some of them were good men, and we lived on peaceful terms with them, but they were not all good. Nearly every year the agent came over from Lapwai and ordered us to the reservation. We always replied that we were satisfied to live in Wallowa. We were careful to refuse the presents or annuities which he offered.

Through all the years since the white man came to Wallowa we have been threatened and taunted by them and the treaty Nez Perce. They have given us no rest. We have had a few good friends among the white men, and they have always advised my people to bear these taunts without fighting. Our young men are quick tempered and I have had great trouble in keeping them from doing rash things. I have carried a heavy load on my back ever since I was a boy. I learned then that we were but few while the white men were many, and that we could not hold our own with them. We were like deer. They were like grizzly bears. We had a small country. Their country was large. We were contented to let things remain as the Great Spirit Chief made them. They were not; and would change the mountains and rivers if they did not suit them.

III.

[At his surrender in the Bear Paw Mountains, 1877]

Tell General Howard that I know his heart. What he told me before I have in my heart. I am tired of fighting. Our chiefs are killed. Looking Glass is dead, tuhul-hil-sote is dead. the old men are all dead. It is the young men who now say yes or no. He who led the young men [Joseph's brother Alikut] is dead. It is cold and we have no blankets. The little children are freezing to death. My people — some of them have run away to the hills and have no blankets and no food. No one knows where they are — perhaps freezing to death. I want to have time to look for my children and see how many of them I can find. Maybe I shall find them among the dead. Hear me, my chiefs, my heart is sick and sad. From where the sun now stands I will fight no more against the white man.

IV

[On a visit to Washington, D.C., 1879]

At last I was granted permission to come to Washington and bring my friend Yellow Bull and our interpreter with me. I am glad I came. I have shaken hands with a good many friends, but there are some things I want to know which no one seems able to explain. I cannot understand how the Government sends a man out to fight us, as it did General Miles, and then breaks his word. Such a government has something wrong about it. I cannot understand why so many chiefs are allowed to talk so many different ways, and promise so many different things. I have seen the Great Father Chief [President Hayes]; the Next Great Chief [Secretary of the Interior]; the Commissioner Chief; the Law Chief; and many other law chiefs [Congressmen] and they all say they are my friends, and that I shall have justice, but while all their mouths talk right I do not understand why nothing is done for my people. I have heard talk and talk but nothing is done. Good words do not last long unless they amount to something. Words do not pay for my dead people. They do not pay for my country now overrun by white men. They do not protect my father's grave. They do not pay for my horses and cattle. Good words do not give me back my children. Good words will not make good the promise of your war chief, General Miles. Good words will not give my people a home where they can live in peace and take care of themselves. I am tired of talk that comes to nothing. It makes my heart sick when I remember all the good words and all the broken promises. There has been too much talking by men who had no right to talk. Too many misinterpretations have been made; too many misunderstandings have come up between the white men and the Indians. If the white man wants to live in peace with the Indian he can live in peace. There need be no trouble. Treat all men alike. Give them the same laws. Give them all an even chance to live and grow. All men were made by the same Great Spirit Chief. They are all brothers. The earth is the mother of all people, and all people should have equal rights upon it. You might as well expect all rivers to run backward as that any man who was born a free man should be contented penned up and denied liberty to go where he pleases. If you tie a horse to a stake, do you expect he will grow fat? If you pen an Indian up on a small spot of earth and compel him to stay there, he will not be contented nor will he grow and prosper. I have asked some of the Great White Chiefs where they get their authority to say to the Indian that he shall stay in one place, while he sees white men going where they please. They cannot tell me.

I only ask of the Government to be treated as all other men are treated. If I cannot go to my own home, let me have a home in a country where my people will not die so fast. I would like to go to Bitter Root Valley. There my people would be happy; where they are now they are dying. Three have died since I left my camp to come to Washington.

When I think of our condition, my heart is heavy. I see men of my own race treated as outlaws and driven from country to country, or shot down like animals.

I know that my race must change. We cannot hold our own with the white men as we are. We only ask an even chance to live as other men live. We ask to be recognized as men. We ask that the same law shall work alike on all men. If an Indian breaks the law, punish him by the law. If a white man breaks the law, punish him also.

Let me be a free man, free to travel, free to stop, free to work, free to trade where I choose, free to choose my own teachers, free to follow the religion of my fathers, free to talk, think and act for myself — and I will obey every law or submit to the penalty.

Whenever the white man treats the Indian as they treat each other then we shall have no more wars. We shall be all alike — brothers of one father and mother, with one sky above us and one country around us and one government for all. Then the Great Spirit Chief who rules above will smile upon this land and send rain to wash out the bloody spots made by brothers' hands upon the face of the earth. For this time the Indian race is waiting and praying. I hope no more groans of wounded men and women will ever go to the ear of the Great Spirit Chief above, and that all people may be one people.

Hin-mah-too-yah-lat-kekht has spoken for his people.

Part IV:
The Progressive Era

DOCUMENT 21

TR Articulates a New Nationalism

Context: A progressive reformer from New York, Theodore Roosevelt served as president of the United States from 1901-1909. He would later lose to Democrat Woodrow Wilson in the election of 1912. This speech, delivered in 1910, synthesized the various strands of Roosevelt's progressive philosophy. Roosevelt was heavily influenced by Herbert Croly, a political philosopher who advocated using Hamiltonian means (activist government) to achieve Jeffersonian ends (democratic idealism).

Questions to Consider: In what ways did Roosevelt's "New Nationalism" contain both conservative and liberal elements? Why would many Americans living in the era of big business find Roosevelt's message appealing? Do you agree with Roosevelt's conclusion that "good character" is an essential part of public service?

Theodore Roosevelt, "The New Nationalism" (1910)

We come here to-day to commemorate one of the epoch-making events of the long struggle for the rights of man—the long struggle for the uplift of humanity. Our country—this great republic—means nothing unless it means the triumph of a real democracy, the triumph of popular government, and, in the long run, of an economic system under which each man shall be guaranteed the opportunity to show the best that there is in him. That is why the history of America is now the central feature of the history of the world; for the world has set its face hopefully toward our democracy; and, O my fellow citizens, each one of you carries on your shoulders not only the burden of doing well for the sake of your own country, but the burden of doing well and of seeing that this nation does well for the sake of mankind.

The issue is joined, and we must fight or fail. In every wise struggle for human betterment one of the main objects, and often the only object, has been to achieve in large measure equality of opportunity. In the struggle for this great end, nations rise from barbarism to civilization, and through it people press forward from one stage of enlightenment to the next. One of the chief factors in progress is the destruction of special privilege. The essence of any struggle for healthy liberty has always been, and must always be, to take from some one man or class of men the right to enjoy power, or wealth, or position, or immunity, which has not been earned by service to his or their fellows. That is what you fought for in the Civil War, and that is what we strive for now.

At many stages in the advance of humanity, this conflict between the men who possess more than they have earned and the men who have earned more than they possess is the central condition of progress. In our day it appears as the struggle of free men to gain and hold the right of self-government as against the special interests, who twist the methods of free government into machinery for defeating the popular will. At every stage, and under all circumstances, the essence of the struggle is to equalize opportunity, destroy privilege, and give to the life and citizenship of every individual the highest possible value both to himself and to the commonwealth. That is nothing new. . . .

Practical equality of opportunity for all citizens, when we achieve it, will have two great results. First, every man will have a fair chance to make of himself all that in him lies; to reach the highest point to which his capacities, unassisted by special privilege of his own and unhampered by the special privilege of others, can carry him, and to get for himself and his family substantially what he has earned. Second, equality of opportunity means that the commonwealth will get from every citizen the highest service of which he is capable. No man who carries the burden of the special privileges of another can give to the commonwealth that service to which it is fairly entitled.

I stand for the square deal. But when I say that I am for the square deal, I mean not merely that I stand for fair play under the present rules of the game, but that I stand for having those rules changed so as to work for a more substantial equality of opportunity and of reward for equally good service. One word of warning, which, I think, is hardly necessary in Kansas. When I say I want a square deal for the poor man, I do not mean that I want a square deal for the man who remains poor because he has not got the energy to work for himself. . . .

Now, this means that our government, national and state, must be freed from the sinister influence or control of special interests. Exactly as the special interests of cotton and slavery threatened our political integrity before the Civil War, so now the great special business interests too often control and corrupt the men and methods of government for their own profit. We must drive the special interests out of politics. That is one of our tasks to-day. Every special interest is entitled to justice—full, fair, and complete, and, now, mind you, if there were any attempt by mob violence to plunder and work harm to the special interest, whatever it may be, that I most dislike, and the wealthy man, whomsoever he may be, for whom I have the greatest contempt, I would fight for him, and you would if you were worth your salt. He should have justice. For every special interest is entitled to justice, but not one is entitled to a vote in Congress, to a voice on the bench, or to representation in any public office. The Constitution guarantees protection to property, and we must make that promise good. But it does not give the right of suffrage to any corporation.

The true friend of property, the true conservative, is he who insists that property shall be the servant and not the master of the commonwealth; who insists that the creature of man's making shall be the servant and not the master of the man who made it. The citizens of the United States must effectively control the mighty commercial forces which they have themselves called into being.

There can be no effective control of corporations while their political activity remains. To put an end to it will be neither a short nor an easy task, but it can be done.

We must have complete and effective publicity of corporate affairs, so that the people may know beyond peradventure whether the corporations obey the law and whether their management entitles them to the confidence of the public. It is necessary that laws should be passed to prohibit the use of corporate funds directly or indirectly for political purposes; it is still more necessary that such laws should be thoroughly enforced. Corporate expenditures for political purposes, and especially such expenditures by public service corporations, have supplied one of the principal sources of corruption in our political affairs.

It has become entirely clear that we must have government supervision of the capitalization, not only of public service corporations, including, particularly, railways, but of all corporations doing an interstate business. I do not wish to see the nation forced into the ownership of the railways if it can possibly be avoided, and the only alternative is thoroughgoing and effective regulation, which shall be based on a full knowledge of all the facts, including a physical valuation of property. This physical valuation is not needed, or, at least, is very rarely needed, for fixing rates; but it is needed as the basis of honest capitalization. We have come to recognize that franchises should never be granted except for a limited time, and never without proper provision for compensation to the public. It is my personal belief that the same kind and degree of control and supervision which should be exercised over public service corporations should be extended also to combinations which control necessaries of life, such as meat, oil, and coal, or which deal in them on an important scale. I have no doubt that the ordinary man who has control of them is much like ourselves. I have no doubt he would like to do well, but I want to have enough supervision to help him realize that desire to do well.

I believe that the officers, and, especially, the directors, of corporations should be held personally responsible when any corporation breaks the law.

Combinations in industry are the result of an imperative economic law which cannot be repealed by political legislation. The effort at prohibiting all combination has substantially failed. The way out lies, not in attempting to prevent such combinations, but in completely controlling them in the interest of the public welfare. For that purpose the Federal Bureau of Corporations is an agency of first importance. Its powers, and, therefore, its efficiency, as well as that of the Interstate Commerce Commission, should be largely increased. We have a right to expect from the Bureau of Corporations and from the Interstate Commerce Commission a very high grade of public service. We should be as sure of the proper conduct of the interstate railways and the proper management of interstate business as we are now sure of the conduct and management of the national banks, and we should have as effective supervision in one case as in the other. The Hepburn Act, and the amendment to the Act in the shape in which it finally passed Congress at the last session, represent a long step in advance, and we must go yet further.

The absence of effective state, and, especially, national, restraint upon unfair money getting has tended to create a small class of enormously wealthy and economically powerful men, whose chief object is to hold and increase their power. The prime need is to change the conditions which enable these men to accumulate power which it is not for the general welfare that they should hold or exercise. We grudge no man a fortune which represents his own power and sagacity, when exercised with entire regard to the welfare of his fellows. Again, comrades over there, take the lesson from your own experience. Not only did you not grudge, but you gloried in the promotion of the great generals who gained their promotion by leading the army to victory. So it is with us. We grudge no man a fortune in civil life if it is honorably obtained and well used. It is not even enough that it should have been gained without doing damage to the community. We should permit it to be gained only so long as the gaining represents benefit to the community. This, I know, implies a policy of a far more active governmental interference with social and economic conditions in this country than we have yet had, but I think we have got to face the fact that such an increase in governmental control is now necessary.

No man should receive a dollar unless that dollar has been fairly earned. Every dollar received should represent a dollar's worth of service rendered—not gambling in stocks, but service rendered. The really big fortune, the swollen fortune, by the mere fact of its size acquires qualities which differentiate it in kind as well as in degree from what is possessed by men of relatively small means. Therefore, I believe in a graduated income tax on big fortunes, and in another tax which is far more easily collected and far more effective—a graduated inheritance tax on big fortunes, properly safeguarded against evasion and increasing rapidly in amount with the size of the estate. . . .

Of conservation I shall speak more at length elsewhere. Conservation means development as much as it does protection. I recognize the right and duty of this generation to develop and use the natural resources of our land; but I do not recognize the right to waste them, or to rob, by wasteful use, the generations that come after us. I ask nothing of the nation except that it so behave as each farmer here behaves with reference to his own children. That farmer is a poor creature who skins the land and leaves it worthless to his children. The farmer is a good farmer who, having enabled the land to support himself and to provide for the education of his children, leaves it to them a little better than he found it himself. I believe the same thing of a nation. Moreover, I believe that the natural resources must be used for the benefit of all our people, and not monopolized for the benefit of the few, and here again is another case in which I am accused of taking a revolutionary attitude. People forget now that one hundred years ago there were public men of good character who advocated the nation selling its public lands in great quantities, so that the nation could get the most money out of it, and giving it to the men who could cultivate it for their own uses. We took the proper democratic ground that the land should be granted in small sections to the men who were actually to till it and live on it. Now, with the water power, with the forests, with the mines, we are brought face to face with the fact that there are many people who will go with us in conserving the resources only if they are to be allowed to exploit them for their benefit. That is one of the fundamental reasons why the special interests should be driven out of politics. Of all the questions which can come before this nation, short of the actual preservation of its existence in a great war, there is none which compares in importance with the great central task of leaving this land even a better land for our descendants than it is for us, and training them into a better race to inhabit the land and pass it on. Conservation is a great moral issue, for it involves the patriotic duty of insuring the safety and continuance of the nation. Let me add that the health and vitality of our people are at least as well worth conserving as their forests, waters, lands, and minerals, and in this great work the national government must bear a most important part. . . .

Nothing is more true than that excess of every kind is followed by reaction; a fact which should be pondered by reformer and reactionary alike. We are face to face with new conceptions of the relations of property to human welfare, chiefly because certain advocates of the rights of property as against the rights of men have been pushing their claims too far. The man who wrongly holds that every human right is secondary to his profit must now give way to the advocate of human welfare, who rightly maintains that every man holds his property subject to the general right of the community to regulate its use to whatever degree the public welfare may require it.

But I think we may go still further. The right to regulate the use of wealth in the public interest is universally admitted. Let us admit also the right to regulate the terms and conditions of labor, which is the chief element of wealth, directly in the interest of the common good. The fundamental thing to do for every man is to give him a chance to reach a place in which he will make the greatest possible contribution to the public welfare. Understand what I say there. Give him a chance, not push him up if he will not be pushed. Help any man who stumbles; if he lies down, it is a poor job to try to carry him; but if he is a worthy man, try your best to see that he gets a chance to show the worth that is in him. No man can be a good citizen unless he has a wage more than sufficient to cover the bare cost of living, and hours of labor short enough so that after his day's work is done he will have time and energy to bear his share in the management of the community, to help in carrying the general load. We keep countless men from being good citizens by the conditions of life with which we surround them. We need comprehensive workmen's compensation acts, both state and national laws to regulate child labor and work for women, and, especially, we need in our common schools not merely education in book learning, but also practical training for daily life and work. We need to enforce better sanitary conditions for our workers and to extend the use of safety appliances for our workers in industry and commerce, both within and between the states. Also, friends, in the interest of the working-man himself we need to set our faces like flint against mob violence just as against corporate greed; against violence and injustice and lawlessness by wage workers just as much as against lawless cunning and greed and selfish arrogance of employers. If I could ask but one thing of my fellow countrymen, my request would be that, whenever they go in for reform, they remember the two sides, and that they always exact justice from one side as much as from the other. I have small use for the public servant who can always see and denounce the corruption of the capitalist, but who cannot persuade himself, especially before election, to say a word about lawless mob violence. And I have equally small use for the man, be he a judge on the bench, or editor of a great paper, or wealthy and influential private citizen, who can see clearly enough and denounce the lawlessness of mob violence, but whose eyes are closed so that he is blind when the question is one of corruption in business on a gigantic scale.

Also remember what I said about excess in reformer and reactionary alike. If the reactionary man, who thinks of nothing but the rights of property, could have his way, he would bring about a revolution; and one of my chief fears in connection with progress comes because I do not want to see our people, for lack of proper leadership, compelled to follow men whose intentions are excellent, but whose eyes are a little too wild to make it really safe to trust them. Here in Kansas there is one paper which habitually denounces me as the tool of Wall Street, and at the same time frantically repudiates the statement that I am a Socialist on the ground that that is an unwarranted slander of the Socialists.

National efficiency has many factors. It is a necessary result of the principle of conservation widely applied. In the end it will determine our failure or success as a nation. National efficiency has to do, not only with natural resources and with men, but it is equally concerned with institutions. The state must be made efficient for the work which concerns only the people of the state; and the nation for that which concerns all the people. There must remain no neutral ground to serve as a refuge for lawbreakers, and especially for lawbreakers of great wealth, who can hire the vulpine legal cunning which will teach them how to avoid both jurisdictions. It is a misfortune when the national legislature fails to do its duty in providing a national remedy, so that the only national activity is the purely negative activity of the judiciary in forbidding the state to exercise power in the premises.

I do not ask for over-centralization; but I do ask that we work in a spirit of broad and far-reaching nationalism when we work for what concerns our people as a whole. We are all Americans. Our common interests are as broad as the continent. I speak to you here in Kansas exactly as I would speak in New York or Georgia, for the most vital problems are those which affect us all alike. The national government belongs to the whole American people, and where the whole American people are interested, that interest can be guarded effectively only by the national government. The betterment which we seek must be accomplished, I believe, mainly through the national government.

The American people are right in demanding that New Nationalism, without which we cannot hope to deal with new problems. The New Nationalism puts the national need before sectional or personal advantage. It is impatient of the utter confusion that results from local legislatures attempting to treat national issues as local issues. It is still more impatient of the impotence which springs from over-division of governmental powers, the impotence which makes it possible for local selfishness or for legal cunning, hired by wealthy special interests, to bring national activities to a deadlock. This New Nationalism regards the executive power as the steward of the public welfare. It demands of the judiciary that it shall be interested primarily in human welfare rather than in property, just as it demands that the representative body shall represent all the people rather than any one class or section of the people. I believe in shaping the ends of government to protect property as well as human welfare. Normally, and in the long run, the ends are the same; but whenever the alternative must be faced, I am for men and not for property, as you were in the Civil War. I am far from underestimating the importance of dividends; but I rank dividends below human character. Again, I do not have any sympathy with the reformer who says he does not care for dividends. Of course, economic welfare is necessary, for a man must pull his own weight and be able to support his family. I know well that the reformers must not bring upon the people economic ruin, or the reforms themselves will go down in the ruin. But we must be ready to face temporary disaster, whether or not brought on by those who will war against us to the knife. Those who oppose all reform will do well to remember that ruin in its worst form is inevitable if our national life brings us nothing better than swollen fortunes for the few and the triumph in both politics and business of a sordid and selfish materialism.

If our political institutions were perfect, they would absolutely prevent the political domination of money in any part of our affairs. . . .

One of the fundamental necessities in a representative government such as ours is to make certain that the men to whom the people delegate their power shall serve the people by whom they are elected, and not the special interests. I believe that every national officer, elected or appointed, should be forbidden to perform any service or receive any compensation, directly or indirectly, from interstate corporations; and a similar provision could not fail to be useful within the states. The object of government is the welfare of the people. The material progress and prosperity of a nation are desirable chiefly so far as they lead to the moral and material welfare of all good citizens. Just in proportion as the average man and woman are honest, capable of sound judgment and high ideals, active in public affairs, but, first of all, sound in their home life, and the father and mother of healthy children whom they bring up well—just so far, and no farther, we may count our civilization a success. We must have—I believe we have already—a genuine and permanent moral awakening, without which no wisdom of legislation or administration really means anything; and, on the other hand, we must try to secure the social and economic legislation without which any improvement due to purely moral agitation is necessarily evanescent. Let me again illustrate by a reference to the [northern] Grand Army [of the Civil War]. You could not have won simply as a disorderly and disorganized mob. You needed generals; you needed careful administration of the most advanced type; and a good commissary—the cracker line. You well remember that success was necessary in many different lines in order to bring about general success. You had to have the administration at Washington good, just as you had to have the administration in the field; and you had to have the work of the generals good. You could not have triumphed without that administration and leadership; but it would all have been worthless if the average soldier had not had the right stuff in him. He had to have the right stuff in him, or you could not get it out of him.

In the last analysis, therefore, vitally necessary though it was to have the right kind of organization and the right kind of generalship, it was even more vitally necessary that the average soldier should have the fighting edge, the right character. So it is in our civil life. No matter how honest and decent we are in our private lives, if we do not have the right kind of law and the right kind of administration of the law, we cannot go forward as a nation. That is imperative; but it must be an addition to, and not a substitution for, the qualities that make us good citizens. In the last analysis, the most important elements in any man's career must be the sum of those qualities which, in the aggregate, we speak of as character. If he has not got it, then no law that the wit of man can devise, no administration of the law by the boldest and strongest executive, will avail to help him. We must have the right kind of character—character that makes a man, first of all, a good man in the home, a good father, a good husband—that makes a man a good neighbor. You must have that, and, then, in addition, you must have the kind of law and the kind of administration of the law which will give to those qualities in the private citizen the best possible chance for development. The prime problem of our nation is to get the right type of good citizenship, and, to get it, we must have progress, and our public men must be genuinely progressive.

DOCUMENT 22

Jane Addams Analyzes the Motivations of the Settlement House Movement

Context: The settlement house movement attempted to connect members of the upper and middle classes with the urban poor. By 1910, more than 400 settlement homes existed in the United States. The majority of residents were much like Jane Addams: idealistic, educated women seeking to make a difference. In 1899, Addams and Ellen Gates Starr moved to Chicago and founded Hull House, which quickly became the best-known settlement house. Hull House provided a wide array of services to the many immigrants in the surrounding neighborhoods. Addams's energy and idealism made her one of the most admired figures during the Progressive era.

Questions to Consider: According to Addams, what three impulses motivated the settlement house movement? In what ways would the settlement house movement revitalize American democracy? Compare and contrast Addams's understanding of the settlement house movement with TR's New Nationalism. What aspirations did TR and Addams share? In what ways did their approach to reform differ?

Jane Addams, Subjective Necessity For Social Settlements (From *Twenty Years at Hull-House with Autobiographical Notes*. (c.1919): 113-127.

This paper is an attempt to analyze the motives which underlie a movement based, not only upon conviction, but upon genuine emotion, wherever educated young people are seeking an outlet for that sentiment for universal brotherhood, which the best spirit of our times is forcing from an emotion into a motive. These young people accomplish little toward the solution of this social problem, and bear the brunt of being cultivated into unnourished, oversensitive lives. They have been shut off from the common labor by which they live which is a great source of moral and physical health. They feel a fatal want of harmony between their theory and their lives, a lack of coördination between thought and action. I think it is hard for us to realize how seriously many of them are taking to the notion of human brotherhood, how eagerly they long to give tangible expression to the democratic ideal. These young men and women, longing to socialize their democracy, are animated by certain hopes which may be thus loosely formulated; that if in a democratic country nothing can be permanently achieved save through the masses of the people, it will be impossible to establish a higher political life than the people themselves crave; that it is difficult to see how the notion of a higher civic life can be fostered save through common intercourse; that the blessings which we associate with a life of refinement and cultivation can be made universal and must be made universal if they are to be permanent; that the good we secure for ourselves is precarious and uncertain, is floating in mid-air, until it is secured for all of us and incorporated into our common life. It is easier to state these hopes than to formulate the line of motives, which I believe to constitute the trend of the subjective pressure toward the Settlement. There is something primordial about these motives, but I am perhaps overbold in designating them as a great desire to share the race life. We all bear traces of the starvation struggle which for so long made up the life of the race. Our very organism holds memories and glimpses of that long life of our ancestors, which still goes on among so many of our contemporaries. Nothing so deadens the sympathies and shrivels the power of enjoyment as the persistent keeping away from the great opportunities for helpfulness and a continual ignoring of the starvation struggle which makes up the life of at least half the race. To shut one's self away from that half of the race life is to shut one's self away from the most vital part of it; it is to live out but half the humanity to which we have been born heir and to use but half our faculties. We have all had longings for a fuller life which should include the use of these faculties. These longings are the physical complement of the "Intimations of Immortality," on which no ode has yet been written. To portray these would be the work of a poet, and it is hazardous for any but a poet to attempt it.

You may remember the forlorn feeling which occasionally seizes you when you arrive early in the morning a stranger in a great city: the stream of laboring people goes past you as you gaze through the plate-glass window of your hotel; you see hard working men lifting great burdens; you hear the driving and jostling of huge carts and your heart sinks with a sudden sense of futility. The door opens behind you and you turn to the man who brings you in your breakfast with a quick sense of human fellowship. You find yourself praying that you may never lose your hold on it all. A more poetic prayer would be that the great mother breasts of our common humanity, with its labor and suffering and its homely comforts, may never be withheld from you. You turn helplessly to the waiter and feel that it would be almost grotesque to claim from him the sympathy you crave because civilization has placed you apart, but you resent your position with a sudden sense of snobbery. Literature is full of portrayals of these glimpses: they come to shipwrecked men on rafts; they overcome the differences of an incongruous multitude when in the presence of a great danger or when moved by a common enthusiasm. They are not, however, confined to such moments, and if we were in the habit of telling them to each other, the recital would be as long as the tales of children are, when they sit down on the green grass and confide to each other how many times they have remembered that they lived once before. If these childish tales are the stirring of inherited impressions, just so surely is the other the striving of inherited powers.

"It is true that there is nothing after disease, indigence and a sense of guilt, so fatal to health and to life itself as the want of a proper outlet for active faculties." I have seen young girls suffer and grow sensibly lowered in vitality in the first years after they leave school. In our attempt then to give a girl pleasure and freedom from care we succeed, for the most part, in making her pitifully miserable. She finds "life" so different from what she expected it to be. She is besotted with innocent little ambitions, and does not understand this apparent waste of herself, this elaborate preparation, if no work is provided for her. There is a heritage of noble obligation which young people accept and long to perpetuate. The desire for action, the wish to right wrong and alleviate suffering haunts them daily. Society smiles at it indulgently instead of making it of value to itself. The wrong to them begins even farther back, when we restrain the first childish desires for "doing good", and tell them that they must wait until they are older and better fitted. We intimate that social obligation begins at a fixed date, forgetting that it begins at birth itself. We treat them as children who, with strong-growing limbs, are allowed to use their legs but not their arms, or whose legs are daily carefully exercised that after a while their arms may be put to high use. We do this in spite of the protest of the best educators, Locke and Pestalozzi. We are fortunate in the meantime if their unused members do not weaken and disappear. They do sometimes. There are a few girls who, by the time they are "educated", forget their old childish desires to help the world and to play with poor little girls "who haven't playthings". Parents are often inconsistent: they deliberately expose their daughters to knowledge of the distress in the world; they send them to hear missionary addresses on famines in India and China; they accompany them to lectures on the suffering in Siberia; they agitate together over the forgotten region of East London. In addition to this, from babyhood the altruistic tendencies of these daughters are persistently cultivated. They are taught to be self-forgetting and self-sacrificing, to consider the good of the whole before the good of the ego. But when all this information and culture show results, when the daughter comes back from college and begins to recognize her social claim to the "submerged tenth", and to evince a disposition to fulfill it, the family claim is strenuously asserted; she is told that she is unjustified, ill-advised in her efforts. If she persists, the family too often are injured and unhappy unless the efforts are called missionary and the religious zeal of the family carry them over their sense of abuse. When this zeal does not exist, the result is perplexing. It is a curious violation of what we would fain believe a fundamental law—that the final return of the deed is upon the head of the doer. The deed is that of exclusiveness and caution, but the return, instead of falling upon the head of the exclusive and cautious, falls upon a young head full of generous and unselfish plans. The girl loses something vital out of her life to which she is entitled. She is restricted and unhappy; her elders meanwhile, are unconscious of the situation and we have all the elements of a tragedy.

We have in America a fast-growing number of cultivated young people who have no recognized outlet for their active faculties. They hear constantly of the great social maladjustment, but no way is provided for them to change it, and their uselessness hangs about them heavily. Huxley declares that the sense of uselessness is the severest shock which the human system can sustain, and that if persistently sustained, it results in atrophy of function. These young people have had advantages of college, of European travel, and of economic study, but they are sustaining this shock of inaction. They have pet phrases, and they tell you that the things that make us all alike are stronger than the things that make us different. They say that all men are united by needs and sympathies far more permanent and radical than anything that temporarily divides them and sets them in opposition to each other. If they affect art, they say that the decay in artistic expression is due to the decay in ethics, that art when shut away from the human interests and from the great mass of humanity is self-destructive. They tell their elders with all the bitterness of youth that if they expect success from them in business or politics or in whatever lines their ambition for them has run, they must let them consult all of humanity; that they must let them find out what the people want and how they want it. It is only the stronger young people, however, who formulate this. Many of them dissipate their energies in so-called enjoyment. Others not content with that, go on studying and go back to college for their second degrees; not that they are especially fond of study, but because they want something definite to do, and their powers have been trained in the direction of mental accumulation. Many are buried beneath this mental accumulation with lowered vitality and discontent. Walter Besant says they have had the vision that Peter had when he saw the great sheet let down from heaven, wherein was neither clean nor unclean. He calls it the sense of humanity. It is not philanthropy nor benevolence, but a thing fuller and wider than either of these.

This young life, so sincere in its emotion and good phrases and yet so undirected, seems to me as pitiful as the other great mass of destitute lives. One is supplementary to the other, and some method of communication can surely be devised. Mr. Barnett, who urged the first Settlement, Toynbee Hall, in East London—recognized this need of outlet for the young men of Oxford and Cambridge, and hoped that the Settlement would supply the communication. It is easy to see why the Settlement movement originated in England, where the years of education are more constrained and definite than they are here, where class distinctions are more rigid. The necessity of it was greater there, but we are fast feeling the pressure of the need and meeting the necessity for Settlements in America. Our young people feel nervously the need of putting theory into action, and respond quickly to the Settlement form of activity.

Other motives which I believe make toward the Settlement are the result of a certain renaissance going forward in Christianity. The impulse to share the lives of the poor, the desire to make social service, irrespective of propaganda, express the spirit of Christ, is as old as Christianity itself. We have no proof from the records themselves that the early Roman Christians, who strained their simple art to the point of grotesqueness in their eagerness to record a "good news" on the walls of the catacombs, considered this good news a religion. Jesus had no set of truths labeled Religious. On the contrary, his doctrine was that all truth is one, that the appropriation of it is freedom. His teaching had no dogma to mark it off from truth and action in general. He himself called it a revelation–a life. These early Roman Christians received the Gospel message, a command to love all men, with a certain joyous simplicity. The image of the Good Shepherd is blithe and gay beyond the gentlest shepherd of Greek mythology; the hart no longer pants, but rushes to the water brooks. The Christians looked for the continuous revelation, but believed what Jesus said, that this revelation, to be retained and made manifest, must be put into terms of action; that action is the only medium man has for receiving and appropriating truth; that the doctrine must be known through the will.

That Christianity has to be revealed and embodied in the line of social progress is a corollary to the simple proposition, that man's action is found in his social relationships in the way in which he connects with his fellows; that his motives for action are the zeal and affection with which he regards his fellows. By this simple process was created a deep enthusiasm for humanity; which regarded man as at once the organ and the object of revelation; and by this process came about the wonderful fellowship, the true democracy of the early Church, that so captivates the imagination. The early Christians were preëminently nonresistant. They believed in love as a cosmic force. There was no iconoclasm during the minor peace of the Church. They did not yet denounce nor tear down temples, nor preach the end of the world. They grew to a mighty number, but it never occurred to them, either in their weakness or in their strength, to regard other men for an instant as their foes or as aliens. The spectacle of the Christians loving all men was the most astounding Rome had ever seen. They were eager to sacrifice themselves for the weak, for children, and for the aged; they identified themselves with slaves and did not avoid the plague; they longed to share the common lot that they might receive the constant revelation. It was a new treasure which the early Christians added to the sum of all treasures, a joy hitherto unknown in the world—the joy of finding the Christ which lieth in each man, but which no man can unfold save in fellowship. A happiness ranging from the heroic to the pastoral enveloped them. They were to possess a revelation as long as life had new meaning to unfold, new action to propose.

I believe that there is a distinct turning among many young men and women toward this simple acceptance of Christ's message. They resent the assumption that Christianity is a set of ideas which belong to the religious consciousness, whatever that may be. They insist that it cannot be proclaimed and instituted apart from the social life of the community and that it must seek a simple and natural expression in the social organism itself. The Settlement movement is only one manifestation of that wider humanitarian movement which throughout Christendom, but pre-eminently in England, is endeavoring to embody itself, not in a sect, but in society itself.

I believe that this turning, this renaissance of the early Christian humanitarianism, is going on in America, in Chicago, if you please, without leaders who write or philosophize, without much speaking, but with a bent to express in social service and in terms of action the spirit of Christ. Certain it is that spiritual force is found in the Settlement movement, and it is also true that this force must be evoked and must be called into play before the success of any Settlement is assured. There must be the overmastering belief that all that is noblest in life is common to men as men, in order to accentuate the likenesses and ignore the differences which are found among the people whom the Settlement constantly brings into juxtaposition. It may be true, as the Positivists insist, that the very religious fervor of man can be turned into love for his race, and his desire for a future life into content to live in the echo of his deeds; Paul's formula of seeking for the Christ which lieth in each man and founding our likenesses on him, seems a simpler formula to many of us.

In a thousand voices singing the Hallelujah Chorus in Handel's "Messiah," it is possible to distinguish the leading voices, but the differences of training and cultivation between them and the voices in the chorus, are lost in the unity of purpose and in the fact that they are all human voices lifted by a high motive. This is a weak illustration of what a Settlement attempts to do. It aims, in a measure, to develop whatever of social life its neighborhood may afford, to focus and give form to that life, to bring to bear upon it the results of cultivation and training; but it receives in exchange for the music of isolated voices the volume and strength of the chorus. It is quite impossible for me to say in what proportion or degree the subjective necessity which led to the opening of Hull-House combined the three trends: first, the desire to interpret democracy in social terms; secondly, the impulse beating at the very source of our lives, urging us to aid in the race progress; and, thirdly, the Christian movement toward humanitarianism. It is difficult to analyze a living thing; the analysis is at best imperfect. Many more motives may blend with the three trends; possibly the desire for a new form of social success due to the nicety of imagination, which refuses worldly pleasures unmixed with the joys of self-sacrifice; possibly a love of approbation, so vast that it is not content with the treble clapping of delicate hands, but wishes also to hear the bass notes from toughened palms, may mingle with these.

The Settlement then, is an experimental effort to aid in the solution of the social and industrial problems which are engendered by the modern conditions of life in a great city. It insists that these problems are not confined to any one portion of a city. It is an attempt to relieve, at the same time, the overaccumulation at one end of society and the destitution at the other; but it assumes that this overaccumulation and destitution is most sorely felt in the things that pertain to social and educational privileges. From its very nature it can stand for no political or social propaganda. It must, in a sense, give the warm welcome of an inn to all such propaganda, if perchance one of them be found an angel. The only thing to be dreaded in the Settlement is that it lose its flexibility, its power of quick adaptation, its readiness to change its methods as its environment may demand. It must be open to conviction and must have a deep and abiding sense of tolerance. It must be hospitable and ready for experiment. It should demand from its residents a scientific patience in the accumulation of facts and the steady holding of their sympathies as one of the best instruments for that accumulation. It must be grounded in a philosophy whose foundation is on the solidarity of the human race, a philosophy which will not waver when the race happens to be represented by a drunken woman or an idiot boy. Its residents must be emptied of all conceit of opinion and all self-assertion, and ready to arouse and interpret the public opinion of their neighborhood. They must be content to live quietly side by side with their neighbors, until they grow into a sense of relationship and mutual interests. Their neighbors are held apart by differences of race and language which the residents can more easily overcome. They are bound to see the needs of their neighborhood as a whole, to furnish data for legislation, and to use their influence to secure it. In short, residents are pledged to devote themselves to the duties of good citizenship and to the arousing of the social energies which too largely lie dormant in every neighborhood given over to industrialism. They are bound to regard the entire life of their city as organic, to make an effort to unify it, and to protest against its over-differentiation.

It is always easy to make all philosophy point one particular moral and all history adorn one particular tale; but I may be forgiven the reminder that the best speculative philosophy sets forth the solidarity of the human race; that the highest moralists have taught that without the advance and improvement of the whole, no man can hope for any lasting improvement in his own moral or material individual condition; and that the subjective necessity for Social Settlements is therefore identical with that necessity, which urges us on toward social and individual salvation.

Jacob Riis Exposes Poverty in New York City

Context: Jacob Riis was a Danish-born photographer and journalist. He was part of a journalistic movement called "muckraking," which sought to instigate political change by exposing corporate abuses, political corruption, and social evils. Effectively combining the written word with photographs to publicize poverty in the New York City, Riis became a particularly influential reformer. "The Problem of Children" is a chapter of *How the Other Half Lives* (1890), which became a landmark in the social reform literature.

Questions to Consider: How did Riis portray immigrant culture? Who did Riis blame for the condition of immigrant children? Why do you think Riis focused so heavily on the plight of children to arouse reform? Do you see any connections between Riis and abolitionist reformers of the previous generation? How did Riis's rhetoric strengthen and weaken his advocacy for immigrants?

"The Problem of the Children" (1890)

The problem of the children becomes, in these swarms, to the last degree perplexing. Their very number make one stand aghast. I have already given instances of the packing of the child population in East Side tenements. They might be continued indefinitely until the array would be enough to startle any community. For, be it remembered, these children with the training they receive—or do not receive—with the instincts they inherit and absorb in their growing up, are to be our future rulers, if our theory of government is worth anything. More than a working majority of our voters now register from the tenements. I counted the other day the little ones, up to ten years or so, in a Bayard Street tenement . . . I tried to count the children that swarmed there, but could not. Sometimes I have doubted that anybody knows just how many there are about. Bodies of drowned children turn up in the rivers right along sin summer whom no one seems to know anything about. When last spring some workmen, while moving a pile of lumber on a North River pier, found under the last plank the body of a little lad crushed to death, no one had missed a boy, though his parents afterward turned up. The truant officer assuredly does not know, though he spends his life trying to find out, somewhat illogically, perhaps, since the department that employs him admits that thousands of poor children are crowded out of the schools year by year for want of room. . ...

The old question, what to do with the boy, assumes a new and serious phase in the tenements. Under the best conditions found there, it is not easily answered. In nine cases out of ten he would make an excellent mechanic, if trained early to work at a trade, for he is neither dull nor slow, but the short-sighted despotism of the trades unions has practically closed that avenue to him. Trade-schools, however excellent, cannot supply the opportunity thus denied him, and at the outset the boy stands condemned by his own to low and ill-paid drudgery, held down by the hand that of all should labor to raise him. Home, the greatest factor of all in the training of the young, means nothing to him but a pigeon-hole in a coop along with so many other human animals. Its influence is scarcely of the elevating kind, if it have any. The very games at which he takes a hand in the street become polluting in its atmosphere. With no steady hand to guide him, the boy takes naturally to idle ways. Caught in the street by the truant officer, or by the agents of the Children's Societies, peddling, perhaps, or begging, to help out the family resources; he runs the risk of being sent to a reformatory, where contact with vicious boys older than himself soon develop the latent possibilities for evil that lie hidden in him. The city has no Truant Home in which to keep him, and all efforts of the children's friends to enforce school attendance are paralyzed by this want. The risk of the reformatory is too great. What is done in the end is to let him take chances—with the chances all against him. The result is the rough young savage, familiar from the street.

Rough as he is, if any one doubt that this child of common clay have in him the instinct of beauty, of love for the ideal of which his life has no embodiment, let him put the matter to the test. Let him take into a tenement block a handful of flowers from the fields and watch the brightened faces, the sudden abandonment of play and fight that go ever hand in hand where there is no elbow-room, the wild entreaty for "posies," the eager love with which the little messengers of peace are shielded, once possessed; then let him change his mind. I have seen an armful of daisies keep the peace of a block better than a policeman and his club, seen instincts awaken under their gentle appeal, whose very existence the soil in which they grew made seem a mockery. ...

With such human instincts and cravings, forever unsatisfied, turned into a haunting curse; with appetite ground to keenest edge by a hunger that is never fed, the children of the poor grow up in joyless homes to lives of wearisome toil that claims them at an age when the play of their happier fellows has but just begun. Has a yard of turf been laid and a vine been coaxed to grow within their reach, they are banished and barred out from it as from a heaven that is not for such as they. I came upon a couple of youngsters in a Mulberry Street yard a while ago that were chalking on the fence their first lesson in "writin'." And this is what they wrote: "Keeb of te Grass." They had it by heart, for there was not, I verily believe, a green sod within a quarter of a mile. Home to them is an empty name. ...

A little fellow who seemed clad in but a single rag was among the flotsam and jetsam stranded at Police Headquarters one day last summer. No one knew where he came from or where he belonged. ... The examination went on after this fashion:

"Where do you go to church, my boy?"

"We don't have no clothes to go to church." And indeed his appearance, as he was, in the door of any New York church would have caused a sensation.

"Well, where do you go to school, then?"

"I don't go to school," with a snort of contempt.

"Where do you buy your bread?"

"We don't buy no bread; we buy beer," said the boy, and it was eventually the saloon that led the police as a landmark to his "home." It was worthy of the boy. As he had said, his only bed was a heap of dirty straw on the floor, his daily diet a crust in the morning, nothing else.

Into the rooms of the Children's Aid Society were led two little girls whose father had "busted up the house "and put them on the street after their mother died. Another, who was turned out by her stepmother "because she had five of her own and could not afford to keep her," could not remember ever having been in church or Sunday-school, and only knew the name of Jesus through hearing people swear by it. She had no idea what they meant. These were specimens of the overflow from the tenements of our home-heathen that are growing up in New York's streets to-day, while tender-hearted men and women are busying themselves with the socks and the hereafter of well-fed little Hottentots thousands of miles away. According to Canon Taylor, of York, one hundred and nine missionaries in the four fields of Persia, Palestine, Arabia, and Egypt spent one year and sixty thousand dollars in converting one little heathen girl. If there is nothing the matter with those missionaries, they might come to New York with a good deal better prospect of success. ...

Nothing is now better understood than that the rescue of the children is the key to the problem of city poverty, as presented for our solution today; that character may be formed where to reform it would be a hopeless task. The concurrent testimony of all who have to undertake it at a later stage: that the young are naturally neither vicious nor hardened, simply weak and undeveloped, except by the bad influences of the street, makes this duty all the more urgent as well as hopeful. Helping hands are held out on every side. To private charity the municipality leaves the entire care of its proletariat of tender years, lulling its conscience to sleep with liberal appropriations of money to foot the bills. Indeed, it is held by those whose opinions are entitled to weight that it is far too liberal a paymaster for its own best interests and those of its wards. It deals with the evil in the seed to a limited extent in gathering in the outcast babies from the streets. To the ripe fruit the gates of its prisons, its reformatories, and its workhouses are opened wide the year round. What the showing would be at this end of the line were it not for the barriers wise charity has thrown across the broad highway to ruin—is building day by day—may be measured by such results as those quoted above in the span of a single life.

DOCUMENT 24

Anzia Yezierska Describes Conflict between Immigrants and Reformers

Context: During the Progressive Period, tens of millions of emigrants left Eastern and Southern Europe to live in the United States. Anzia Yezierska's family emigrated from Poland when she was a young child. She worked to help support her large family by selling newspapers, which was a common experience for many immigrant children. After winning a scholarship to the American Academy in 1907, she became a successful writer, often focusing on the experiences of immigrant women. This story is drawn from her book *Hungry Hearts*, which was published in 1920.

Questions to Consider: In what ways is the title of the story ("The Free Vacation House") ironic? What does the vacation house come to symbolize? What does this story reveal about the motives of Progressive Reformers? Is it fair to characterize all reformers in this light? To what extent do you think Yezierska would have agreed with Andrew Carnegie's conception of charity? How might have Jane Addams and Jacob Riis reacted to this story?

"The Free Vacation House" (1920)

How came it that I went to the free vacation house was like this:

One day the visiting teacher from the school comes to find out for why don't I get the children ready for school in time; for why are they so often late.

I let out on her my whole bitter heart. I told her my head was on wheels from worrying. When I get up in the morning, I don't know on what to turn first: should I nurse the baby, or make Sam's breakfast, or attend on the older children. I only got two hands.

"My dear woman," she says, "you are about to have a nervous breakdown. You need to get away to the country for a rest and vacation."

"Gott im Himmel!" says I. "Don't I know I need a rest? But how? On what money can I go to the country?"

"I know of a nice country place for mothers and children that will not cost you anything. It is free."

"Free! I never heard from it."

"Some kind people have made arrangements so no one need pay," she explains.

Later, in a few days, I just finished up with Masha and Mendel and Frieda and Sonya to send them to school, and I was getting Aby ready for kindergarten, when I hear a knock on the door, and a lady comes in. She had a white starched dress like a nurse and carried a black satchel in her hand.

"I am from the Social Betterment Society," she tells me. "You want to go to the country?"

Before I could say something, she goes over to the baby and pulls out the rubber nipple from her mouth, and to me she says, "You must not get the child used to sucking this; it is very unsanitary."

"Gott im Himmel!" I beg the lady. "Please don't begin with that child, or she'll holler my head off. She must have the nipple. I'm too nervous to hear her scream like that."

When I put the nipple back again in the baby's mouth, the lady takes herself a seat, and then takes out a big black book from her satchel. Then she begins to question me. What is my first name? How old I am? From where come I? How long I'm already in this country? Do I keep any boarders? What is my husband's first name? How old he is? How long he is in this country? By what trade he works? How much wages he gets for a week? How much money do I spend out for rent? How old are the children, and everything about them.

"My goodness!" I cry out. "For why is it necessary all this to know? For why must I tell you all my business? What difference does it make already if I keep boarders, or I don't keep boarders? If Masha had the whooping-cough or Sonya had the measles? Or whether I spend out for my rent ten dollars or twenty? Or whether I come from Schnipishock or Kovner Gubernie?

"We must make a record of all the applicants, and investigate each case," she tells me. "There are so many who apply to the charities, we can help only those who are the most worthy."

"Charities!" I scream out. "Ain't the charities those who help the beggars out? I ain't no beggar. I'm not asking for no charity. My husband, he works."

"Miss Holcomb, the visiting teacher, said that you wanted to go to the country, and I had to make out this report before investigating your case."

"Oh! Oh!" I choke and bit my lips. "Is the free country from which Miss Holcomb told me, is it from the charities? She was telling me some kind people made arrangements for any mother what needs to go there."

"If your application is approved, you will be notified," she says to me, and out she goes.

When she is gone I think to myself, I'd better knock out from my head this idea about the country. For so long I lived, I didn't know nothing about the charities. For why should I come down among the beggars now?

Then I looked around me in the kitchen. On one side was the big wash-tub with clothes, waiting for me to wash. On the table was a pile of breakfast dishes yet. In the sink was the potatoes, waiting to be peeled. The baby was beginning to cry for the bottle. Aby was hollering and pulling me to take him to kindergarten. I felt if I didn't get away from here for a little while, I would land in a crazy house, or from the window jump down. Which was worser, to land in a crazy house, jump from the window down, or go to the country from the charities?

In about two weeks later around comes the same lady with the satchel again in my house.

"You can go to the country to-morrow," she tells me. "And you must come to the charity building to-morrow at nine o'clock sharp. Here is a card with the address. Don't lose it, because you must hand it to the lady in the office."

I look on the card, and there I see my name wrote; and by it, in big printed letters, that word "CHARITY."

"Must I go to the charity office?" I ask, feeling my heart to sink. "For why must I come there?"

"It is the rule that everybody comes to the office first, and from there they are taken to the country."

I shivered to think how I would feel, suppose somebody from my friends should see me walking to the charity office with my children. They wouldn't know that it is only for the country I go there. They might think I go to beg. Have I come down so low as to be seen by the charities? But what's the use? Should I knock my head on the walls? I had to go.

When I come to the office, I already found a crowd of women and children sitting on long benches and waiting. I took myself a seat with them, and we were sitting and sitting and looking on one another, sideways and crosswise, and with lowered eyes, like guilty criminals. Each one felt like hiding herself from all the rest. Each one felt black with shame in the face.

We may have been sitting and waiting for an hour or more. But every second was seeming years to me. The children began to get restless. Mendel wanted water. The baby on my arms was falling asleep. Aby was crying for something to eat.

"For why are we sittin' here like fat cats?" says the woman next to me. "Ain't we going to the country today yet?"

At last a lady comes to the desk and begins calling us our names, one by one. I nearly dropped to the floor when over she begins to ask: Do you keep boarders? How much do you spend out for rent? How much wages does your man get for a week?

Did n't the nurse tell them all about us already? It was bitter enough to have to tell the nurse everything, but in my own house nobody was hearing my troubles, only the nurse. But in the office there was so many strangers all around me. For why should everybody have to know my business? At every question I wanted to holler out: "Stop! Stop! I don't want no vacations! I'll better run home with my children." At every question I felt like she was stabbing a knife into my heart. And she kept on stabbing me more and more, but I could not help it, and they were all looking at me. I couldn't move from her. I had to answer everything.

When she got through with me, my face was red like fire. I was burning with hurts and wounds. I felt like everything was bleeding in me.

When all the names was already called, a man doctor with a nurse comes in, and tells us to form a line, to be examined. I wish I could ease out my heart a little, and tell in words how that doctor looked on us, just because we were poor and had no money to pay. He only used the ends, from his finger-tips to examine us with. From the way he was afraid to touch us or come near us, he made us feel like we had some catching sickness that he was trying not to get on him.

The doctor got finished with us in about five minutes, so quick he worked. Then we was told to walk after the nurse, who was leading the way for us through the street to the car. Everybody what passed us in the street turned around to look on us. I kept down my eyes and held down my head and I felt like sinking into the sidewalk. All the time I was trembling for fear somebody what knows me might yet pass and see me. For why did they make us walk through the street, after the nurse, like stupid cows? Were n't all of us smart enough to find our way without the nurse? Why should the whole world have to see that we are from the charities?

When we got into the train, I opened my eyes, and lifted up my head, and straightened out my chest, and again began to breathe. It was a beautiful, sun-shiny day. I knocked open the window from the train, and the fresh-smelling country air rushed upon my face and made me feel so fine! I looked out from the window and instead of seeing the iron fire-escapes with garbage-cans and bed-clothes, that I always seen when from my flat I looked – instead of seeing only walls and wash-lines between walls, I saw the blue sky, and green grass, and trees and flowers.

Ah, how grand I felt, just on the sky to look! Ah, how grand I felt just to see the green grass – and the free space – and no houses!

"Get away from me, my troubles!" I said. "Leave me rest a minute. Leave me breathe and straighten out my bones. Forget the unpaid butcher's bill. Forget the rent. Forget the wash-tub and the cook-stove and the pots and pans. Forget the charities!"

"Tickets, please," calls the train conductor.

I felt knocked out from heaven all at once. I had to point to the nurse who held our tickets, and I was feeling the conductor looking on me as if to say, "Oh, you are only from the charities."

By the time we came to the vacation house I already forgot all about my knock-down. I was again filled with the beauty of the country. I never in all my life yet seen such a swell house like that vacation house. Like the grandest palace it looked. All round the front, flowers from all colors was smelling out the sweetest per-fume. Here and there was shady trees with comfortable chairs under them to sit down on.

When I only came inside, my mouth opened wide and my breathing stopped still from wonder. I never yet seen such an order and such a cleanliness. From all the corners from the room, the cleanliness was shining like a looking-glass. The floor was so white scrubbed you could eat on it. You couldn't find a speck of dust on nothing, if you was looking for it with eyeglasses on.

I was beginning to feel happy and glad that I come, when, Gott im Himmel! again a lady begins to ask us out the same questions what the nurse already asked me in my home and what was asked over again in the charity office. How much wages my husband makes out for a week? How much money I spend out for rent? Do I keep boarders?

We were hungry enough to faint. So worn out was I from excitement, and from the long ride, that my knees were bending under me ready to break from tiredness. The children were pulling me to pieces, nagging me for a drink, for something to eat and such like. But still we had to stand out the whole list of questionings. When she already got through asking us out everything, she gave to each of us a tag with our name written on it. She told us to tie the tag on our hand. Then like tagged horses at a horse sale in the street, they marched us into the dining-room.

There was rows of long tables, covered with the pure-white oil-cloth. A vase with bought flowers was standing on the middle from each table. Each person got a clean napkin for himself. Laid out by the side from each person's plate was a silver knife and fork and spoon and teaspoon. When we only sat ourselves down, girls with white starched aprons was passing around the eatings.

I soon forgot again all my troubles. For the first time in ten years I sat down to a meal what I did not have to cook or worry about. For the first time in ten years I sat down to the table like a somebody. Ah, how grand it feels, to have handed you over the eatings and everything you need. Just as I was beginning to like it and let myself feel good, in comes a fat lady all in white, with a teacher's look on her face. I could tell already, right away by the way she looked on us, that she was the boss from this place.

"I want to read you the rules from this house, before you leave this room," says she to us.

Then she began like this: We dassen't stand on the front grass where the flow-ers are. We dassen't stay on the front porch. We dassen't sit on the chairs under the shady trees. We must stay always in back and sit on those long wooden benches there. We dassen't come in the front sitting-room or walk on the front steps that have carpet on it – we must walk on the back iron steps. Everything on the front from the house must be kept perfect for the show for visitors. We dassen't lay down on the beds in the daytime, the beds must always be made up perfect for the show for visitors.

"Gott im Himmel!" thinks I to myself; "ain't there going to be no end to the things we dassen't do in this place?"

But still she went on. The children over two years dassen't stay around by the mothers. They must stay by the nurse in the play-room. By the meal-times, they can see their mothers. The children dassen't run around the house or tear up flowers or do anything. They dassen't holler or play rough in the play-room. They must always behave and obey the nurse.

We must always listen to the bells. Bell one was for getting up. Bell two, for getting babies' bottles. Bell three, for coming to breakfast. Bell four, for bathing the babies. If we come later, after the ring from the bell, then we'll not get what we need. If the bottle bell rings and we don't come right away for the bottle, then the baby don't get no bottle. If the breakfast bell rings, and we don't come right away down to the breakfast, then there won't be no breakfast for us.

When she got through with reading the rules, I was wondering which side of the house I was to walk on. At every step was some rule what said don't more here, and don't go there, don't stand there, and don't sit there. If I tried to remember the endless rules, it would only make me dizzy in the head. I was thinking for why, with so many rules, didn't they also have already another rule, about how much air in our lungs to breathe.

On every few days there came to the house swell ladies in automobiles. It was for them that the front from the house had to be always perfect. For them was all the beautiful smelling flowers. For them the front porch, the front sitting-room, and the easy stairs with the carpet on it.

Always when the rich ladies came the fat lady, what was the boss from the vacation house, showed off to them the front. Then she took them over to the back to look on us, where we was sitting together, on long wooden benches, like prisoners. I was always feeling cheap like dirt, and mad that I had to be there, when they smiled down on us.

"How nice for these poor creatures to have a restful place like this," I heard one lady say.

The next day I already felt like going back. The children what had to stay by the nurse in the play-room didn't like it neither.

"Mamma," says Mendel to me, "I wisht I was home and out in the street. They don't let us do nothing here. It's worser than school."

"Ain't it a play-room?" asks I. "Don't they let you play?"

"Gee wiss! play-room, they call it! The nurse hollers on us all the time. She don't let us do nothing."

The reason why I stayed out the whole two weeks is this: I think to myself, so much shame in the face I suffered to come here, let me at least make the best from it already. Let me at least save up for two weeks what I got to spend out for grocery and butcher for my back bills to pay out. And then also think I to myself, if I go back on Monday, I got to do the big washing; on Tuesday waits for me the ironing; on Wednesday, the scrubbing and cleaning, and so goes it on. How bad it is already in this place, it's a change from the very sameness of what I'm having day in and day out at home. And so I stayed out this vacation to the bitter end.

But at last the day for going out from this prison came. On the way riding back, I kept thinking to myself: "This is such a beautiful vacation house. For why do they make it so hard for us? When a mother needs a vacation, why must they tear the insides out from her first, by making her come down to the charity office? Why drag us from the charity office through the streets? And when we live through the shame of the charities and when we come already to the vacation house, for why do they boss the life out of us with so many rules and bells? For why don't they let us lay down our heads on the bed when we are tired? For why must we always stick in the back, like dogs what have got to be chained in one spot? If they would let us walk around free, would we bite off something from the front part of the house?

"If the best part of the house what is comfortable is made up for show for visitors, why ain't they keeping the whole business for a show for visitors? For why do they have to fool in worn-out mothers, to make them think they'll give them a rest? Do they need the worn-out mothers as part of the show? I guess that is it, already."

When I got back in my home, so happy and thankful I was I could cry from thankfulness. How good it was feeling for me to be able to move around my own house, like I pleased. I was always kicking that my rooms was small and narrow, but now my small rooms seemed to grow so big like the park. I looked out from my window on the fire-escapes, full with bedding and garbage-cans, and on the wash-lines full with the clothes. All these ugly things was grand in my eyes. Even the high brick walls all around made me feel like a bird that just jumped out of a cage. And I cried out, "Gott sei dank! Gott sei dank!"

DOCUMENT 25

Booker T. Washington Advocates Economic Advancement

Context: Facing mounting violence and increasingly discriminatory laws, African Americans in the Progressive Era had few viable strategies for economic and political advancement. Booker T. Washington, a former slave and well-known educator, proposed a strategy focusing on economic success. Washington outlined his views at the Atlanta Exposition, a large fair that promoted the business prospects of the New South. Washington's speech made him the most influential African American since Frederick Douglass. Washington met frequently with powerful politicians and industrialists, and even dined with TR at the White House in 1901.

Questions to Consider: What sort of training and education for African Americans did Washington propose? Did Washington's speech echo any elements of free labor ideology? Why do you think that many whites reacted favorably to Washington's remarks? To what extent did Washington accept segregation as a fact of life? Would Frederick Douglass have agreed with Washington's strategies?

Booker T. Washington, "The Atlanta Exposition Speech" (1895)

The Atlanta Exposition, at which I had been asked to make an address as a representative of the Negro race, as stated in the last chapter, was opened with a short address from Governor Bullock. After other interesting exercises, including an invocation from Bishop Nelson, of Georgia, a dedicatory ode by Albert Howell, Jr., and addresses by the President of the Exposition and Mrs. Joseph Thompson, the President of the Woman's Board, Governor Bullock introduced me with the words, "We have with us to-day a representative of Negro enterprise and Negro civilization."

When I arose to speak, there was considerable cheering, especially from the colored people. As I remember it now, the thing that was uppermost in my mind was the desire to say something that would cement the friendship of the races and bring about hearty cooperation between them. So far as my outward surroundings were concerned, the only thing that I recall distinctly now is that when I got up, I saw thousands of eyes looking intently into my face. The following is the address which I delivered:

Mr. President and Gentlemen of the Board of Directors and Citizens

One-third of the population of the South is of the Negro race. No enterprise seeking the material, civil, or moral welfare of this section can disregard this element of our population and reach the highest success. I but convey to you, Mr. President and Directors, the sentiment of the masses of my race when I say that in no way have the value and manhood of the American Negro been more fittingly and generously recognized than by the managers of this magnificent Exposition at every stage of its progress. It is a recognition that will do more to cement the friendship of the two races than any occurrence since the dawn of our freedom.

Not only this, but the opportunity here afforded will awaken among us a new era of industrial progress. Ignorant and inexperienced, it is not strange that in the first years of our new life we began at the top instead of at the bottom; that a seat in Congress or the state legislature was more sought than real estate or industrial skill; that the political convention of stump speaking had more attraction than starting a dairy farm or truck garden.

A ship lost at sea for many days suddenly sighted a friendly vessel. From the mast of the unfortunate vessel was seen a signal, "Water, water; we die of thirst!" The answer from the friendly vessel at once came back, "Cast down your bucket where you are." A second time the signal, "Water, water; send us water!" ran up from the distressed vessel, and was answered, "Cast down your bucket where you are." And a third and fourth signal for water was answered, "Cast down your bucket where you are." The captain of the distressed vessel, at last heeding the injunction, cast down his bucket, and it came up full of fresh, sparkling water from the mouth of the Amazon River. To those of my race who depend on bettering their condition in a foreign land or who underestimate the importance of cultivating friendly relations with the Southern white man, who is their next-door neighbor, I would say: "Cast down your bucket where you are"—cast it down in making friends in every manly way of the people of all races by whom we are surrounded.

Cast it down in agriculture, mechanics, in commerce, in domestic service, and in the professions. And in this connection it is well to bear in mind that whatever other sins the South may be called to bear, when it comes to business, pure and simple, it is in the South that the Negro is given a man's chance in the commercial world, and in nothing is this Exposition more eloquent than in emphasizing this chance. Our greatest danger is that in the great leap from slavery to freedom we may overlook the fact that the masses of us are to live by the productions of our hands, and fail to keep in mind that we shall prosper in proportion as we learn to dignify and glorify common labour and put brains and skill into the common occupations of life; shall prosper in proportion as we learn to draw the line between the superficial and the substantial, the ornamental gewgaws of life and the useful. No race can prosper till it learns that there is as much dignity in tilling a field as in writing a poem. It is at the bottom of life we must begin, and not at the top. Nor should we permit our grievances to overshadow our opportunities.

To those of the white race who look to the incoming of those of foreign birth and strange tongue and habits for the prosperity of the South, were I permitted I would repeat what I say to my own race, "Cast down your bucket where you are." Cast it down among the eight millions of Negroes whose habits you know, whose fidelity and love you have tested in days when to have proved treacherous meant the ruin of your firesides. Cast down your bucket among these people who have, without strikes and labor wars, tilled your fields, cleared your forests, built your railroads and cities, and brought forth treasures from the bowels of the earth, and helped make possible this magnificent representation of the progress of the South. Casting down your bucket among my people, helping and encouraging them as you are doing on these grounds, and to education of head, hand, and heart, you will find that they will buy your surplus land, make blossom the waste places in your fields, and run your factories. While doing this, you can be sure in the future, as in the past, that you and your families will be surrounded by the most patient, faithful, law-abiding, and unresentful people that the world has seen. As we have proved our loyalty to you in the past, in nursing your children, watching by the sick-bed of your mothers and fathers, and often following them with tear-dimmed eyes to their graves, so in the future, in our humble way, we shall stand by you with a devotion that no foreigner can approach, ready to lay down our lives, if need be, in defense of yours, interlacing our industrial, commercial, civil, and religious life with yours in a way that shall make the interests of both races one. In all things that are purely social we can be as separate as the fingers, yet one as the hand in all things essential to mutual progress.

There is no defense or security for any of us except in the highest intelligence and development of all. If anywhere there are efforts tending to curtail the fullest growth of the Negro, let these efforts be turned into stimulating, encouraging, and making him the most useful and intelligent citizen. Effort or means so invested will pay a thousand per cent. interest. These efforts will be twice blessed—"blessing him that gives and him that takes."

There is no escape through law of man or God from the inevitable:

The laws of changeless justice bind Oppressor with oppressed;
And close as sin and suffering joined
We march to fate abreast.

Nearly sixteen millions of hands will aid you in pulling the load upward, or they will pull against you the load downward. We shall constitute one-third and more of the ignorance and crime of the South, or one-third its intelligence and progress; we shall contribute one-third to the business and industrial prosperity of the South, or we shall prove a veritable body of death, stagnating, depressing, retarding every effort to advance the body politic. Gentlemen of the Exposition, as we present to you our humble effort at an exhibition of our progress, you must not expect overmuch. Starting thirty years ago with ownership here and there in a few quilts and pumpkins and chickens (gathered from miscellaneous sources), remember the path that has led from these to the inventions and production of agricultural implements, buggies, steam-engines, newspapers, books, statuary, carving, paintings, the management of drug-stores and banks, has not been trodden without contact with thorns and thistles. While we take pride in what we exhibit as a result of our independent efforts, we do not for a moment forget that our part in this exhibition would fall far short of your expectations but for the constant help that has come to our educational life, not only from the Southern states, but especially from Northern philanthropists, who have made their gifts a constant stream of blessing and encouragement.

The wisest among my race understand that the agitation of questions of social equality is the extremest folly, and that progress in the enjoyment of all the privileges that will come to us must be the result of severe and constant struggle rather than of artificial forcing. No race that has anything to contribute to the markets of the world is long in any degree ostracized. It is important and right that all privileges of the law be ours, but it is vastly more important that we be prepared for the exercises of these privileges. The opportunity to earn a dollar in a factory just now is worth infinitely more than the opportunity to spend a dollar in an opera-house.

In conclusion, may I repeat that nothing in thirty years has given us more hope and encouragement, and drawn us so near to you of the white race, as this opportunity offered by the Exposition; and here bending, as it were, over the altar that represents the results of the struggles of your race and mine, both starting practically empty-handed three decades ago, I pledge that in your effort to work out the great and intricate problem which God has laid at the doors of the South, you shall have at all times the patient, sympathetic help of my race; only let this be constantly in mind, that, while from representations in these buildings of the product of field, of forest, of mine, of factory, letters, and art, much good will come, yet far above and beyond material benefits will be that higher good, that, let us pray God, will come, in a blotting out of sectional differences and racial animosities and suspicions, in a determination to administer absolute justice, in a willing obedience among all classes to the mandates of law. This, coupled with our material prosperity, will bring into our beloved South a new heaven and a new earth.

DOCUMENT 26

W.E.B. Du Bois Criticizes Booker T. Washington

Context: W. E. B. Du Bois was one of the most accomplished Americans of the twentieth century. He graduated from Fisk University in 1888, and become the first African American to earn a Ph.D. from Harvard University in 1895. Du Bois had an extraordinary career as a historian and sociologist, eventually writing one of the most important histories of Reconstruction (*Black Reconstruction*, 1935). Du Bois, however, did not confine himself to the ivory tower of academics. He helped start the NAACP, and severed as editor of the organization's newspaper *The Crisis* for 24 years. His best-known book, *The Souls of Black Folk* (1903) reflected both his academic interests and lifelong political activism.

Questions to Consider: To what extent did Du Bois's criticisms reflect his own experiences as an accomplished scholar? Do you agree with Du Bois's argument that political power and voting rights were necessary preconditions for black economic advancement? How did Du Bois's critique of Washington's economic program reflect some of the same attitudes toward wealth and accumulation that TR and Jane Addams expressed?

W. E. B. Du Bois, "Of Mr. Booker T. Washington and Others" (From *The Souls of Black Folk* (1903))

From birth till death enslaved;
in word, in deed, unmanned!
Hereditary bondsmen! Know ye not
Who would be free themselves must strike the blow?
BYRON

Easily the most striking thing in the history of the American Negro since 1876 is the ascendancy of Mr. Booker T. Washington. It began at the time when war memories and ideals were rapidly passing; a day of astonishing commercial development was dawning; a sense of doubt and hesitation overtook the freedmen's sons—then it was that his leading began. Mr. Washington came, with a single definite program, at the psychological moment when the nation was a little ashamed of having bestowed so much sentiment on Negroes, and was concentrating its energies on Dollars. His program of industrial education, conciliation of the South, and submission and silence as to civil and political rights, was not wholly original; the Free Negroes from 1830 up to wartime had striven to build industrial schools, and the American Missionary Association had from the first taught various trades; and Price and others had sought a way of honorable alliance with the best of the Southerners. But Mr. Washington first indissolubly linked these things; he put enthusiasm, unlimited energy, and perfect faith into this program, and changed it from a by-path into a veritable Way of Life. And the tale of the methods by which he did this is a fascinating study of human life.

It startled the nation to hear a Negro advocating such a program after many decades of bitter complaint; it startled and won the applause of the South, it interested and won the admiration of the North; and after a confused murmur of protest, it silenced if it did not convert the Negroes themselves.

To gain the sympathy and cooperation of the various elements comprising the white South was Mr. Washington's first task; and this, at the time Tuskegee was founded, seemed, for a black man, well-nigh impossible. And yet ten years later it was done in the word spoken at Atlanta: "In all things purely social we can be as separate as the five fingers, and yet one as the hand in all things essential to mutual progress." This "Atlanta Compromise" is by all odds the most notable thing in Mr. Washington's career. The South interpreted it in different ways: the radicals received it as a complete surrender of the demand for civil and political equality; the conservatives, as a generously conceived working basis for mutual understanding. So both approved it, and today its author is certainly the most distinguished Southerner since Jefferson Davis, and the one with the largest personal following.

Next to this achievement comes Mr. Washington's work in gaining place and consideration in the North. Others less shrewd and tactful had formerly essayed to sit on these two stools and had fallen between them; but as Mr. Washington knew the heart of the South from birth and training, so by singular insight he intuitively grasped the spirit of the age which was dominating the North. And so thoroughly did he learn the speech and thought of triumphant commercialism, and the ideals of material prosperity that the picture of a lone black boy poring over a French grammar amid the weeds and dirt of a neglected home soon seemed to him the acme of absurdities. One wonders what Socrates and St. Francis of Assisi would say to this.

And yet this very singleness of vision and thorough oneness with his age is a mark of the successful man. It is as though Nature must needs make men narrow in order to give them force. So Mr. Washington's cult has gained unquestioning followers, his work has wonderfully prospered, his friends are legion, and his enemies are confounded. Today he stands as the one recognized spokesman of his ten million fellows, and one of the most notable figures in a nation of seventy millions. One hesitates, therefore, to criticize a life which, beginning with so little has done so much. And yet the time is come when one may speak in all sincerity and utter courtesy of the mistakes and shortcomings of Mr. Washington's career, as well as of his triumphs, without being thought captious or envious, and without forgetting that it is easier to do ill than well in the world.

The criticism that has hitherto met Mr. Washington has not always been of this broad character. In the South especially has he had to walk warily to avoid the harshest judgments—and naturally so, for he is dealing with the one subject of deepest sensitiveness to that section. Twice—once when at the Chicago celebration of the Spanish-American War he alluded to the color-prejudice that is "eating away the vitals of the South," and once when he dined with President Roosevelt—has the resulting Southern criticism been violent enough to threaten seriously his popularity. In the North the feeling has several times forced itself into words, that Mr. Washington's counsels of submission overlooked certain elements of true manhood, and that his educational program was unnecessarily narrow. Usually, however, such criticism has not found open expression, although, too, the spiritual sons of the Abolitionists have not been prepared to acknowledge that the schools founded before Tuskegee, by men of broad ideals and self-sacrificing spirit, were wholly failures or worthy of ridicule. While, then, criticism has not failed to follow Mr. Washington, yet the prevailing public opinion of the land has been but too willing to deliver the solution of a wearisome problem into his hands, and say, "If that is all you and your race ask, take it."

Among his own people, however, Mr. Washington has encountered the strongest and most lasting opposition, amounting at times to bitterness, and even today continuing strong and insistent even though largely silenced in outward expression by the public opinion of the nation. Some of this opposition is, of course, mere envy; the disappointment of displaced demagogues and the spite of narrow minds. But aside from this, there is among educated and thoughtful colored men in all parts of the land a feeling of deep regret, sorrow, and apprehension at the wide currency and ascendancy which some of Mr. Washington's theories have gained. . . .

Now in the past the American Negro has had instructive experience in the choosing of group leaders, founding thus a peculiar dynasty which in the light of present conditions is worth while studying. When sticks and stones and beasts form the sole environment of a people, their attitude is largely one of determined opposition to and conquest of natural forces. But when to earth and brute is added an environment of men and ideas, then the attitude of the imprisoned group may take three main forms—a feeling of revolt and revenge; an attempt to adjust all thought and action to the will of the greater group; or, finally, a determined effort at self-realization and self-development despite environing opinion. The influence of all of these attitudes at various times can be traced in the history of the American Negro, and in the evolution of his successive leaders. . . .

The disappointment and impatience of the Negroes at the persistence of slavery and serfdom voiced itself in two movements. The slaves in the South, aroused undoubtedly by vague rumors of the Haitian revolt, made three fierce attempts at insurrection—in 1800 under Gabriel in Virginia, in 1822 under Vesey in Carolina, and in 1831 again in Virginia under the terrible Nat Turner. In the Free States, on the other hand, a new and curious attempt at self-development was made. In Philadelphia and New York color-prescription led to a withdrawal of Negro communicants from white churches and the formation of a peculiar socio-religious institution among the Negroes known as the African Church, an organization still living and controlling in its various branches over a million of men. . . .

. . . [A] new period of self-assertion and self-development dawned. To be sure, ultimate freedom and assimilation was the ideal before the leaders, but the assertion of the manhood rights of the Negro by himself was the main reliance, and John Brown's raid was the extreme of its logic. After the war and emancipation, the great form of Frederick Douglass, the greatest of American Negro leaders, still led the host. Self-assertion, especially in political lines, was the main program, and behind Douglass came Elliot, Bruce, and Langston, and the Reconstruction politicians, and, less conspicuous but of greater social significance Alexander Crummell and Bishop Daniel Payne.

Then came the Revolution of 1876, the suppression of the Negro votes, the changing and shifting of ideals, and the seeking of new lights in the great night. Douglass, in his old age, still bravely stood for the ideals of his early manhood— ultimate assimilation through self-assertion, and no other terms. But Booker T. Washington arose as essentially the leader not of one race but of two—a compromiser between the South, the North, and the Negro. Naturally the Negroes resented, at first bitterly, signs of compromise which surrendered their civil and political rights, even though this was to be exchanged for larger chances of economic development. The rich and dominating North, however, was not only weary of the race problem, hut was investing largely in Southern enterprises, and welcomed any method of peaceful cooperation. Thus, by national opinion, the Negroes began to recognize Mr. Washington's leadership; and the voice of criticism was hushed.

Mr. Washington represents in Negro thought the old attitude of adjustment and submission; but adjustment at such a peculiar time as to make his program unique. This is an age of unusual economic development, and Mr. Washington's program naturally takes an economic cast, becoming a gospel of Work and Money to such an extent as apparently almost completely to overshadow the higher aims of life. Moreover, this is an age when the more advanced races are coming in closer contact with the less developed races, and the race-feeling is therefore intensified; and Mr. Washington's program practically accepts the alleged inferiority of the Negro races. Again, in our own land, the reaction from the sentiment of war time has given impetus to race— prejudice against Negroes, and Mr. Washington withdraws many of the high demands of Negroes as men and American citizens. In other periods of intensified prejudice all the Negro's tendency to self-assertion has been called forth; at this period a policy of submission is advocated. In the history of nearly all other races and peoples the doctrine preached at such crises has been that manly self-respect is worth more than lands and houses, and that a people who voluntarily surrender such respect, or cease striving for it, are not worth civilizing.

In answer to this, it has been claimed that the Negro can survive only through submission. Mr. Washington distinctly asks that black people give up, at least for the present, three things:

First, political power,

Second, insistence on civil rights,

Third, higher education of Negro youth,

and concentrate all their energies on industrial education, the accumulation of wealth, and the conciliation of the South. This policy has been courageously and insistently advocated for over fifteen years, and has been triumphant for perhaps ten years. As a result of this tender of the palm-branch, what has been the return? In these years there have occurred:

1. The disfranchisement of the Negro.

2. The legal creation of a distinct status of civil inferiority for the Negro.

3. The steady withdrawal of aid from institutions for the higher training of the Negro.

These movements are not, to be sure, direct results of Mr. Washington's teachings; but his propaganda has, without a shadow of doubt, helped their speedier accomplishment. The question then comes: Is it possible, and probable, that nine millions of men can make effective progress in economic lines if they are deprived of political rights, made a servile caste, and allowed only the most meagre chance for developing their exceptional men? If history and reason give any distinct answer to these questions, it is an emphatic No. And Mr. Washington thus faces the triple paradox of his career:

1. He is striving nobly to make Negro artisans business men and property-owners; but it is utterly impossible, under modern competitive methods, for workingmen and property-owners to defend their rights and exist without the right of suffrage.

2. He insists on thrift and self-respect, but at the same time counsels a silent submission to civic inferiority such as is bound to sap the manhood of any race in the long run.

3. He advocates common-school and industrial training, and depreciates institutions of higher learning; but neither the Negro common-schools, nor Tuskegee itself, could remain open a day were it not for teachers trained in Negro colleges, or trained by their graduates.

This triple paradox in Mr. Washington's position is the object of criticism by two classes of colored Americans. One class is spiritually descended from Toussaint the Savior, through Gabriel, Vesey, and Turner, and they represent the attitude of revolt and revenge; they hate the white South blindly and distrust the white race generally, and so far as they agree on definite action, think that the Negro's only hope lies in emigration beyond the borders of the United States. And yet, by the irony of fate, nothing has more effectually made this program seem hopeless than the recent course of the United States toward weaker and darker peoples in the West Indies, Hawaii, and the Philippines— for where in the world may we go and be safe from lying and brute Force?

The other class of Negroes who cannot agree with Mr. Washington has hitherto said little aloud. They deprecate the sight of scattered counsels, of internal disagreement; and especially they dislike making their just criticism of a useful and earnest man an excuse for a general discharge of venom from small-minded opponents. Nevertheless, the questions involved are so fundamental and serious that it is difficult to see how men like the Grimkes, Kelly Miller, J.W.E. Bowen, and other representatives of this group, can much longer be silent. Such men feel in conscience bound to ask of this nation three things.

1. The right to vote.

2. Civic equality.

3. The education of youth according to ability.

They acknowledge Mr. Washington's invaluable service in counseling patience and courtesy in such demands; they do not ask that ignorant black men vote when ignorant whites are debarred, or that any reasonable restrictions in the suffrage should not be applied; they know that the low social level or the mass of the race is responsible for much discrimination against it, but they also know, and the nation knows, that relentless color-prejudice is more often a cause than a result of the Negro's degradation; they seek the abatement of this relic or barbarism, and not its systematic encouragement and pampering by all agencies of social power from the Associated Press to the Church of Christ. They advocate, with Mr. Washington, a broad system of Negro common schools supplemented by thorough industrial training; but they are surprised that a man of Mr. Washington's insight cannot see that no such educational system ever has rested or can rest on any other basis than that of the well-equipped college and university, and they insist that there is a demand for a few such institutions throughout the South to train the best of the Negro youth as teachers, professional men, and leaders.

This group of men honor Mr. Washington for his attitude of conciliation toward the white South; they accept the "Atlanta Compromise" in its broadest interpretation; they recognize, with him, many signs of promise, many men of high purpose and fair judgment, in this section; they know that no easy task has been laid upon a region already tottering under heavy burdens. But, nevertheless, they insist that the way to truth and right lies in straightforward honesty, not in indiscriminate flattery; in praising those of the South who do well and criticizing uncompromisingly those who do ill; in taking advantage of the opportunities at hand and urging their fellows to do the same, but at the same time in remembering that only a firm adherence to their higher ideals and aspirations will ever keep those ideals within the realm of possibility. They do not expect that the free right to vote, to enjoy civic rights, and to be educated, will come in a moment; they do not expect to see the bias and prejudices of years disappear at the blast of a trumpet; but they are absolutely certain that the way for a people to gain their reasonable rights is not by voluntarily throwing them away and insisting that they do not want them; that the way for a people to gain respect is not by continually belittling and ridiculing themselves; that, on the contrary, Negroes must insist continually, in season and out of season, that voting is necessary to modern manhood, that color discrimination is barbarism, and that black boys need education as well as white boys.

In failing thus to state plainly and unequivocally the legitimate demands of their people, even at the cost of opposing an honored leader, the thinking classes of American Negroes would shirk a heavy responsibility—a responsibility to themselves, a responsibility to the struggling masses, a responsibility to the darker races of men whose future depends so largely on this American experiment, but especially a responsibility to this nation—this common Fatherland. It is wrong to encourage a man or a people in evil-doing; it is wrong to aid and abet a national crime simply because it is unpopular not to do so. The growing spirit of kindliness and reconciliation between the North and South after the frightful difference of a generation ago ought to be a source of deep congratulation to all, and especially to those whose mistreatment caused the war; but if that reconciliation is to be marked by the industrial slavery and civic death of those same black men, with permanent legislation into a position of inferiority, then those black men, if they are really men, are called upon by every consideration of patriotism and loyalty to oppose such a course by all civilized methods, even though such opposition involves disagreement with Mr. Booker T. Washington. We have no right to sit silently by while the inevitable seeds are sown for a harvest of disaster to our children, black and white.

First, it is the duty of black men to judge the South discriminatingly. The present generation of Southerners are not responsible for the past, and they should not be blindly hated or blamed for it. Furthermore, to no class is the indiscriminate endorsement of the recent course of the South toward Negroes more nauseating than to the best thought of the South. The South is not "solid"; it is a land in the ferment of social change, wherein forces of all kinds are fighting for supremacy; and to praise the ill the South is today perpetrating is just as wrong as to condemn the good. Discriminating and broad-minded criticism is what the South needs—needs it for the sake of her own white sons and daughters, and for the insurance of robust, healthy mental and moral development.

Today even the attitude of the Southern whites toward the blacks is not, as so many assume, in all cases the same; the ignorant Southerner hates the Negro, the workingmen fear his competition, the money-makers wish to use him as a laborer, some of the educated see a menace in his upward development, while others—usually the sons of the masters—wish to help him to rise. National opinion has enabled this last class to maintain the Negro common schools, and to protect the Negro partially in property, life, and limb. Through the pressure of the money-makers, the Negro is in danger of being reduced to semi-slavery, especially in the country districts; the workingmen, and those of the educated who fear the Negro, have united to disfranchise him, and some have urged his deportation; while the passions of the ignorant are easily aroused to lynch and abuse any black man. . . .

It would be unjust to Mr. Washington not to acknowledge that in several instances he has opposed movements in the South which were unjust to the Negro; he sent memorials to the Louisiana and Alabama constitutional conventions, he has spoken against lynching, and in other ways has openly or silently set his influence against sinister schemes and unfortunate happenings. Notwithstanding this, it is equally true to assert that on the whole the distinct impression left by Mr. Washington's propaganda is, first, that the South is justified in its present attitude toward the Negro because of the Negro's degradation; secondly, that the prime cause of the Negro's failure to rise more quickly is his wrong education in the past; and, thirdly, that his future rise depends primarily on his own efforts. Each of these propositions is a dangerous half-truth. The supplementary truths must never be lost sight of: first, slavery and race-prejudice are potent if not sufficient causes of the Negro's position; second, industrial and common-school training were necessarily slow in planting because they had to await the black teachers trained by higher institutions—it being extremely doubtful if any essentially different development was possible, and certainly a Tuskegee was unthinkable before 1880; and, third, while it is a great truth to say that the Negro must strive and strive mightily to help himself, it is equally true that unless his striving be not simply seconded, but rather aroused and encouraged, by the initiative of the richer and wiser environing group, he cannot hope for great success.

In his failure to realize and impress this last point, Mr. Washington is especially to be criticized. His doctrine has tended to make the whites, North and South, shift the burden of the Negro problem to the Negro's shoulders and stand aside as critical and rather pessimistic spectators; when in fact the burden belongs to the nation, and the hands of none of us are clean if we bend not our energies to righting these great wrongs.

The South ought to be led, by candid and honest criticism, to assert her better self and do her full duty to the race she has cruelly wronged and is still wronging. The North—her co-partner in guilt—cannot salve her conscience by plastering it with gold. We cannot settle this problem by diplomacy and suaveness, by "policy" alone. If worse comes to worst, can the moral fibre of this country survive the slow throttling and murder of nine millions of men?

The black men of America have a duty to perform, a duty stern and delicate—a forward movement to oppose a part of the work of their greatest leader. So far as Mr. Washington preaches Thrift, Patience, and Industrial Training for the masses, we must hold up his hands and strive with him, rejoicing in his honors and glorying in the strength of this Joshua called of God and of man to lead the headless host. But so far as Mr. Washington apologizes for injustice, North or South, does not rightly value the privilege and duty of voting, belittles the emasculating effects of caste distinctions, and opposes the higher training and ambition of our brighter minds—so far as he, the South, or the Nation, does this—we must unceasingly and firmly oppose them. By every civilized and peaceful method we must strive for the rights which the world accords to men, clinging unwaveringly to those great words which the sons of the Fathers would fain forget: "We hold these truths to be self-evident: That all men are created equal; that they are endowed by their Creator with certain unalienable rights; that among these are life, liberty, and the pursuit of happiness."

DOCUMENT 27

Ida B. Wells Condemns Lynching

Context: Lynching had been part of southern life for several generations, but in the 1890s it reached epidemic proportions. Between 1890 and 1910, nearly 100 blacks were lynched every year. Ida B. Wells was one of the nation's most outspoken critics of lynching. Born a slave in 1862, Wells became a school teacher and civil rights leader in Memphis, Tennessee. When a white mob lynched three of her friends in 1892, she helped organize a black boy-cott of white-owned businesses and wrote scathing editorials in her own newspaper. After a mob ransacked her newspaper office, she left Memphis and eventually settled in Chicago. Her best known publication was *Southern Horrors: Lynch Law in All Its Phases* (1892).

Questions to Consider: Why did Wells stress that lynching was a national prob-lem, instead of merely a regional one? Why did Wells argue that rape was not the alleged offense in most lynchings? What pragmatic reasons did Wells give for ending lynching? How did her rhetoric try to win the support of white Americans? How did Wells' strategy for mobilizing the support of whites compare to Booker T. Washington's tactics?

Ida B. Wells, "Lynch Law in America" (1900)

Our country's national crime is *lynching*. It is not the creature of an hour, the sudden outburst of uncontrolled fury, or the unspeakable brutality of an insane mob. It represents the cool, calculating deliberation of intelligent people who openly avow that there is an "unwritten law" that justifies them in putting hu-man beings to death without complaint under oath, without trial by jury, without opportunity to make defense, and without right of appeal. . . . No emergency called for lynch law. It asserted its sway in defiance of law and in favor of anarchy. . . . In the thirty years of its existence [it has marked] the inhuman butchery of more than ten thousand men, women, and children by shooting, drowning, hanging, and burning them alive. Not only this, but so potent is the force of example that the lynching mania has spread throughout the North and middle West. It is now no uncommon thing to read of lynchings north of Mason and Dixon's line, and those most responsible for this fashion gleefully point to these instances and assert that the North is no better than the South.

This is the work of the "unwritten law" about which so much is said, and in whose behest butchery is made a pastime and national savagery condoned. The first statute of this "unwritten law" was written in the blood of thousands of brave men who thought that a government that was good enough to create a citizenship was strong enough to protect it. Under the authority of a national law that gave every citizen the right to vote, the newly-made citizens chose to exercise their suffrage. But the reign of the national law was short-lived and illusionary. Hardly had the sentences dried upon the statute-books before one Southern State after another raised the cry against "negro domination" and proclaimed there was an "unwritten law" that justified any means to resist it.

The method then inaugurated was the outrages by the "red-shirt" bands of Louisiana, South Carolina, and other Southern States, which were succeeded by the Ku-Klux Klans. These advocates of the "unwritten law" boldly avowed their purpose to intimidate, suppress, and nullify the negro's right to vote. In support of its plans the Ku-Klux Klans, the "red-shirt" and similar organizations proceeded to beat, exile, and kill negroes until the purpose of their organization was accomplished and the supremacy of the "unwritten law" was effected. Thus lynchings began in the South, rapidly spreading into the various States until the national law was nullified and the reign of the "unwritten law" was supreme. Men were taken from their homes by "red-shirt" bands and stripped, beaten, and exiled; others were assassinated when their political prominence made them obnoxious to their political opponents; while the Ku-Klux barbarism of election days, reveling in the butchery of thousands of colored voters, furnished records in Congressional investigations that are a disgrace to civilization.

The alleged menace of universal suffrage having been avoided by the absolute suppression of the negro vote, the spirit of mob murder should have been satisfied and the butchery of negroes should have ceased. But men, women, and children were the victims of murder by individuals and murder by mobs, just as they had been when killed at the demands of the "unwritten law" to prevent "negro domination." Negroes were killed for disputing over terms of contracts with their employers. If a few barns were burned some colored man was killed to stop it. If a colored man resented the imposition of a white man and the two came to blows, the colored man had to die, either at the hands of the white man then and there or later at the hands of a mob that speedily gathered. If he showed a spirit of courageous manhood he was hanged for his pains, and the killing was justified by the declaration that he was a "saucy nigger." Colored women have been murdered because they refused to tell the mobs where relatives could be found for "lynching bees." Boys of fourteen years have been lynched by white representatives of American civilization. In fact, for all kinds of offenses—and, for no offenses—from murders to misdemeanors, men and women are put to death without judge or jury; so that, although the political excuse was no longer necessary, the wholesale murder of human beings went on just the same. A new name was given to the killings and a new excuse was invented for so doing.

Again the aid of the "unwritten law" is invoked, and again it comes to the rescue. During the last ten years a new statute has been added to the "unwritten law." This statute proclaims that for certain crimes or alleged crimes no negro shall be allowed a trial; that no white woman shall be compelled to charge an assault under oath or to submit any such charge to the investigation of a court of law. The result is that many men have been put to death whose innocence was afterward established; and to-day, under this reign of the "unwritten law," no colored man, no matter what his reputation, is safe from lynching if a white woman, no matter what her standing or motive, cares to charge him with insult or assault. ... No matter that our laws presume every man innocent until he is proved guilty; no matter that it leaves a certain class of individuals completely at the mercy of another class; no matter that it encourages those criminally disposed to blacken their faces and commit any crime in the calendar so long as they can throw suspicion on some negro, as is frequently done, and then lead a mob to take his life; no matter that mobs make a farce of the law and a mockery of justice; no matter that hundreds of boys are being hardened in crime and schooled in vice by the repetition of such scenes before their eyes—if a white woman declares herself insulted or assaulted, some life must pay the penalty, with all the horrors of the Spanish Inquisition and all the barbarism of the Middle Ages. The world looks on and says it is well.

Not only are two hundred men and women put to death annually, on the average, in this country by mobs, but these lives are taken with the greatest publicity. In many instances the leading citizens aid and abet by their presence when they do not participate, and the leading journals inflame the public mind to the lynching point with scare-head articles and offers of rewards. Whenever a burning is advertised to take place, the railroads run excursions, photographs are taken, and the same jubilee is indulged in that characterized the public hangings of one hundred years ago. There is, however, this difference: in those old days the multitude that stood by was permitted only to guy or jeer. The nineteenth century lynching mob cuts off ears, toes, and fingers, strips off flesh, and distributes portions of the body as souvenirs among the crowd. If the leaders of the mob are so minded, coal-oil is poured over the body and the victim is then roasted to death. This has been done in Texarkana and Paris, Tex., in Bardswell, Ky., and in Newman, Ga. In Paris the officers of the law delivered the prisoner to the mob. The mayor gave the school children a holiday and the railroads ran excursion trains so that the people might see a human being burned to death. In Texarkana, the year before, men and boys amused themselves by cutting off strips of flesh and thrusting knives into their helpless victim. At Newman, Ga., of the present year, the mob tried every conceivable torture to compel the victim to cry out and confess, before they set fire to the faggots that burned him. But their trouble was all in vain—he never uttered a cry, and they could not make him confess.

This condition of affairs were brutal enough and horrible enough if it were true that lynchings occurred only because of the commission of crimes against women—as is constantly declared by ministers, editors, lawyers, teachers, statesmen, and even by women themselves. It has been to the interest of those who did the lynching to blacken the good name of the helpless and defenseless victims of their hate. For this reason they publish at every possible opportunity this excuse for lynching, hoping thereby not only to palliate their own crime but at the same time to prove the negro a moral monster and unworthy of the respect and sympathy of the civilized world. But this alleged reason adds to the deliberate injustice of the mob's work. Instead of lynchings being caused by assaults upon women, the statistics show that not one-third of the victims of lynchings are even charged with such crimes.

Indeed, the record for the last twenty years shows exactly the same or a smaller proportion who have been charged with this horrible crime. Quite a number of the one-third alleged cases of assault that have been personally investigated by the writer have shown that there was no foundation in fact for the charges; yet the claim is not made that there were no real culprits among them. The negro has been too long associated with the white man not to have copied his vices as well as his virtues. But the negro resents and utterly repudiates the efforts to blacken his good name by asserting that assaults upon women are peculiar to his race. The negro has suffered far more from the commission of this crime against the women of his race by white men than the white race has ever suffered through *his* crimes. Very scant notice is taken of the matter when this is the condition of affairs. What becomes a crime deserving capital punishment when the tables are turned is a matter of small moment when the negro woman is the accusing party.

But since the world has accepted this false and unjust statement, and the burden of proof has been placed upon the negro to vindicate his race, he is taking steps to do so. The Anti-Lynching Bureau of the National Afro-American Council is arranging to have every lynching investigated and publish the facts to the world, as has been done in the case of Sam Hose, who was burned alive last April at Newman, Ga. The detective's report showed that Hose killed Cranford, his employer, in self-defense, and that, while a mob was organizing to hunt Hose to punish him for killing a white man, not till twenty-four hours after the murder was the charge of rape, embellished with psychological and physical impossibilities, circulated. That gave an impetus to the hunt, and the Atlanta *Constitution's* reward of $500 keyed the mob to the necessary burning and roasting pitch. Of five hundred newspaper clippings of that horrible affair, nine-tenths of them assumed Hose's guilt—simply because his murderers said so, and because it is the fashion to believe the negro peculiarly addicted to this species of crime. All the negro asks is justice—a fair and impartial trial in the courts of the country. That given, he will abide the result.

But this question affects the entire American nation, and from several points of view: First, on the ground of consistency. Our watchword has been "the land of the free and the home of the brave." Brave men do not gather by thousands to torture and murder a single individual, so gagged and bound he cannot make even feeble resistance or defense. Neither do brave men or women stand by and see such things done without compunction of conscience, nor read of them without protest. Our nation has been active and outspoken in its endeavors to right the wrongs of the Armenian Christian, the Russian Jew, the Irish Home Ruler, the native women of India, the Siberian exile, and the Cuban patriot. Surely it should be the nation's duty to correct its own evils!

Second, on the ground of economy. To those who fail to be convinced from any other point of view touching this momentous question, a consideration of the economic phase might not be amiss. It is generally known that mobs in Louisiana, Colorado, Wyoming, and other States have lynched subjects of other countries. When their different governments demanded satisfaction, our country was forced to confess her inability to protect said subjects in the several States because of our State-rights doctrines, or in turn demand punishment of the lynchers. This confession, while humiliating in the extreme, was not satisfactory; and, while the United States cannot protect, she can pay. This she has done, and it is certain will have to do again in the case of the recent lynching of Italians in Louisiana. The United States already has paid in indemnities for lynching nearly a half million dollars.

Third, for the honor of Anglo-Saxon civilization. No scoffer at our boasted American civilization could say anything more harsh of it than does the American white man himself who says he is unable to protect the honor of his women without resort to such brutal, inhuman, and degrading exhibitions as characterize "lynching bees." The cannibals of the South Sea Islands roast human beings alive to satisfy hunger. The red Indian of the Western plains tied his prisoner to the stake, tortured him, and danced in fiendish glee while his victim writhed in the flames. His savage, untutored mind suggested no better way than that of wreaking vengeance upon those who had wronged him. These people knew nothing about Christianity and did not profess to follow its teachings; but such primary laws as they had they lived up to. No nation, savage or civilized, save only the United States of America, has confessed its inability to protect its women save by hanging, shooting, and burning alleged offenders.

Finally, for love of country. No American travels abroad without blushing for shame for his country on this subject. And whatever the excuse that passes current in the United States, it avails nothing abroad. With all the powers of government in control; with all laws made by white men, administered by white judges, jurors, prosecuting attorneys, and sheriffs; with every office of the executive department filled by white men—no excuse can be offered for exchanging the orderly administration of justice for barbarous lynchings and "unwritten laws." Our country should be placed speedily above the plane of confessing herself a failure at self-government. This cannot be until Americans of every section, of broadest patriotism and best and wisest citizenship, not only see the defect in our country's armor but take the necessary steps to remedy it. Although lynchings have steadily increased in number and barbarity during the last twenty years, there has been no single effort put forth by the many moral and philanthropic forces of the country to put a stop to this wholesale slaughter. Indeed, the silence grows more marked as the years go by.

DOCUMENT 28

Elizabeth Cady Stanton Justifies Complete Equality

Context: Elizabeth Cady Stanton had been a leader of the suffrage movement for more than forty years when she delivered this address. Stanton had become increasingly isolated within the women's rights movement. While she continued to advocate a radical agenda of complete equality, most suffrage leaders wanted to focus exclusively on suffrage. To their eyes, Stanton's radical stands were more of a hindrance than a help. Stanton resigned from the presidency of the major suffrage organization after giving this address.

Questions to Consider: What were Stanton's justifications for women's equality? What are the connections, if any, between "The Solitude of Self" and Stanton's ideals expressed at the Seneca Falls convention? To what extent was Stanton's message outside the main currents of Progressive ideology? How would have William Graham Sumner and Andrew Carnegie reacted to this speech?

Elizabeth Cady Stanton, "The Solitude of Self" (1892)

(Address Delivered by Mrs. Stanton Before the Committee of the Judiciary of the United States Congress Monday, January 18, 1892).

The point I wish plainly to bring before you on this occasion is the individuality of each human soul; our Protestant idea, the right of individual conscience and judgment-our republican idea, individual citizenship. In discussing the rights of woman, we are to consider, first, what belongs to her as an individual, in a world of her own, the arbiter of her own destiny, an imaginary Robinson Crusoe with her woman Friday on a solitary island. Her rights under such circumstances are to use all her faculties for her own safety and happiness.

Secondly, if we consider her as a citizen, as a member of a great nation, she must have the same rights as all other members, according to the fundamental principles of our Government.

Thirdly, viewed as a woman, an equal factor in civilization, her rights and duties are still the same-individual happiness and development.

Fourthly, it is only the incidental relations of life, such as mother, wife, sister, daughter, that may involve some special duties and training. In the usual discussion in regard to woman's sphere, such as men as Herbert Spencer, Frederic Harrison, and Grant Allen uniformly subordinate her rights and duties as an individual, as a citizen, as a woman, to the necessities of these incidental relations, some of which a large class of woman may never assume. In discussing the sphere of man we do not decide his rights as an individual, as a citizen, as a man by his duties as a father, a husband, a brother, or a son, relations some of which he may never fill. Moreover he would be better fitted for these very relations and whatever special work he might choose to do to earn his bread by the complete development of all his faculties as an individual.

Just so with woman. The education that will fit her to discharge the duties in the largest sphere of human usefulness will best fit her for whatever special work she may be compelled to do.

The isolation of every human soul and the necessity of self-dependence must give each individual the right, to choose his own surroundings.

The strongest reason for giving woman all the opportunities for higher education, for the full development of her faculties, forces of mind and body; for giving her the most enlarged freedom of thought and action; a complete emancipation from all forms of bondage, of custom, dependence, superstition; from all the crippling influences of fear, is the solitude and personal responsibility of her own individual life. The strongest reason why we ask for woman a voice in the government under which she lives; in the religion she is asked to believe; equality in social life, where she is the chief factor; a place in the trades and professions, where she may earn her bread, is because of her birthright to self-sovereignty; because, as an individual, she must rely on herself. No matter how much women prefer to lean, to be protected and supported, nor how much men desire to have them do so, they must make the voyage of life alone, and for safety in an emergency they must know something of the laws of navigation. To guide our own craft, we must be captain, pilot, engineer; with chart and compass to stand at the wheel; to match the wind and waves and know when to take in the sail, and to read the signs in the firmament over all. It matters not whether the solitary voyager is man or woman.

Nature having endowed them equally, leaves them to their own skill and judgment in the hour of danger, and, if not equal to the occasion, alike they perish.

The appreciate the importance of fitting every human soul for independent action, think for a moment of the immeasurable solitude of self. We come into the world alone, unlike all who have gone before us; we leave it alone under circumstances peculiar to ourselves. No mortal ever has been, no mortal over will be like the soul just launched on the sea of life. …

Again we ask complete individual development for the general good; for the consensus of the competent on the whole round of human interest; on all questions of national life, and here each man must bear his share of the general burden. …

We ask no sympathy from others in the anxiety and agony of a broken friendship or shattered love. When death sunders our nearest ties, alone we sit in the shadows of our affliction. Alike mid the greatest triumphs and darkest tragedies of life we walk alone. On the divine heights of human attainments, eulogized land worshiped as a hero or saint, we stand alone. In ignorance, poverty, and vice, as a pauper or criminal, alone we starve or steal; alone we suffer the sneers and rebuffs of our fellows; alone we are hunted and hounded thro dark courts and alleys, in by-ways and highways; alone we stand in the judgment seat; alone in the prison cell we lament our crimes and misfortunes; alone we expiate them on the gallows. In hours like these we realize the awful solitude of individual life, its pains, its penalties, its responsibilities; hours in which the youngest and most helpless are thrown on their own resources for guidance and consolation. Seeing then that life must ever be a march and a battle, that each soldier must be equipped for his own protection, it is the height of cruelty to rob the individual of a single natural right.

To throw obstacle in the way of a complete education is like putting out the eyes; to deny the rights of property, like cutting off the hands. To deny political equality is to rob the ostracized of all self-respect; of credit in the market place; of recompense in the world of work; of a voice among those who make and administer the law; a choice in the jury before whom they are tried, and in the judge who decides their punishment. Shakespeare's play of Titus and Andronicus contains a terrible satire on woman's position in the nineteenth century-"Rude men" (the play tells us) "seized the king's daughter, cut out her tongue, out off her hands, and then bade her go call for water and wash her hands." What a picture of woman's position. Robbed of her natural rights, handicapped by law and custom at every turn, yet compelled to fight her own battles, and in the emergencies of life to fall back on herself for protection. …

The young wife and mother, at the head of some establishment with a kind husband to shield her from the adverse winds of life, with wealth, fortune and position, has a certain harbor of safety, occurs against the ordinary ills of life. But to manage a household, have an influence in society, keep her friends and the affections of her husband, train her children and servants well, she must have rare common sense, wisdom, diplomacy, and a knowledge of human nature. To do all this she needs the cardinal virtues and the strong points of character that the most successful statesman possesses.

An uneducated woman, trained to dependence, with no resources in herself must make a failure of any position in life. But society says women do not need a knowledge of the world, the liberal training that experience in public life must give, all the advantages of collegiate education; but when for the lock of all this, the woman's happiness is wrecked, alone she bears her humiliation; and the attitude of the weak and the ignorant in indeed pitiful in the wild chase for the price of life they are ground to powder.

In age, when the pleasures of youth are passed, children grown up, married and gone, the hurry and hustle of life in a measure over, when the hands are weary of active service, when the old armchair and the fireside are the chosen resorts, then men and women alike must fall back on their own resources. If they cannot find companionship in books, if they have no interest in the vital questions of the hour, no interest in watching the consummation of reforms, with which they might have been identified, they soon pass into their dotage. The more fully the faculties of the mind are developed and kept in use, the longer the period of vigor and active interest in all around us continues. If from a lifelong participation in public affairs a woman feels responsible for the laws regulating our system of education, the discipline of our jails and prisons, the sanitary conditions of our private homes, public buildings, and thoroughfares, an interest in commerce, finance, our foreign relations, in any or all of these questions, here solitude will at least be respectable, and she will not be driven to gossip or scandal for entertainment. ...

Whatever the theories may be of woman's dependence on man, in the supreme moments of her life he can not bear her burdens. Alone she goes to the gates of death to give life to every man that is born into the world. No one can share her fears, on one mitigate her pangs; and if her sorrow is greater than she can bear, alone she passes beyond the gates into the vast unknown. ...

But when ... women are recognized as individuals, responsible for their own environments, thoroughly educated for all the positions in life they may be called to fill; with all the resources in themselves that liberal though and broad culture can give; guided by their own conscience an judgment; trained to self-protection by a healthy development of the muscular system and skill in the use of weapons of defense, and stimulated to self-support by the knowledge of the business world and the pleasure that pecuniary independence must ever give; when women are trained in this way they will, in a measure, be fitted for those hours of solitude that come alike to all, whether prepared or otherwise. As in our extremity we must depend on ourselves, the dictates of wisdom point of complete individual development. ...

Is it, then, consistent to hold the developed woman of this day within the same narrow political limits as the dame with the spinning wheel and knitting needle occupied in the past? No! no! Machinery has taken the labors of woman as well as man on its tireless shoulders; the loom and the spinning wheel are but dreams of the past; the pen, the brush, the easel, the chisel, have taken their places, while the hopes and ambitions of women are essentially changed.

We see reason sufficient in the outer conditions of human being for individual liberty and development, but when we consider the self dependence of every human soul we see the need of courage, judgment, and the exercise of every faculty of mind and body, strengthened and developed by use, in woman as well as man.

Whatever may be said of man's protecting power in ordinary conditions, mid all the terrible disasters by land and sea, in the supreme moments of danger, alone, woman must ever meet the horrors of the situation; the Angel of Death even makes no royal pathway for her. Man's love and sympathy enter only into the sunshine of our lives. In that solemn solitude of self, that links us with the immeasurable and the eternal, each soul lives alone forever. ... There is a solitude, which each and every one of us has always carried with him, more inaccessible than the ice-cold mountains, more profound than the midnight sea; the solitude of self. Our inner being, which we call our self, no eye nor touch of man or angel has ever pierced. It is more hidden than the caves of the gnome; the sacred adytum of the oracle; the hidden chamber of Eleusinian mystery, for to it only omniscience is permitted to enter. Such is individual life. Who, I ask you, can take, dare take, on himself the rights, the duties, the responsibilities of another human soul?

DOCUMENT 29

Jane Addams Extends Domestic Ideology to Municipal Government

Context: Like many settlement house residents, Jane Addams was a strong proponent of women's rights, especially suffrage While some supporters of suffrage used racial arguments to justify their position—the votes of white women would offset the votes blacks and immigrants—Addams had a more inclusive vision of suffrage.

Questions to Consider: What general ideas and attitudes did Addams use to justify suffrage? How did Addams use her Hull House experience to shape her arguments? How did Addams' arguments for suffrage differ from those of Elizabeth Cady Stanton? To what extent did Addams argue that men and women are inherently different in their political outlooks?

Jane Addams, "Why Women Should Vote" (1915)

Reprinted in *Woman Suffrage: History, Arguments, and Results* (New York: National Woman Suffrage Publishing Co., Revised Edition, May, 1917).

For many generations it has been believed that woman's place is within the walls of her own home, and it is indeed impossible to imagine the time when her duty there shall be ended or to forecast any social change which shall release her from that paramount obligation. This paper is an attempt to show that many women to-day are failing to discharge their duties to their own households properly simply because they do not perceive that as society grows more complicated it is necessary that woman shall extend her sense of responsibility to many things outside of her own home if she would continue to preserve the home in its entirety. One could illustrate in many ways. A woman's simplest duty, one would say, is to keep her house clean and wholesome, and to feed her children properly. Yet if she lives in a tenement house, as so many of my neighbors do, she cannot fulfill these simple obligations by her own efforts because she is utterly dependent upon the city administration for the conditions which render decent living possible. Her basement will not be dry, her stairways will not be fireproof, her house will not be provided with sufficient windows to give light and air, nor will it be equipped with sanitary plumbing, unless the Public Works Department sends inspectors who constantly insist that these elementary decencies be provided. Women who live in the country sweep their own dooryards and may either feed the refuse of the table to a flock of chickens or allow it innocently to decay in the open air and sunshine. In a crowded city quarter, however, if the street is not cleaned by the city authorities, no amount of private sweeping will keep the tenement free from grime; if the garbage is not properly collected and destroyed, a tenement house mother may see her children sicken and die of diseases from which she alone is powerless to shield them, although her tenderness and devotion are unbounded. She cannot even secure untainted meat for her household, she cannot provide fresh fruit, unless the meat has been inspected by city officials, and the decayed fruit, which is so often placed upon sale in the tenement districts, has been destroyed in the interests of public health. In short, if woman would keep on with her old business of caring for her house and rearing her children, she will have to have some conscience in regard to public affairs lying quite outside of her immediate household. The individual conscience and devotion are no longer effective.

Chicago one spring had a spreading contagion of scarlet fever just at the time that the school nurses had been discontinued because business men had pronounced them too expensive. If the women who sent their children to the schools had been sufficiently public-spirited and had been provided with an implement through which to express that public spirit, they would have insisted that the schools be supplied with nurses in order that their own children might be protected from contagion. In other words, if women would effectively continue their old avocations they must take part in the slow upbuilding of that code of legislation which is alone sufficient to protect the home from the dangers incident to modern life. One might instance the many deaths of children from contagious diseases the germs of which had been carried in tailored clothing. Country doctors testify as to the outbreak of scarlet fever in remote neighborhoods each autumn, after the children have begun to wear the winter overcoats and cloaks which have been sent from infected city sweatshops. That their mothers mend their stockings and guard them from "taking cold" is not a sufficient protection, when the tailoring of the family is done in a distant city under conditions which the mother cannot possibly control. The sanitary regulation of sweatshops by city officials is all that can be depended upon to prevent such needless destruction. Who shall say that women are not concerned in the enactment and enforcement of such legislation if they would preserve their homes?

Even women who take no part in public affairs, in order that they may give themselves entirely to their own families, sometimes going so far as to despise those other women who are endeavoring to secure protective legislation, may illustrate this point. The Hull-House neighborhood was at one time suffering from a typhoid epidemic. A careful investigation was made by which we were able to establish a very close connection between the typhoid and a mode of plumbing which made it most probable that the infection had been carried by flies. Among the people who had been exposed to the infection was a widow who had lived in the ward for a number of years, in a comfortable little house which she owned.

Although the Italian immigrants were closing in all around her, she was not willing to sell her property and to move away, until she had finished the education of her children. In the meantime she held herself quite aloof from her Italian neighbors and could never be drawn into any of the public efforts to protect them by securing a better code of tenement house sanitation. Her two daughters were sent to an Eastern college; one June, when one of them had graduated and the other still had two years before she took her degree, they came to the spotless little house, and to their self-sacrificing mother for the Summer's holidays. They both fell ill, not because their own home was not clean, not because their mother was not devoted, but because next door to them and also in the rear were wretched tenements, and because the mother's utmost efforts could not keep the infection out of her own house. One daughter died, and one recovered, but was an invalid for two years following. This is, perhaps, a fair illustration of the futility of the individual conscience when woman insists upon isolating her family from the rest of the community and its interests. The result is sure to be a pitiful failure.

One of the interesting experiences in the Chicago campaign for inducing the members of the Charter Convention to recommend municipal franchise for women in the provisions of the new charter was the unexpected enthusiasm and help which came from large groups of foreign-born women. The Scandinavian women represented in many Lutheran Church societies said quite simply that in the old country they had had the municipal franchise upon the same basis as men for many years; all the women living under the British Government, in England, Australia or Canada, pointed out that Chicago women were asking now for what the British women had long ago. But the most unexpected response came from the foreign colonies in which women had never heard such problems discussed, and took the prospect of the municipal ballot as a simple device-which it is-to aid them in their daily struggle with adverse city conditions. The Italian women said that the men engaged in railroad construction were away all summer and did not know anything about their household difficulties.

. . . If women follow only the lines of their traditional activities, here are certain primary duties which belong to even the most conservative women, and which no one woman or group of women can adequately discharge unless they join the more general movements looking toward social amelioration through legal enactment.

The first of these, of which this article has already treated, is woman's responsibility for the members of her own household that they may be properly fed and clothed and surrounded by hygienic conditions. The second is a responsibility for the education of children: (a) that they may be provided with good books; (b) that they may be kept free from vicious influences on the street; (c) that when working they may be protected by adequate child-labor legislation.

(a) The duty of a woman toward the schools which her children attend is so obvious that it is not necessary to dwell upon it. But even this simple obligation cannot be effectively carried out without some form of social organization, as the mothers school clubs and mothers congresses testify, and to which the most conservative women belong because they feel the need of wider reading and discussion concerning the many problems of childhood. It is, therefore, perhaps natural that the public should have been more willing to accord a vote to women in school matters than in any other, and yet women have never been members of a Board of Education in sufficient numbers to influence largely actual school curriculi. If they had been kindergartens, domestic science courses and school playgrounds would be far more numerous than they are. More than one woman has been convinced of the need of the ballot by the futility of her efforts in persuading a business man that young children need nurture in something besides the three r's. Perhaps, too, only women realize the influence which the school might exert upon the home if a proper adaptation to actual needs were considered. An Italian girl who has had lessons in cooking at the public school will help her mother to connect the entire family with American food and household habits. That the mother has never baked bread in Italy-only mixed it in her own house and then taken it out to the village oven-makes it all the more necessary that her daughter should understand the complications of a cooking-stove. The some thing is true of the girl who learns to sew in the public school, and more than anything else, perhaps, of the girl who receives the first simple instruction in the care of little children, that skillful care which every tenement house baby requires if he is to be pulled through his second summer. The only time, to my knowledge, that lessons in the care of children were given in the public schools of Chicago was one summer when the vacation schools were being managed by a volunteer body of women. The instructions was eagerly received by the Italian girls, who had been "little mothers" to younger children ever since they could remember.

As a result of this teaching I recall a young girl who carefully explained to her Italian mother that the reason the babies in Italy were so healthy and the babies in Chicago were so sickly was not, as her mother had always firmly insisted, because her babies in Italy had goat's milk and her babies in America had cow's milk, but because the milk in Italy was clean and the milk in Chicago was dirty. She said that when you milked your own goat before the door you knew that the milk was clean, but when you bought milk from the grocery store after it had been carried for many miles in the country, "you couldn't tell whether or not it was fit for baby to drink until the men from the City Hall, who had watched it all the way, said that it was all right." She also informed her mother that the "City Hall wanted to fix up the milk so that it couldn't make the baby sick, but that they hadn't quite enough votes for it yet."

 . . .(b) But women are also beginning to realize that children need attention outside of school hours; that much of the petty vice in cities is merely the love of pleasure gone wrong, the over-restrained boy or girl seeking improper recreation and excitement. It is obvious that a little study of the needs of children, a sympathetic understanding of the conditions under which they go astray, might save hundreds of them. Women traditionally have had an opportunity to observe the plays of children and the needs of youth, and yet in Chicago, at least, they had done singularly little in this vexed problem of juvenile delinquency until they helped to inaugurate the Juvenile Court movement a dozen years ago. The Juvenile Court Committee, made up largely of women, paid the salaries of the probation officers connected with the court for the first six years of its existence, and after the salaries were cared for by the county the same organization turned itself into a Juvenile Protective League, and through a score of paid officers are doing valiant service in minimizing some of the dangers of city life which boys and girls encounter.

This Protective League, however, was not formed until the women had had a civic training through their semi-official connection with the Juvenile Court. This is, perhaps, an illustration of our inability to see the duty "next to hand" until we have become alert through our knowledge of conditions in connection with the larger duties. We would all agree that social amelioration must come about through the efforts of many people who are moved thereto by the compunction and stirring of the individual conscience, but we are only beginning to understand that the individual conscience will respond to the special challenge largely in proportion as the individual is able to see the social conditions because he has felt responsible for their improvement. Because this body of women assumed a public responsibility they have seen to it that every series of pictures displayed in the five-cent theatre is subjected to a careful censorship before it is produced, and those series suggesting obscenity and criminality have been practically eliminated. The police department has performed this and many other duties to which it was oblivious before, simply because these women have made it realize that it is necessary to protect and purify those places amusement which are crowded with young people every night. This is but the negative side of the policy pursued by the public authorities in the fifteen small parks of Chicago, each of which is provided with halls in which young people may meet nightly for social gatherings and dances. The more extensively the modern city endeavors on the one hand to control and on the other hand to provide recreational facilities for its young people, the more necessary it is that women should assist in their direction and extension. After all, a care for wholesome and innocent amusement is what women have for many years assumed. When the reaction comes on the part of taxpayers, women's votes may be necessary to keep the city to its beneficent obligations towards its own young people.

(c) As the education of her children has been more and more transferred to the school, so that even children four years old go to the kindergarten, the woman has been left in a household of constantly narrowing interests, not only because the children are away, but also because one industry after another is slipping from the household into the factory. Ever since steam power has been applied to the processes of weaving and spinning woman's traditional work has been carried on largely outside of the home. The clothing and household linen are not only spun and woven, but also usually sewed by machinery; the preparation of many foods has also passed into the factory and necessarily a certain number of women have been obliged to follow their work there; although it is doubtful, in spite of the large number of factory girls, whether women now are doing as large a proportion of the world's work as they used to do. Because many thousands of those working in factories and shops are girls between the ages of fourteen and twenty-two, there is a necessity that older women should be interested in the conditions of industry. The very fact that these girls are not going to remain in industry permanently makes it more important that some one should see to it that they shall not be incapacitated for their future family life because they work for exhausting hours and under unsanitary conditions.

If woman's sense of obligation had enlarged as the industrial condition changed, she might naturally and almost imperceptibly have inaugurated the movements for social amelioration in the line of factory legislation and shop sanitation. That she has not done so is doubtless due to the fact that her conscience is slow to recognize any obligation outside of her own family circle, and because she was so absorbed in her own household that she failed to see what the conditions outside actually were. It would be interesting to know how far the consciousness that she had no vote and could not change matters operated in this direction. After all, we see only those things to which our attention has been drawn, we feel responsibility for those things which are brought to us as matters of responsibility. If conscientious women were convinced that it was a civic duty to be informed in regard to these grave industrial affairs, and then to express the conclusions which they had reached by depositing a piece of paper in a ballot-box, one cannot imagine that they would shirk simply because the action ran counter to old traditions.

. . . [m]any busy women who would be glad to use the ballot to further public measures in which they are interested and for which they have been working for years. It offends the taste of such a woman to be obliged to use indirect "influence" when she is accustomed to well-bred, open action in other affairs, and she very much resents the time spent in persuading a voter to take her point of view, and possibly to give up his own quite as honest and valuable as hers, although different because resulting from a totally different experience. Public-spirited women who wish to use the ballot, as I know them, do not wish to do the work of me nor to take over men's affairs. They simply want an opportunity to do their own work and to take care of those affairs which naturally and historically belong to women, but which are constantly being overlooked and slighted in our political institutions.

In a complex community like the modern city all points of view need to be represented; the resultants of diverse experiences need to be pooled, if the community would make for sane and balanced progress. If it would meet fairly each problem as it arises, whether it be connected with a freight tunnel having to do largely with business men, or with the increasing death rate among children under five years of age, a problem in which women are vitally concerned, or with the question of more adequate street-car transfers, in which both men and women might be said to be equally interested, it must not ignore the judgments of its entire adult population.

To turn the administration of our civic affairs wholly over to men may mean that the American city will continue to push forward in its commercial and industrial development, and continue to lag behind in those things which make a city healthful and beautiful. After all, woman's traditional function has been to make her dwelling-place both clean and fair. Is that dreariness in city life, that lack of domesticity which the humblest farm dwelling presents, due to a withdrawal of one of the naturally co-operating forces? If women have in any sense been responsible for the gentler side of life which softens and blurs some of its harsher conditions, may they not have a duty to perform in our American cities?

In closing, may I recapitulate that if woman would fulfill her traditional responsibility to her own children; if she would educate and protect from danger factory children who must find their recreation on the street; if she would bring the cultural forces to bear upon our materialistic civilization; and if she would do it all with the dignity and directness fitting one who carries on her immemorial duties, then she must bring herself to the use of the ballot-that latest implement for self-government. May we not fairly say the American women need this implement in order to preserve the home?

DOCUMENT 30

Belle Kearney Equates Suffrage with White Supremacy

Context: The women's suffrage movement originated from the abolitionist agitation of the 1830s and 1840s. Recall the Frederick Douglass, the escaped slave, eloquently spoke on behalf of women's suffrage at the 1848 Seneca Falls convention. By the Progressive period, though, the orientation of the movement had changed. While some suffrage supporters still advocated complete equality of all races, others argued that the greater propensity of white women to vote would effectively dilute the political power of immigrants and African Americans. Belle Kearney, a white Mississippi suffragist who addressed the 1903 NAWSA convention, typified racist appeals for women's suffrage.

Questions to Consider: How, according to Kearney, would women's suffrage help maintain white supremacy in the South? Why would women's suffrage help stimulate progress among poor whites? Why did Kearney consider the Tuskegee Institute and other black vocational schools as a threat to white supremacy? From the standpoint of practical politics, did Kearney's embrace of racism ultimately help or hurt the suffrage cause?

Belle Kearney, "The South and Woman Suffrage" (1903)

By degrees, slavery became the bone of contention in politics. In course of time it would probably have been abolished by the Southerners themselves, if they had been left to work out their own destiny and that of the black man in bonds, but a conflict of ideas gathered to a storm-center between the Puritan of the North and the Cavalier of the South, and the institution was wiped out in blood.

The world is scarcely beginning to realize the enormity of the situation that faces the South in its grapple with the race question which was thrust upon it at the close of the Civil War, when 4,500,000 ex-slaves, illiterate and semi-barbarous, were enfranchised. Such a situation has no parallel in history. In forging a path out of the darkness, there were no precedents to lead the way. All that has been and is being accomplished is pioneer statecraft. The South has struggled under its death-weight for nearly forty years, bravely and magnanimously.

The Southern States are making a desperate effort to maintain the political supremacy of Anglo-Saxonism by amendments to their constitutions limiting the right to vote by a property and educational qualification. If the United States government had been wise enough to enact such a law when the negro was first enfranchised, it would have saved years of bloodshed in the South, and such experiences of suffering and horror among the white people here as no other were ever subjected to in an enlightened nation.

The present suffrage laws in the different Southern States can be only temporary measures for protection. Those who are wise enough to look beneath the surface will be compelled to realize the fact that they act as a stimulus to the black man to acquire both education and property, but no incentive is given to the poor whites; for it is understood, in a general way, that any man whose skin is fair enough to let the blue veins show through, may be allowed the right of franchise.

The industrial education that the negro is receiving at Tuskegee and other schools is only fitting him for power, and when the black man becomes necessary to a community by reason of his skill and acquired wealth, and the poor white man, embittered by his poverty and humiliated by his inferiority, finds no place for himself or his children, then will come the grapple between the races.

To avoid this unspeakable culmination, the enfranchisement of women will have to be effected, and an educational and property qualification for the ballot be made to apply, without discrimination, to both sexes and to both races. It will spur the poor white to keep up with the march of progression, and enable him to hold his own. The class that is not willing to measure its strength with that of an inferior is not fit to survive.

The enfranchisement of women would insure immediate and durable white supremacy, honestly attained; for, upon unquestionable authority, it is stated that "in every Southern State but one, there are more educated women than all the illiterate voters, white and black, native and foreign, combined." As you probably know, of all the women in the South who can read and write, ten out of every eleven are white. When it comes to the proportion of property between the races, that of the white outweighs that of the black immeasurably. The South is slow to grasp the great fact that the enfranchisement of women would settle the race question in politics.

The civilization of the North is threatened by the influx of foreigners with their imported customs; by the greed of monopolistic wealth, and the unrest among the working classes; by the strength of the liquor traffic, and by encroachments upon religious belief.

Some day the North will be compelled to look to the South for redemption from these evils, on account of the purity of its Anglo-Saxon blood, the simplicity of its social and economic structure, the great advance in prohibitory law, and the maintenance of the sanctity of its faith, which has been kept inviolate. Just as surely as the North will be forced to turn to the South for the nation's salvation, just so surely will the South be compelled to look to its Anglo-Saxon women as the medium through which to retain the supremacy of the white race over the African. . . .

Anglo-Saxonism is the standard of the ages to come. It is, above all else, the granite foundation of the South. Upon that its civilization will mount; upon that it will stand unshaken. . . . Thank God the black man was freed! I wish for him all possible happiness and all possible progress, but not in encroachments upon the holy of holies of the Anglo-Saxon race. . . .